Excerpts from YOUR LAST GOODBYE

Recently in New York, blindfolded and barefooted communicants were guided up and down flights of stairs, tossed bodily in the air and then crawled on hands and knees over bread crumbs . . . they were guided downstairs, admitted individually into the bathroom where blindfolds were removed. A smiling confessor, draped in toilet paper, flushed away their sins in a symbolic "declamation of absolution."

chapter 1

* * *

Since October, 1968, medical guidelines for life have changed. It was then that a woman stroke victim was rushed to Houston where her still beating heart was removed and transplanted into a patient. Now doctors are talking of brain transplants to perpetuate personalities of famous (or infamous) people.

chapter 2

* * *

One group of Crazies arrived at Harvard, and then things started to fall apart when the five—including two girls—took off their clothes . . .

chapter 3

* * *

High priests of finance meet secretly once each month in Basel, Switzerland and control money affairs of the world.

chapter 4

* * *

The vice president of a 17-theater chain, dickering for the rights to show the pornographic film "I AM CURIOUS" stated: "I know how much money I can make with this picture in Texas . . . about $2 million."

Our nation is pursuing wildly after the same decay that weakened and eventually destroyed the ancient Greco-Roman empires.

chapter 5

* * *

The bankruptcy of the United States is probably the Number One objective of World Communism. As of December 31, 1967, the public debt of the United States was $345,947,345,000. On the same date the debt of *all* other nations of the world was $302,128,345,000. Thus our country actually owes $43,819,000,000 more than all the rest of the world combined!

chapter 6

* * *

There are over 500 "sky spies" now circling the earth . . . some of which can photograph in clear detail a man walking along a street —from 100 miles up!

chapter 7

* * *

Above are some of the startling facts you will read in the first 7 chapters of YOUR LAST GOODBYE. But you'll read more! For there are 14 fact-filled challenging chapters that will bring you to the GREATEST DECISION IN YOUR LIFE!

DEDICATION

First, to my wife, Mary, who continually provides encouragement bathed in a foundation of prayer. Without such backing it would have been impossible for me to write YOUR LAST GOODBYE simply, clearly . . . so everyone could understand.

To our children, Dennis, Doreen, Diane, Duane and Dawn, who have accepted Christ as their personal Saviour and Lord . . . and have the abiding assurance of an eternity in Heaven with their parents and with our blessed Lord.

and to

YOU, the READER, that this book will bring you face to face with the greatest decision of your LIFE. My sincere prayer is that when you read the last chapter . . . you might choose LIFE!

YOUR LAST GOODBYE

by Salem Kirban

Each additional printing of YOUR LAST GOODBYE is completely updated with the most recent statistics and current news events that have prophetic significance.

First Printing _____September, 1969
Second Printing _____January, 1971
Third Printing _____May, 1971
Fourth Printing _____January, 1973
Fifth Printing _____October, 1973
Sixth Printing _____February, 1974

Published by SALEM KIRBAN Inc., Kent Road, Huntingdon Valley, Penna. 19006. Copyright © 1969, 1973 by Salem Kirban. Printed in the United States of America. All rights reserved, including the right to reproduce this book or portions thereof in any form.

Library of Congress Catalog Card No. 70-87000

ISBN 0-912582-06-5

ACKNOWLEDGMENTS

The Amplified New Testament, By Permission of The Lockman Foundation.

To Bob Krauss and Bill Goggins, artists, who were able to capture the central theme of God's prophecies of the Millennium and New Heavens and New Earth and graphically portray them in easy-to-read charts.

To Dennis and Eileen Kirban, who quickly typed the original manuscript from reels of dictated tape.

To Dr. Gary Cohen, Professor of Greek and New Testament at Biblical School of Theology, Hatfield, Pennsylvania, who carefully checked the final manuscript to assure its accuracy to the Scriptures.

To U.S. NEWS & WORLD REPORT, NEWSWEEK, TIME, NATIONAL OBSERVER, Beirut DAILY STAR, JERUSALEM POST, FORTUNE and the ILLUS-TRATED LONDON NEWS for providing comprehensive coverage of current news events.

To World Wide Photos, United Press International and many photographers throughout the world who supplied the dramatic photographs that appear in this book.

4

CONTENTS

Why I Wrote This Book

It was the summer of 1938.

We lived in a little country town in Pennsylvania with a very funny name . . . Schultzville . . . in a big, rambling house.

No, we didn't own the house. These were depression days. Work was scarce but I was only a little boy of eleven and the cares of this world didn't seem to affect me.

Although, looking back, I can see where trying to make ends meet was a constant burden to my mother and to my stepfather who would walk miles in the open country from one house to another selling Singer sewing machines.

We were poor. But then so was everyone else. But I never realized it. I felt like the richest person on earth . . . and while home in the country during my summer vacations . . . I was as happy as a lark.

I only came home once a year—every July and August— from Girard College. Girard College is a school for fatherless boys in Philadelphia. It's not really a college but rather an elementary and high school.

My parents were too poor to afford the bus fare for me to come home during the Christmas vacation . . . so I always counted the days till good ole' summer.

I loved Girard College . . . but I also loved my country home. I can remember as a child seeing inscribed in stone on the Chapel in Girard College the words of its founder, Stephen Girard:

> When death comes to me it will find me busy, unless I am asleep. If I thought I was going to die tomorrow, I should nevertheless plant a tree today.

It didn't mean too much to me than . . . but it does now.

And the education and discipline I learned at Girard College prepared me for the world outside . . . a world that constantly reminded me that it did not owe me a living but rather, as an adult, I owed the world a contribution.

It's funny. In those days in the country in Schultzville a penny meant a great deal to me. I can remember my mother swinging back and forth on our old fashion swing on the front yard sewing or shelling peas . . . and my sitting next to her begging for one cent. I didn't realize it at the time but her giving me the penny represented a real sacrifice . . . for in those days when we had nothing . . . a penny was like a $1 bill.

Photo taken in 1938 shows my mother and me in Schultzville, Penna. country home.

Guaranteed wage increases? More pay for less hours of work? Negative Income Tax? School riots?

These things just didn't exist. We were simply thankful we could breathe God's air and enjoy God's handiwork. To us College was a privilege. And if we could meet the standards . . . and they were very choosy in those days with high standards . . . for some odd reason . . . call it patriotism or whatever, we would count it a privilege to be able to go to college. In fact we regarded it as a privilege even to get a job. I can remember when my brother Lafayette graduated from Girard College in 1938 how difficult it was to get any kind of a job.

But we were happy. No air pollution, nor population explosion was ours . . . just good fresh country air, and an artesian well that even in mid-summer was clear and sparkling cold.

Even a little pond and a few chickens were mine, along with my prize garden.

Once in a while we even had hamburger for supper.

This was Heaven.

A dear old couple took an interest in the three Kirban children . . . my sister Elsie, my brother Lafayette and me.

On weekends Mr. and Mrs. Ellison would take us up to Montrose Bible Conference. I can remember sitting in the big tabernacle with the sawdust floor and wooden roof and listening to such greats as Will Houghton as he taught us that chorous "Lead me to some soul today . . . oh teach me Lord just how to pray . . . friends of mine are lost in sin . . . and cannot find their way."

Then there was W. Graham Scroggie from England and Herbert Lockyer and the prophetic messages from David L. Cooper. There was William Ward Ayer and E. Schuyler English.

And can I ever forget Henry Ironsides as he led all of us singing "There shall be showers of blessing" as the rain came down in torrents on the wooden tabernacle roof?

It was here I accepted Christ as my personal Saviour and Lord. This was Heaven to me.

And then there was Prince. How we got him, I don't remember. But he was a lovable collie. And he provided that extra special love that a boy often needs. I remember learning to ride a two-wheeler with Prince running after me. For some reason I didn't learn to steer and my first ride headed me right into the big tree on our front lawn.

I remember Prince and myself playing hide and seek.

And as little boys sometimes do . . . I remember getting mad for some reason. Anyway that day I decided to hide from the family.

About 50 feet from the house was a cornfield and I ran to it and hid among the tall corn.

Came supper time and mom got worried because I didn't show up. The whole family was calling for me . . . but I did not answer.

Then mom, in her wisdom, called Prince and told Prince to find me. In a moment Prince was bounding up the path and stood still right where I was sitting barking his fool head off! I can remember how embarrassed I was . . . and how happy mom was.

Prince was wonderful. And I loved him. This was Heaven!

Then one day about noon I found Prince lying at the kitchen steps. And he couldn't get up. I didn't know it then . . . but he was paralyzed . . . apparently he had eaten some poison. When he saw me he lifted his head and wagged his tail.

And I cried.

He loved my stepfather. And early that evening when my stepfather pulled in the drive with his Model "T" I ran to him and told him about Prince.

He and I walked over to the doorstep. Prince looked up at me and Dad and then with all the strength his body could muster, he wagged his tail . . . and died!

And I cried!

The sky had fallen in for me. My own Prince dead. Why? Sadly, the next day, my sister Elsie, my brother Lafayette and I tenderly carried Prince up to the cornfield near the place where Prince found me . . . we buried him . . . put a homemade wooden cross over the freshly dug grave . . . just as the sun set over the hill.

And then we walked back home.

And secretly for many a day, I would go up to visit Prince

My brother Lafayette playing tennis on our front lawn in Schultzville, Penna. Note Prince, our collie, to left of photo. Taken 1938.

and talk to him . . . but he did not bark . . . no tail wagged . . .
Prince was gone.

It was then I realized the reality of death.

Time has a way of erasing sorrow and I grew up, graduated from Girard College, served in World War II in the U.S.
Navy and began my career of writing and advertising.

One day, my dear wife, Mary and our five children went
on a little outing on a late Sunday afternoon for a picnic.

Coming back home . . . the phone rang . . . it was my sister
Elsie telling me that mom had had a stroke.

I rushed over and followed the ambulance to the hospital.
For two days we took turns standing by her bedside but all of
us knew this vigil was hopeless.

It was late one evening. Just my brother Lafayette and I
were in the private waiting room. I walked into the intensive
care unit where mom lay. I can remember looking at her still
form, breathing only by mechanical assistance. I can remember touching her arm and whispering a prayer: "Oh, God, thou
hast said you will heal the sick. You have said 'Ask and you
shall receive that your joy may be made full' . . . Lord I am
asking . . . raise up my mom."

That night mom died.

And I cried.

And the realities of a life hereafter struck home.

Is there a Heaven? Where do people go when they die?

I thought things on this earth went on forever . . . but now
the realities of life were closing in.

And then, some time later, when I went on a private fact-
finding tour around the world . . . and viewed the silent dead –
young Americans slain in the prime of youth – I realized that
somehow I had to get the message of God's love across.

It was then I wrote GUIDE TO SURVIVAL, the book
that covers in detail the Rapture (when believers are caught
up to meet Christ in the air) and the dreaded Tribulation
Period . . . when Antichrist will cause tragedy to cover the face
of the earth.

But somehow the Lord made me restless . . . as though my
mission was only half complete.

What kind of a writer was I? Should I simply convey the Rapture and the awesomeness of the Tribulation and lose the central message of God's redeeming love – the message that God has prepared for all those who believe in Him a New Heaven and a New Earth?

Of course not . . . I must go on! There was no time to lose. But what could I write about? The Bible has so much to say about the Tribulation Period and not much about Heaven, I thought. How could I ever fill a book.

I told God . . . this is your book . . . you will have to guide the thoughts. Two weeks ago, I sat down at the typewriter . . . and for a solid two weeks God kept my fingers pounding the keys . . . revealing as I studied the Bible truths that to me had previously been hidden. Everything seemed to fall in place automatically. I searched the Scriptures. I found hundreds of occurrences of the word "Heaven" in the Scriptures.

One of the greatest blessings I received was discovering through God's Word that we will know our loved ones in Heaven. What a grand reunion that will be!

And what a comfort it is to me to know that right now my loved ones who have left the night of this world are enjoying the dawn of Heaven with Christ. No intermediate place. For God's Word makes this very clear.

Sad to say, many once firmly-rooted churches and organizations who accepted the Scriptures as the Word of God now think it necessary to compete with the world in its own jargon, in its surface Christianity, in its permissiveness, in its music with a beat . . . in order to bring Christ down to their level to "win" them. How sad!

But listen, dear friend, God doesn't need this crutch. Christ comes with His own glory. Well is it said of Christ in Revelation 5:12

> . . . Worthy is the Lamb that was slain to receive power, and riches, and wisdom, and strength, and honour, and glory and blessing.
>
> *(Revelation 5:12 King James Version)*

But Christ's challenge to us today is not to change Him so

as to make Him more acceptable. No, rather it is to "Preach the Word . . . for the time will come when they will not endure sound doctrine . . ." (*II Timothy 4:2*)

Unfortunately that time has come. And that is why God seeks fearless men and women who still stand true . . . when others are preaching a counterfeit gospel.

Yes, it was Stephen Girard who said, "If I thought I was going to die tomorrow, I should nevertheless plant a tree today."

This book, YOUR LAST GOODBYE, is my Tree.

And in it is the Tree of Life . . . Christ Jesus.

> Blessed is the man that trusteth in the Lord, and whose hope the Lord is.
> For he shall be as a tree planted by the waters. . . .
> Blessed are they that wash their robes [in the blood of Christ through faith], that they may have right to the tree of life. . . .
> *(Jeremiah 17:7,8; Revelation 22:14)*

The prayer of my wife Mary and me is that you might find the Tree of Life, Christ Jesus . . . and by accepting Him in your heart as personal Saviour and Lord . . . join us and our family someday in the Millennial reign with Christ and enter into the New Heaven and New Earth for endless eternity.

If this book, YOUR LAST GOODBYE, accomplishes this . . . it will have been more than worth the effort of this writer.

And to the Christian, may YOUR LAST GOODBYE, give you an even greater insight to your wonderful inheritance that awaits you.

And as we approach the end of this world's night, may we welcome in God's glorious dawn!

Salem Kirban

Huntingdon Valley, Pennsylvania
U.S.A.

April, 1969

Explanation Of Terms Used In This Book

Apocalypse

Apocalypse comes from the identical Greek word, *apokalipsis*, which is *apo*, "from" *kalipsis*, "that which is hidden." Hence it means "Revelation," and it is so used as the first word in the book of the same name, that is, in the Book of *Revelation*, also called, The *Apocalypse* (Revelation 1:1).

Covenant

Covenant is the word for a binding agreement, a treaty, or a pact made with a solemn oath. God in His grace has made certain covenants with mankind. In Genesis 9:8-17 God makes a covenant with man not to destroy the world again by a flood. The rainbow is given as the token of this covenant. In Genesis 17:1-14 God makes a covenant with Abraham to bless him and his seed and to give them Canaan (Palestine). Circumcision was given as the sign of this covenant. The Law given to Moses at Sinai was God's covenant with Israel (Exodus 24:7-8), and the Ark which held the two tablets of the Law was called the Ark of the Covenant (Numbers 10:33). God promised in Jeremiah 31:34 to make a New Covenant with Israel someday. Christ's death was this New Covenant (Testament) sealed with His blood (I Corinthians 11:25).

Day of the Lord

Day of the Lord, DAY OF GOD, DAY OF RETRIBUTION are kindred expressions which denote time periods in which God will be supreme, destroy and judge the wicked, and reward them for their wickedness. Paul in I Thessalonians 5:2 speaks of the Day of the Lord as the coming 7 year awful Tribulation period when God, before the Millennium begins will pour out His wrath on a world which is following the Antichrist. Peter in II Peter 3:10 uses this same expression referring to the final destruction of the earth prior to the formation of the new earth. Jeremiah 46:10, however, uses the expression "the Day of the Lord God of Hosts" to refer to God's destroying Pharaoh Necho's army which took place in 605 B.C.

Eschatology

Eschatology is from the Greek words *eschatos*, "last," and *logos*, "word; knowledge," hence it refers to Knowledge of the Last Things—the study of the prophecies which tell of the future consumation of this world.

Heaven

Heaven refers in the Scriptures to (a) the far off starry heavens, Genesis 1:1; (b) the atmospheric heavens in which the birds fly, Jeremiah 4:25; and to (c) the place wherein God specially manifests His presence, Matthew 6:9. This Third Heaven is where the redeemed have an eternal place prepared for them (2 Corinthians 5:1; John 14:2). Before Christ's resurrection it was sometimes called "Abraham's Bosom" or "Paradise" (Luke 16:22; 23:43). In the New Testament it is especially marked by the fact that here the believer is alive and "present with the Lord" (2 Corinthians 5:8). In the future, after the millennium and after sin is forever done away with, God will make a "New Heaven and a New Earth"

(Revelation 21:1). Upon this New Earth the heavenly New Jerusalem will descend wherein (i.e., on the New Earth and in this New city) the redeemed will dwell throughout all eternity with Christ (Revelation 21 and 22).

Immortality

Immortality is the state of living forever. The Bible indeed makes it clear that human souls are immortal. Man's sin has brought to man spiritual death (separation from God) as well as physical death (separation of the soul from the body); but Christ's substitutionary death on the cross has made forgiveness and true immortality (union forever with God) possible to those who will repent and trust Him. Both those who now die in Christ (believers) and the Old Testament saints have everlasting life; they are conscious today, they are in joy and peace present with Christ awaiting their resurrection bodies (John 11:25-26; Matthew 22:31-32; Luke 16:19-31; 2 Corinthians 5:8; 1 Corinthians 15:35-58). These are immortal in the true sense of the word! Those, however, who die in unbelief are now in hell, the unseen world, awaiting consciously their resurrection, final judgment, and final fate of being sent to dwell in the "Lake of Fire" forever and ever. Here they are not annihilated, for their souls remain alive (Mark 9:48; Revelation 20:10). Hence these "lost souls" are in this sense also immortal. But, since the Lake of Fire involves eternal separation from God, they are spiritually *eternally dead!* Hence the Lake of Fire is rightly given the awful title of "The Second Death" (Revelation 20:10-15)! Thus only the redeemed, the saved, have true immortality—for these are *both* eternally conscious (as are the lost) and eternally with God (which the lost are not).

Millennium

Millennium is from the Latin, *mille*, "thousand," and *annum*, "year." It thus refers to the prophesied coming 1000 year period when Christ shall reign on the earth with a rod of iron (Revelation 20:4; 12:5; etc.). Satan shall be bound at this time and a period of earthly peace shall prevail (Revelation 20:1-10). In the Old Testament this period is described as the period of the Kingdom of Heaven (Daniel 2:44; 7:13-14). Isaiah 11 is the key O.T. passage which tells of the peace and righteousness of this time. Israel shall be restored and converted, and it shall have an honored place in this Millennial Kingdom (Zechariah 8:20-23; Acts 1:6).

Pre-Millennialism

Pre-Millennialism (*pre*, "before," the *mille annum*, "1000 year") advocates that the Second Coming of Christ will occur *before* the *millennium*. In fact, it believes that the 1000 year Kingdom Age of the earth (the *Millennium*) cannot be started until Christ, the King, comes again personally and visibly. Matthew 25:21-34 indeed shows that the Second Coming of Christ is the event which does inaugurate this 1000 year reign of Christ (Revelation 19:11-20:6).

Post-Millennialism

Post-Millennialism (*post*, "after," the *mille annum*, "1000 year") advocates that the Second Coming of Christ will be *after* the Church has led the world into conversion and 1000 years of earthly bliss. This opinion, once popular when it seemed as if the missionary message was going to bring the whole world to Christ, has today been largely abandoned. It is now clear that until Christ comes there will be no 1000 year millennial peace.

Amillennialism

Amillennialism comes from the Greco-Latin, *a*, "no," and *mille-annum*, "thousand year." Thus those who hold to this school of thought say that there will be No *Future* Millennial reign of Christ on the Earth. They say that the prophecies of the millennial kingdom are *not* literal; but rather that they refer figuratively to the happy state of the Church *today*. They understand Satan to be bound *today* "so that he should deceive the nations no more" (Revelation 20:3) (When one compares, however, the state of the nations and the church today with Revelation 20:3 it is difficult to defend the amillennial notion that Satan is today bound "so that he should deceive the nations no more").

Mystery

Mystery (*musterion* in the Greek) is a term used in the New Testament which can only be truly understood in the light of its Greco-Roman usage in the ancient world. There it referred to a secret known only to the *initiated* members of a secret or exclusive group—for example, the "mystery religions" of the time were those with secret oaths, rites, laws, and books. Hence in the New Testament a "mystery" is a truth, plan, or program of God which has been either kept secret in prior ages or which, though hinted at in the Old Testament, is yet too profound for the human mind to fully grasp. To the disciples and believers, the initiated, these are revealed (Matthew 13:11; Luke 8:10; Romans 11:25; I Corinthians 4:1; Ephesians 5:32; 6:19; Colossians 1:26).

Pre-, Mid-, Post-Tribulationist

Pre-, Mid-, Post-Tribulationist is a person who is of the persuasion that the Rapture of the Church (1

Thessalonians 4:13-18) is respectively before (Pre), in the midst of (Mid), or after (Post) the Prophecied Tribulation Period—the final 7 year period when Antichrist rises and reigns (Daniel 9:27; Matthew 24:15,21; etc.). Pre-tribulationists believe that since the Church is said to have been delivered from the "wrath to come" (I Thess. 1:9-10; 5:9; Romans 5:9), it, the Church, therefore must be raptured before the Tribulation Period which is the great day of God's wrath (Revelation 6:17). See Genesis 19:22!

Theocracy

Theocracy from the Greek *Theos*, "God," and *-cracy* "rule." Hence, this term denotes a rule or kingdom where God Himself is both the acknowledged supreme leader and the actual supreme leader. This was the case of Old Testament Israel. There the religious laws were as binding as the civil laws—and indeed there was no real distinction between the two. God was worshipped by the state as well as by the individual. God ruled in actuality by His Law being the law of the land, and by His revealing His will to the nation through the High Priest and through His prophets. The Millennium shall be a world-theocracy, and since the Only True God is righteous, holy, good, kind, and loving, the Millennium shall be the earth's Golden Age.

Chapter 1

The Leaves Must Fall

The Circle of Life • Man's Concept of Heaven • Scientists Play God • Prisoners of This World • This Fleeting Game • The Flying Dollar • Bats Live While Others Die • The Counterfeit Gospel • The Bible Returns to School • The Church's New Foundation

The other day I heard a story about a little child. Her mother was very ill. And standing in the kitchen . . . this little child overheard the doctor tell her daddy, "I'm afraid your wife will be leaving this earth when the leaves begin to fall."

This child loved her mother so dearly. And as she looked out the kitchen window on that cool October day she realized that time was short.

Feverishly she ran outside going to every tree she could find on their spacious lawn. Nightime fell and her daddy got worried . . . not seeing her in the house. He ran out calling for his little daughter. And he found her sobbing under a tree. "Why are you crying, honey?"

"Daddy, I heard the doctors say that mommy would go to heaven when the leaves begin to fall. And I've been hurrying as fast as I could today *tying all the leaves* to the branches on our trees. I love mommy so much . . . I don't want the leaves to fall."

Everyday, as we read the newspapers, we witness the finality of life. For everyday not only do we read of famous persons dying but the obituary columns are filled with names of ju.t plain ordinary folk who have gone on and while they are momentarily remembered, they will soon be forgotten. Everyday from the tree of life in today's world, whether it be the warmth of spring, the sunshine of summer, the golden days of fall, or the bitter winds of winter—the leaves from the tree fall and many many thousands die.

In spite of this, people throughout the world want to ignore death and pretend that it does not exist.

THE CIRCLE OF LIFE

Their whole life and energy is spent in building for them a heaven on earth.

From the moment of birth, the proud parents start saving money so their child can go to college. Then comes the nurturing of the child through grammar school and high school. But then what?

After high school, many young people seek to secure a college education and struggle through four or eight years of learning. After that, what?

After they have secured their training, they enter into their chosen field or profession and spend several initial years building up their business. If they are not in a profession, they begin working for a company and building seniority in that company to assure a promotion and retirement nest egg. After that, what?

After that promotion comes, for which they have sought, they strive to build a retirement fund and to set aside enough money to take care of their needs in old age. At the same time, with children coming along, they strive to supply their children with the things that they did not receive. But after that, what?

After years of working, they feel they have reached the "golden age"—the age that everyone looks forward to—the age of retirement. And so retirement comes. They have achieved a fine standing in their community, have attended church regularly, have sent off to school fine sons and daughters, and now what should be a heaven on earth is just around the corner. But after that, what?

After all of this energy is spent, covering a period of perhaps thirty, forty or fifty years, suddenly all of the wealth means nothing, all of the security means nothing, the home, the 20-year mortgage which they finished paying for, means nothing. For suddenly, the world closes round them and the leaves begin to fall. And after that, what?

That's what this book hopes to answer for you.

In my travels throughout the United States and throughout the world. I have seen businessmen feverishly working day and night with their god being the almighty dollar. I have seen them worship this dollar to the point where they have neglected their family, have neglected their dedication to God and in reaching for their supposed ladder of success, have stepped on every other individual who got in their way. For what? For a temporary exposure to the limelight of what the world calls success?

Is all of the struggle and all of this effort for one brief moment in the sun worth the throwing away of an eternity in heaven? What is heaven? Is there such a thing as a real heaven? These questions and many more will be answered in this book . . . YOUR LAST GOODBYE.

MAN'S CONCEPT OF HEAVEN

But for the moment, let us look at some of the plans that man sets forth in order to build his own heaven on earth. It is a heaven without foundation, one that is built on moral decay, and one which will be evidenced by a crumbling away in a few short years. For physical life on this earth is not eternal. It is a temporal thing. And yet so much energy and so much dedication is directed towards attempting to make life on earth a permanent heavenly place.

To some, heaven is financial security and by 1980 it is estimated that more than half the households in the United States will have incomes of more than $10,000 a year. It will be a time when the gross national product of the United States will approach an incredible $2 trillion compared with the present $900 billion.

The greed to make more money is even evident in the type of reading material that reaches the public these days.

The moral decay that is sweeping across the United States because of the laxity of favorable decisions by the Supreme Court has affected every avenue of thinking in this country.

This is a time when book publishers no longer exercise moral restraint or wise judgment before they publish a book.

In many cases, the book publishers are seeking the books with the most lurid sex content – for they realize that books of this nature will sell fast and return to them a handsome profit. Typical of this is the book, *Portnoy's Complaints.*

In less than two months after publication, it had sold 450,000 hard back copies at $6.95 each.

The publisher stated that they never had a book that sold so well, so quickly.

This was not a book that had subtle sex, but in the opinion of Christians, a book which violates public decency.

The sad fact is that this book is bought by people of all income brackets. A conservative book store in Boston sold 200 copies within a very short time to their clientele which is made up primarily of wealthy residents and financial-district businessmen.

One book seller in California stated, "The nicest people come in and ask for this book. People aren't embarrassed to ask for it. Five years ago they would have been, but not today."

This preoccupation with sex reflects the moral condition of our country . . . and the moral leadership of those who allow such things to get in print.

Even women's magazines are taking up the sex trend. *Cosmopolitan's* July, 1969 issue cover lines are:

38 Men Tell A Nice Girl Like You What Turns Them On.
What It's Like to Have a Latin Lover.

Girls and Their Married Men.
I Was Raped!

While the July, 1969 issue of *Mademoiselle* sports on its cover:

Sex: The New Status Symbol . . . What, Why, and Where is Sexy . . . plus a Supersensuous Romantic Novel by Coleete!

A women's magazine editor commented: "We carry sex in every issue. Sex happens to be an important ingredient of life . . . we are trying to produce a magazine that reflects the changes in attitude of young women today."

Troubled by unwanted pregnancies, *Wall Street Journal* reports that an increasing number of women are bringing their problem to a group of ministers who have begun a Consultation Service on Abortion.

In 1968 some 350,000 women were hospitalized in the U.S. after illegal abortions (about 8000 of them died). New York City alone spends about $2.7 million annually for public hospital care after botched abortions by quacks who use coat hangers, kitchen knives, castor oil or gasoline.

This is another reflection on the troubled times we face in today's world.

Christ spoke of an end-time world with chaotic conditions, and today's moral climate heralds the coming of such times. The Lord said,

When these things begin to come to pass, then look up, and lift your heads; for your redemption draweth nigh.
(*Luke 21:28*)

Thus as the world becomes chaotic with wars, famines, lawlessness, unbelief, and *deteriorating morals*, it is a sign that the end is fast approaching.

Many people, of course, are still striving to make this earth a heaven. Even the post office has its problems. It appears that very shortly, even the zip code may be extended by 10 more numbers because of the complexity of the growth of our nation. This complexity even shows in the luxuries which America has taken for granted. This year as some 10 million gleaming new automobiles hit the nation's highways, 7 million vintage models will give their last gasp and limp to the side of the road.

With the drastic drop in scrap metal prices over the last decade, it is becoming a problem on how to get rid of these old cars. Millions of them dot the American landscape. The old car plague has even struck the cities. In New York City, where some 35,500 hulks were left on the streets last year, even the efforts of private contractors and the Sanitation Department could not stem this tide.

In Chicago last year 83,000 automobiles were abandoned and this rate is rising annually by an additional 4,000. At this moment, more than 45 million wrecks are stacked sky-high in junk yards strung across the country. Driving from San Francisco to Fresno, California you can count 29 junk yards!

While this may appear to be a humorous problem, this is typical of the many problems that are being created by modern technological advances. These advances in themselves are a blessing, but the accompanying problems that result become a curse.

Those who would strive to make heaven here on earth find that they are bucking insurmountable problems.

SCIENTISTS PLAY GOD

We have come, however, to the point where many scientists feel they have the right to play God. In a recent article in a national magazine, one scientist wrote,

> Just what do we mean by the word God? In Christian mythology, as represented by the Bible, God is credited with a variety of functions. He is the creator . . . He is the law-giver . . . He is the judge who punishes sinners even when human law fails to do so. He is also a kind of trickster who intervenes in human affairs in a quite arbitrary way so as to test the faith of the righteous; and finally, He is a mediator between sinful man and his destiny.
>
> But such beliefs are justified by faith alone, never by reason, and the true believer is expected to go on reaffirming his faith in the same verbal formula, even if the passage of

Newsweek—James D. Wilson

As some 10 million gleaming new automobiles hit the nation's highways, 7 million vintage models gasp their last and limp to the side of the road. In New York City alone in 1972, 35,500 cars were junked on city streets. "Fields of amber grain" are cluttered with the trash of a nation. Driving from San Francisco to Fresno you can count 29 junk yards.

history and the growth of scientific knowledge should have turned the words into plain nonsense.

We can fly through the air, we can look in on events that are taking place on the other side of the earth, we can transplant organs from corpses to living bodies, we can change one element into another, we can even produce a chemical mimicry of living tissue itself.

The scientist can now play God in his role as wonderworker. We ourselves have to decide what is sin and what is virtue, and we must do so on the basis of our modern knowledge and not on the basis of traditional categories. But unless we teach those of the next generation that they can afford to be atheists only if they assume the moral responsibilities of God, the prospects for the human race are decidedly bleak.

This is a quotation, sadly enough, from a well-known scientist.

Man has failed to make the earth more livable, more permanent, or more peaceful—despite all the modern advances of science and technology. And it is the kind of thinking quoted above which is permeating not only America but the world, saying that man has the ability to do everything. Recent advances in space will make man more sure of himself in being able to conquer not only this world but the universe—and this will be his downfall.

Earth is only a small planet in God's great universe and each day 40,000 tons of meteors and other natural bodies from space enter the earth's atmosphere. Except for the providence of God, these could destroy the earth. But God has created a friction system by means of the air in the earth's atmosphere which burns up most of the daily onslaught of rocks. Those that finally do reach the ground are mostly the size of pebbles or grains of sand.

Providence? Yes! Because this is not true of Mars which has relatively little atmosphere to protect it, and hence much larger meteors crash into that planet and create havoc with it.

PRISONERS OF THIS WORLD

Russia is credited with the largest prison in the world—Kharkov Prison, which at times has accommodated 40,000 prisoners. But what many people don't realize is that as human beings we are prisoners in this world. Born in this world we must confront the problems of the world and live with these problems temporarily at least—for there is no escape outside of death.

This is a world that in spite of its miraculous TV dinners, minute car washes and color television sets, is frought with problems that the ordinary individual would like to forget or ignore. Once in a while the newspapers bring the dramatic facts to life, but only briefly for a moment.

For in this world, the United States must live with its neighbors and vice versa. And this heaven here on earth makes this quite an impossible task for even the most dedicated of presidents.

Several years ago John F. Kennedy, then a senator, estimated that the world's nuclear stockpile represented a mountain of thirty billion tons of TNT—or enough to favor every
human being with 10 tons of TNT! This amount, however,
has grown by billions of tons since then!

Can this be heaven?

The exact size of the United States' nuclear stockpile remains a secret but it can be estimated that it numbers somewhere between 50,000 and 100,000 bombs and warheads. By
the end of 1972 Russia took the lead in Intercontinental Ballistic
Missiles (ICBM's) with 1550 — virtually all equipped with much
heavier warheads than the U.S.

There are at least 1,000 Minutemen missile launchers
buried in the western prairies of the United States. There are
over 40 Polaris submarines carrying 656 hydrogen warheads
and there are 600 long-range bombers, each capable of in-
cinerating the largest city on earth. And yet, sadly enough,
there are many church-going people who believe the world
is getting better and better and that these days are no more
perilous than the days when Christ was born or even the days
of just 10 years ago.

Somehow, they want to bury their head in the sand and
ignore the signs of the time that point to the soon return of our
Lord Jesus Christ.

> And He spake to them a parable; Behold the fig tree,
> and all the trees;
> When they now shoot forth, ye see and know of your own
> selves that summer is now nigh at hand.
> So likewise ye, when ye see these things come to pass,
> know ye that the kingdom of God is nigh at hand.
> (*Luke 21:29-31 King James Version*)

With the noise of war going around, is it no wonder that
Elizabeth Chapman telephoned California from Carhampton,
England and barely spoke a word. Instead she held the phone
outside the door of her home in England and explained to
a visiting reporter, "My sister is 85 years old and her one wish
was to hear the village church bells again." Miss Chapman's
sister, who then lived in Sacramento, California, 6,000 miles

away from the English village where she was born, once again wanted to hear the bells of that old familiar church. And so it was that Mrs. Chapman invested $12.24 to relay the chimes from England across the Atlantic.

THIS FLEETING FAME

Fame has a way of fleeting very fast. This was no more evident than when one day in New York a movie star made a reservation at a luxury hotel. At 5 pm he phoned the hotel to be sure the suite's current occupants would be out by 6 pm.

The hotel manager then called the suite and explained to the occupant how important it was for the suite to be ready for this movie star. "We understand," the man told the manager, "We'll be out in half an hour."

35 minutes later, the manager went upstairs to make sure that all was in order. He walked in and found Lyndon B. Johnson putting on his coat.

"It's quite all right," said the former President, "we're just leaving. . . ."

THE FLYING DOLLAR

No one of course, wants to live in the past. In the early 20's, Americans who were living in Europe woke up in 1922 and found their money was only worth half as much as when they had gone to bed. In fact, they had to tear their bank notes in two because only the half that carried the King's picture was worth anything.

In the Germany of 1923, an American dollar could buy more than 4 trillion marks.

Today we find more and more people putting faith into riches, and in spite of the inflationary dollar, they are striving for a heaven here on earth.

One writer observed that men who do not believe in God have few, if any moral ideals upon which to erect a moral law, and that the decline of the West will arise straight out of its loss of faith in God.

Here in the United States we have men more interested in crime, sexual abuse, power, riches and fame, instead of realizing that these things are temporary and will soon fade away.

This is an age when people are looking for something free and the United States government is having problems meeting all of the requests of its people.

When the Antipoverty Action Committee found itself loaded down with 26,000 gallons of battleship grey paint which it had no use for, an announcement was made in the newspaper that the paint in 5-gallon cans—each weighing 52 pounds—would be available for free distribution.

After waiting 2 hours in line, a crowd rushed the doors of the Philadelphia city warehouse. A line, estimated at about 3,000 people, at first patiently waited to get their free paint, but the situation in time became so chaotic that 30 extra policemen were called to reinforce the 12 already on duty to maintain order. How paradoxical it is that people will stand in line and endure all hardships to get something free and yet, won't accept an eternity in heaven which requires simply a sincere repentance of sin and a belief in the Lord Jesus Christ!

> For whosoever shall call upon the name of the Lord shall be saved.
>
> *(Romans 10:13 King James Version)*

Christ said, "I am the way" *(John 14:6)* and yet people want to build their own avenue to heaven.

BATS LIVE WHILE OTHERS DIE

The world is filled with paradoxes.

The Earl of Cranbrook feeds his pet bats on a special mixture of egg yolk, cream cheese and banana. A well known governor, finding that he was getting on badly with his mongrel, put himself and the dog through a $250 course of psychotherapy at a Beverly Hills canine farm. And another dog, a great Dane, came to its owner's wedding in top hat and tails.

Then there is the New York City dog whose owner listed him in the phone book, "In case his friends wanted to telephone him." And there is the case of a pair of Saint Bernards that followed their master everywhere—in their own chauffeured station wagon.

In a recent book on pets, called *Pets and Their People in the Western World*, the author reveals that some owners take their pet alligators for drives, buy hairpieces for dogs and lace-trimmed nightgowns for cats, give the puma a pint of beer as a nightcap, and buy unnecessary gourmet food. In fact, some owners bury their canaries and pooches under massive marble tombstones in special cemeteries.

And while this lavishness goes on for pets—largely ignored, millions of Americans are hungry and sick in poverty pockets across the nation. In one state where 177 children were examined, 98 were infested with intestinal worms which sometimes grew to a foot in length. And many of these children received only 800 calories a day.

The United States already helps some 15 million of the needy with free surplus food allotments. But studies already in hand suggest that perhaps 10 million persons may be afflicted by malnutrition throughout the United States.

And while 10,000 people die of starvation every day throughout the world, the rats never go hungry in Deshnoukh, India. Food is scarce in this desert town, but the rats in this desert state face no food problem. They are considered to be holy creatures, and they are fed by faithful worshipers. The rodent population of this area is said to outnumber the human population: 25 million rats to 20.1 million people!

A Temple in this Indian village serves as the rat sanctuary. They are fed an average of 250 pounds of grain a day. One elderly priest in the temple warned: "If you should kill a rat here, you will be required to present the temple with a statue of a rat cast in gold or the equivalent in cash."

The priest then added: "This worshiping of the rats goes on day in, day out. They are not ordinary rats. These rats are the divine mounts of the holy Ganesh."

Ganesh is the god of prosperity!

Even prosperous America in this advanced 20th Century still has millions of Americans across the nation who are hungry and sick. Mrs. Annie Chaplin, 82, of South Carolina pumps water for her three-room shack while awaiting a new relief program that will give her free food stamps.

As distasteful as this may seem to Americans — that someone starving would worship a rat as god — this is no more distasteful than the idea that people living in the lap of luxury in the United States should worship a temporal security through their own abilities while neglecting a salvation that could provide for them an eternal life.

THE COUNTERFEIT GOSPEL

While the town's people of Deshnoukh, India worship the rat as their god, many Americans worship the dollar as theirs.

The people are not fully to blame. If their leaders preach a false religion and guide them in ways not scriptural, what can be expected?

Many of the churches today are preaching a materialistic religion . . . one that ignores the fact that Christ is coming again — one that ignores the fact that there is such a thing as a real heaven and a real hell.

Many church leaders, seeking to unify their denominations into one body, are striving to build a heaven on earth. They reject the Second Coming of Christ and the Rapture as simply a storybook allegory found in the Scriptures. Through this leadership they inadvertently help support the official communist view which states:

> The struggle against the Gospel and Christian legend must be conducted ruthlessly and with all the means at the disposal of Communism.

One well-known theologian, invited to speak to an audience of some 4,000 people in Nashville, Tennessee, recently commented that he was "sorry for laymen who are caught between the idea that these may be the last days of the world."

He continued: "I don't believe this is the end of the world. I think the pains of this era are the pangs of a better world."

Unfortunately there are many people throughout America who agree with this statement and many churches, which were once very sound and evangelical, have embraced this position that the world will get better and better and that heaven will soon be here on earth.

One leading churchman said recently that the new theologians seriously doubt that the Bible holds the answers to many modern problems. He went on to explain, "Perhaps, theologically speaking, the Bible is just as dated as anything else. It is first century theology."

This leading churchman went on to predict that the new theology would bring Christians and Jews closer together with less reliance on the Bible and more reliance on man's own abilities to meet today's problems head-on.

A Methodist church conducted a rock and roll mass recently. The "rock" was in the form of a musical combo consisting of guitar, bass drums and organ. The "roll" was a hot dog roll, which with Coca Cola, was used for communion emblems. The Mass was celebrated in the psychedelic room of the church which was painted and decorated with appropriate pictures, posters, and signs!

There appears to be a trend among many Christian groups to pattern their music after the worldly "beat."

At some evangelistic crusades "Christian rock" music and psychedelic lights are used to lure the youth to Christ. In 1972 the Salvation Army's Eastern Territory employed a 13-member teen-age rock band. Ray Steadman-Allen, Head of the Army's International Music Department supports this trend. "Rock is another gimmick...," he said.

Is the Word of God so weak that it needs such crutches? Of course not!

Is it no wonder that a sociologist predicted that religion is on the way out. Christ, concerning this type of latter-day church, well said:

> So then because thou are lukewarm, and neither cold nor hot, I will spue thee out of my mouth.
> (*Revelation 3:16 King James Version*)

Professor Thomas Luckmann of the University of Frankfurt said, "I suggest we live in a period of transition in which a particular social form of religion, institutional specialization, is on the wane." Professor Luckmann was speaking at a symposium on atheism sponsored by the Vatican and the University of California at Berkeley. This was a five-day meeting on "The Culture of the Unbelief."

While the Soviet Communists were angry because some

card-carrying party members are still going to church, in the United States many churches are likewise swinging in the opposite direction.

In one Pennsylvania town a Lutheran church is re-scheduling its services to accommodate the weekend vaca-tioner.

Evening services will be held on Thursdays to "meet the needs of the mobile congregation."

The Pastor decided on the 8 PM Thursday service because he felt the Sabbath need not be any one specific day.

The Thursday evening service will be about 40 minutes, compared to the 60 minutes on Sunday. Traditional as well as contemporary forms of worship are planned.

Easter was celebrated at St. Timothy's Episcopal Church in Chicago by a multi-media Mass with folk-rock music, dancers in the aisles, and psychedelic slides sweeping across the walls and the ceiling. The Easter Sunday service had no name but the pastor stated the theme was "Jesus Christ is busting out."

While in Radio City Music Hall, a program of acrobats and leggy high-kicking dancers perform a simulated Cathedral sequence in which nuns with head dresses shaped like elon-gated goat horns, glide in a procession until they form, at the close, a lily-laden human cross.

In the 11 million Southern Baptist denomination some Southern Baptist professors are up in arms over President W.A. Criswell's book, "Why I Preach That the Bible is Literally True."

Protesting this book, one professor stated:

> We have students here who just aren't going to pay lip service to the narrow orthodoxy of the past. The time is now or maybe never for Southern Baptists to enter the main-stream of theological discussion.

The Roman Catholic Church is feeling the pangs of rebel-lion within its ranks. In a Good Friday message, Pope Paul VI twice scolded rebellious Catholics. The church, he com-plained "suffers, above all, from the restless, critical, indocile and destructive rebellion of so many of our children . . . against

Pope Paul VI bows his head in prayer in Ecumenical Center at Geneva with (from left) M.M. Thomas, of the Indian Church; the Rev. Eugene Carson Blake, secretary general of World Council of Churches; and Pauline Mary Webb, a Methodist from the United Kingdom. This historic photo taken June 10, 1969 in Switzerland reveals another step toward a One World Church.

her institutional existence, her canon law, her tradition . . . and also against her authority."

He continued to state: "She suffers from the defection and the scandel of certain ecclesiastics and religious [persons] who are crucifying the church today."

Rome, known by some as the Eternal City, keeps in its

Vatican some 900 relics festooned with gold and jewels. Most Romans are willing to let old bones lie. But in the past month, the remains of 3 Saints have been stolen and this has the police disturbed.

In recent decades, the church has shied away from using the remains of Saints as relics, because it has been difficult to prevent such relics from being used as idols.

In 1949, for example, the severed right forearm of St. Francis Xavier was sent on tour so that Catholics from Japan to Ireland could view the famous relic. This exposition became so popular that only a last minute intervention by the Vatican in 1965 kept it from going on display at a New Jersey department store.

In this day and age when the world is getting restless and no longer accepts orthodox religion, there is a trend towards new forms of religion cropping up.

Many churches are conducting what they term "underground" services.

In San Francisco's Grace Cathedral, Episcopalians played host recently to other faiths in a 90-minute service that offered jazz, contemporary dancing, and a scriptural recitation.

In New York City, the Catholic archdiocese has inaugurated home masses in about 100 parishes.

Today there are an estimated 2,000 or more "underground" groups meeting regularly and many of these are interfaith.

U.S. News and World Report recently stated that

> Among Catholics, there is bewilderment over the exodus of priests opposed to papal teaching on birth control and priestly celibacy.
> Among Protestants, radical theologies are causing many to wonder whether religion any longer has a worthwhile mission of its own to the world at large.

Recently at St. Clement's Episcopal Church in New York, blindfolded and barefooted communicants were guided up and down flights of stairs, tossed bodily in the air and then they crawled on hands and knees over bread crumbs to simulate "humbler access" to the Lord's Supper.

U.S. News and World Report stated that they were

"guided downstairs;" were admitted individually into the bathroom where blindfolds were removed. A smiling confessor, draped in toilet paper, flushed away their sins in a symbolic "declamation of absolution!"

Also, unorthodox, was the Unitarian church in Shorewood Hills, Wisconsin which recently presented an off-Broadway play, "Paradise Now," in which there was a good deal of swearing, spitting and a "flesh pile" of nudes symbolizing the "sexual revolution." Audience participation was invited, and seven in the church — five men and two women — responded by disrobing.

And while thousands have gone into this direction, there are others that are placing a major emphasis on only one theme, namely, faith healing.

In fact, faith healing has at times become a big business in America. It is, however, true that there are sincere Christian evangelists and pastors who believe themselves to be following the Word of God in their ministry of winning souls . . . who also emphasize the Biblical promise of God with respect to healing (James 5:15).

And their ministry is being done an injustice by those faith healers who see in it simply an excellent way to earn income.

One faith healer works up his audience with what is termed "gospel rock," which is aided by organ, drum and piano combo. Last year, this faith healer evangelist grossed over $2½ million. Headquartered in over 1,000 acres of land, which this organization owns, they print and mail out more than 55 million pieces of literature every year and appear in both radio and television broadcasts.

In another area it should be noted that while people are turning away from Christianity, there is a significant trend towards other religions which have a form of godliness but deny the power thereof (II Timothy 3:5). Is it no wonder that the spiritual condition of America is in a tragic state!

How can an individual strive to follow the Word of God when many leaders take all types of devious means to build their own little religious worlds which have only outward form, but leave the heart within empty.

The one answer to this dilemma, the only answer is found in the Scriptures. Yet the Supreme Court decision which banned prayer and Bible reading in schools, was, perhaps the last barrier between Christ and chaos. We are now reaping chaos across this nation because we have eliminated Christ from area after area of life.

THE BIBLE RETURNS TO SCHOOL

No wonder it was refreshing to read that at 9 o'clock each weekday morning Miss Donna Pomella opens a Bible and quietly reads a passage to her first-grade class at Fifth Street Elementary School in Clairton, Pennsylvania. Then, after the children have risen and bowed their heads, she leads the class in the Lord's Prayer.

Actually this is Scripture being bootlegged into the public schools of the Monongahela Valley, in direct defiance of the U.S. Supreme Court. It has been reported that there is a special excitement to the revival of classroom devotion for the people of Clairton, for after six years of obedience, they are performing knowingly an illegal act. But the classroom scene here is being repeated inconspicuously in countless other communities, whose school boards have simply ignored the mandate of the Court (compare Acts 4:19 and 5:29 with this).

One school official commented, "It's illegal, but they can't put us in jail."

This school board's action may be the opening wedge of a wider revolt against the U.S. Supreme Court's 1962 and 1963 decisions that laws declaring that even voluntary prayers in public schools are unconstitutional. It is interesting to note that up to 50% of private schools in the South still have prayers in the classroom.

One 27 year old lawyer in southeastern Pennsylvania summed it up by saying, "They have been saying that ever since we took God out of our schools, our schools have gone to hell."

Mrs. Jessie Clark reads from Bible to her first-graders at D. Ferd Swaney Elementary School, six miles south of Uniontown, Pennsylvania. Despite a Supreme Court ruling, other schools have also resumed Bible reading and prayer.

Meanwhile, the Pittsburgh office of the American Civil Liberties Union, seeking to locate a local plaintiff to file what it regards as "an open-and-shut lawsuit" to end Clairton's defiance, has only recently been able to recruit a litigant there.

Robert Lafrankie, Superintendent of Schools in Clairton, Pennsylvania, says the root issue is: "Do we have the right to recognize God if we decide to do so?" And it is his view that the matter must be resolved in a better way than the Supreme Court has done.

It is heartwarming to know that there are still citizens who, though without religious leadership, have a deep desire to get back to honoring God publicly—this is true despite the fact that many professional religious leaders are directing their constituents down the paths that will lead to an eternity in hell.

It is odd that the Supreme Court will not ban pornography because it cannot define obscenity and yet it will ban God from public schools because apparently, everyone knows who God is.

Also arising is an insidious approach by a national organization which is seeking to teach sex know-how in public schools, while at the same time advocating a moral relativism. The permissiveness that such a sex course will inculate into young minds can only lead to disaster for tomorrow's generation.

THE CHURCH'S NEW FOUNDATION

In fact, it was only a short time ago that the United Methodist Church voted to drop a long standing requirement that its ministers vow to refrain from drinking and smoking (would that this were their worst offense!). Church is becoming more and more a business establishment rather than an avenue for reaching people for Christ.

Nino Lo Bello recently exposed to the light the financial empire of the Vatican in his book titled "The Vatican Empire." The securities it holds are conservatively estimated at $5.6 billion. In fact, the visible assets of American churches are nearly $80 billion—better than twice the worth of the top five business corporations in the nation. One evangelical church in the midwest owns a controlling interest in an apartment building, an electronics firm, a shopping center, and a plastics company.

In fact, this particular group once owned the Real Firm Girdle Company. The pastor commented "there is nothing unusual about our owning business firms. All churches do. What difference does it make if it's a girdle company or an airplane company?"

Dr. Carl McIntire in his publication *Christian Beacon* recently reported on a 96-page Sunday school publication for Methodist youth . . . an official publication of the United Methodist Church.

Entitled *New Creation* it is directed toward young people 14, 15 and 16 years of age.

McIntire commented: "Never in all my years of dealing with modernism and exposing apostasy in present-day churches has there been produced a document which openly offers an entirely different brand of Christianity. It could never be called Christianity. The entire New Testament is described as a myth; 'Myth & the new testament' heads a chapter in which it is openly confessed that no longer has the New Testament or any part of the Bible any real historical value. . . ."

This Sunday school publication implies that (a) the Bible is not infallible, (b) Christ is not the second person of the Trinity, (c) He was never born of a virgin and (d) the infancy narratives of Matthew and Luke describing the birth of Christ are legends.

Is it no wonder the spiritual climate of America today is such as it is! How can it be any better when its spiritual leadership has counterfeited its calling and placed materialism above Christ and His soul saving message. Christ well said:

> But woe unto you, scribes and Pharisees, hypocrites! for ye shut up the kingdom of heaven against men: for ye neither go in yourselves, neither suffer ye them that are entering to go in.
> Woe unto you, scribes and Pharisees, hypocrites! for ye are like whited sepulchres, which indeed appear beautiful outward, but are within full of dead men's bones, and of all uncleanness.
>
> *(Matthew 23:13,27 King James Version)*

The leaves of religious leadership and of national character are falling, and all around us is a nation of people who are putting more faith and hope and trust in their own personal abilities and postponing the decision that will lead them to heaven or condemn them to hell.

Chapter 2

Too Expensive to Live . . .
Too Expensive to Die

Riots and Ruin • This Dying Air • Trash Rockets to the Sun •
Cost of Hospital Care Rising • To Never Grow Old • Harvest-
ing the Body • Head Transplants Next? • The Deep Freeze •
The Leaves Must Fall

With the modern advances of science, the new miracles
of medicine, the higher income of millions . . . one would expect to find this a world of heaven.

But instead life's cruel utopia (heaven on earth)[1] finds a
growing number of inequities that sometimes make it too
expensive to live and too expensive to die.

RIOTS AND RUIN

The cities are finding it particularly difficult to provide a
heaven on earth for its population. In fact, cities all across the

---

[1] UTOPIA today means "heaven on Earth," but its Greek origin
carries with it an amusing but highly profitable lesson. UTOPIA
comes from two Greek words, *OU*, meaning, "no," and *topos*, "place."
Hence UTOPIA literally means "no place," and that is the point of
the early chapters of this book—that is, Heaven is found *no place* on
this earth!

United States are beefing up their police forces, trying out new weapons and drawing battle plans for the riot season that now comes each year. The Army has even earmarked seven task forces totaling 15,000 men for riot duty and has stock-piled equipment in strategically located depots throughout the United States.

Today, sales of riot-control equipment are booming and experiments with new weapons are under way in many cities. One new device is a machine that dispenses masses of bub-bles that can flood a street and make it impossible for an in-dividual to stand up and difficult for him to breathe. Yet the brochure describes it as physically harmless.

Another device coats streets with a slippery substance which is known as "instant banana peel."

A new gun is being tested for Vietnam warfare as well as for American riots—it is said to shoot through brick walls.

Tank-type vehicles are being developed for police use. Shields and helmets are coming into use to protect police against bricks and bottles hurled by rioters.

In 1968 the Detroit Common Council approved a 7 million dollar request for building up the police and fire departments, with more than $1 million of this earmarked for equipment such as machine guns, rifles, ammunition, gas masks, and grenades.

Between 1960 and 1970 the crime rate rose 144%. A Presidential commission calculated that in a given year each American has one chance in 36 of becoming a victim of crime, one chance in 3,000 of being mauled badly enough to need hospital care, one chance in 20,000 of being murdered.

A Washington working girl was a victim four times in eighteen months. Her assaults consisted of a wallet thief, a purse-snatching, a burglary and street holdup during which "people sat on their front porches watching."

In Brooklyn, one mother and her eight children have to race the thieves for the $569 in welfare checks that keeps them going through the month. When a check arrives in the mailbox, it has to be retrieved before the thugs simply yank the mailbox off the wall and take it away. This individual has commented that she has bought four new mailboxes in the past year.

In 1972 survival alone was a challenge in New York City! New York hires a third of a million people to fight its fires, patrol its streets, teach its children, run its subways, drive its taxis, and pick up its trash. It has over 1 million youngsters in school and over 1 million people on relief.

In fact, some 3 million outsiders enter the city every weekday morning but sleep somewhere else at night.

In the U.S., FBI Reports Show—

Every 30 minutes. . . . **A murder**
Every 12 minutes. . . . **A forcible rape**
Every 1 1/2 minutes . **A robbery**
Every 1 1/2 minutes . **An aggravated assault**
Every minute . . . . **12 serious crimes, including a violent crime**
Every 32 seconds . . . **An auto theft**
Every 17 seconds . . . **A larceny**
Every 14 seconds . . . **A burglary**

Police solved about 20% of all crimes in 1970. In 1960 they solved over 31%.

In a recent poll, where 45,000 persons were interviewed, 78% said they feel unsafe even in their own homes!

Source: Federal Bureau of Investigation
Copyright © 1972 Salem Kirban, Inc.

One city official commented that air pollution is so bad that New York would die if it had the confining weather of Los Angeles. And water pollution is so bad that even the ocean beaches often close.

In February of 1968, the trashmen went on strike and 10,000 tons of refuse piled up.

A Hong Kong flu epidemic hit the city and at the same time the fuel oil delivery men struck, and the result was that some 400,000 New Yorkers were left in unheated apartments at a crucial time.

New York City's problems today will become the problems of other cities tomorrow as they grow and become more complex in their structure. For one out of every 8 people in New York City's 8 million is "on welfare." And these relief rolls are swelling by 20,000 people a month.

In fact, taxpayers in New York City are now paying a tax that has been doubled in the last 10 years. The city's expense budget for the year ahead will be close to 10 billion dollars or 3 billion dollars more than it was in January of 1969. And on top of all this, the crime problem keeps worsening.

The rate of reported crime in 1972 was 21.8% higher than that of 1971. Street terrorism showed a sharper rise—robberies were up 50%.

The cities are actually waging a battle for survival. One Harvard professor noted that, "The serious problems of the city are largely insolvable now and will be for the foreseeable future."

In fact, over 25% of the budget in Philadelphia goes to fight crime. Philadelphians are spending $100 million a year to fight crime in the city, while another $92.5 million a year at the state level is being spent for police protection, courts, correctional institutions, and the rehabilitation of criminals.

THIS DYING AIR

In the cities across the nation, the greatest percentage of funds is spent for police protection. Coupled with this plague of crime, our cities are giving us an inheritance of air pollution. A peculiar product of our civilization and of our carelessness, it is simply human litter. It is heaved into the atmosphere by all of us—from automobile tail pipes, from incinerator stacks, and from power stations and home chimneys. Last year over 143 million tons of such chemical-combustion waste went up and fell right back down on Beautiful America. And there will be more next year. The debris of pollution costs us an estimated $11 billion a year in property damage, and it contributes to the illnesses and deaths of many. Yet surprisingly, practically nothing is being done to stop it.

A recent Public Health Service study showed that air pollution is actually cutting down on the amount of sunlight reaching us on the earth. New York, for example, loses almost 25% of its light to smoke and smog, while Chicago loses about 40%. Industry, as a whole, has now generally agreed to cooperate in solving the problem of air pollution. The National Center for Air Pollution in Washington, D.C., however estimates that even if every industry in the country agreed to cooperate, it would still take 10 years and $2.5 billion more than is now being spent to do the job adequately.

Nevertheless, while in Los Angeles industry accounts for 10% of the bad air—the other 90% comes from that city's four million automobiles.

A recent report on this situation by Look Magazine stated that "Even if stationary sources across the U.S. were to stop polluting immediately, our air would still contain some 150 million tons of contaminants by the end of 1973—all from tailpipes, crankcases, carburetors and fuel tank evaporation."

There are over 90 million motor vehicles on the road today and every year 2.8 million are added, a growth rate three times greater than that of the nation's annual population increase.

You may recall reading in Genesis 19:24-25

> Then the Lord rained upon Sodom and upon Gomorrah brimstone and fire from the Lord out of heaven;
> And he overthrew those cities, and all the plain, and all the inhabitants of the cities, and that which grew upon the ground.

The Book of Genesis called it brimstone; modern chemistry books call it sulphur.

But by any name, it can mean death from the skies.

Sulphur is one of the most pervasive, controversial and costly forms of filth in the city air.

It damages human health as well as plant and animal life.

Death rates from some types of cancer and from heart ailments have been specifically linked to sulphur in the air.

More than 30 million tons of sulphur oxides pour into United States skies every year. Their distribution is grossly uneven. Almost one million tons rise over the Philadelphia metropolitan area, and New York City is twice as badly fumigated.

Asbestos particles are also becoming a major hazard in air pollution, so serious in fact that Drs. Irving Selikoff and E. Cuyler Hammond say this may be a major cause of lung cancer in the future. Up to 50% of people living in large cities were found to have asbestos particles in their lungs. It has also been reported by physicians that air pollution may cause stomach cancer. Death rates from stomach cancer are twice as high in areas where a great amount of "suspended particulate material" is found . . . that is, polluted air.

TRASH ROCKETS TO THE SUN

And along with these problems, we have the problem of trash — trash piling up. To burn it or bury it is no longer enough. Some people have suggested rocketing it to the sun!

The nation will dispose of some 350 million tons of industrial and residential trash this year.

The United States Public Health Service estimates that the average American disposes of 5.3 pounds of household trash each day, compared to 2.7 pounds in 1920.

The nation's annual bill for collecting and disposing of its trash runs over $4.5 billion. This ranks third in community expenditures behind only schools and highways. It is interesting to note that the operating budget for New York City's Department of Saniation alone this year is $139,000,000 or larger than the total state budgets of Alaska, Delaware, Idaho, or South Dakota.

Recently San Francisco approved a plan to ship the city's garbage 375 miles by rail to a desert burying ground.

Scientists at Harvard are investigating the possibility of using incinerator ships to burn trash and dump the residue far at sea.

In the past, trash has been disposed simply by burning it and burying it.

But New York City estimates that its available land-fill area will vanish in 4 to 9 years. Philadelphia has already made plans to ride most of its garbage out of town on the railroads. Reading Railroad flatcars loaded with 1,200 tons of refuse in 3,200 pound bails will soon begin to leave the city each night on a 110 mile one-way trip to northern Pennsylvania.

Dr. Frank P. Dee of Rutgers University suggests that if the problems of solid wastes overflow this world, there is always a possibility, remote, to be sure—of rocketing our garbage into space. He states that the sun would make an excellent incinerator, burning up both the refuse and the rocket fired into it.

However, he may be unaware of the fact that we are already using outer space as a floating junk shop.

Since Sputnik I was launched by the Russians in 1957, about 1,000 satellites and deep-space probes have been sent aloft by the U.S., Russia and other nations. Of that total, 386 are still whirling in space. In addition, there are bits and pieces of space-age debris, spent rocket stages and other hardware—that bring the grand total of man-made objects out in space to 1,607. This figure dates from March 1969, but the total increases almost daily.

With the counterfeit leadership from most of today's large and long established churches, and with the frightening peril that faces our cities—can this be heaven?

Many people, in believing that heaven is here on earth,

point to the recent medical advances that may not only prolong life but in their opinion make life eternal.

COST OF HOSPITAL CARE RISING

America finds itself on the horns of a dilemma. Here is a nation which has found itself spending $5 billion for 120 "flying boxcars" to increase its military mobility. Yet at the same time it discovers that it is difficult to allocate an appropriation to rebuild the transportation systems here on earth which are necessary to make everyday travel a little more easier.

Here is a society capable of creating a habitat for explorers on the moon and yet unprepared to spend whatever is needed to cleanse the polluted waters of the Hudson, the Connecticut, and the Missouri Rivers.

No one will doubt that medical advances have been very significant in our day and age and have contributed greatly to prolonging life and the welfare of the individual.

However, as is usually the trend, when technologies increase, man places less and less reliance on faith in God and more reliance on his own abilities.

And as the population increases even with medical aid becoming more sophisticated, it becomes increasingly difficult to meet the needs of this expanding population. Today, it is estimated that the United States is short 50,000 doctors and 85,000 nurses. One way or another, Americans this year will spend more than $80 billion for health care. This represents an outlay of $400 for every American man, woman and child. About a decade ago, only $26 billion was spent for health care.

Today, we find the government has made possible medicare for the elderly and medicaid for the needy. And yet these still do not answer the problems.

The death rate in the country still runs at 9.5 per 1,000 population, which is just about what it was a decade ago. This appears puzzling because up until 1954 the death rate was in steady decline in this country.

What is more surprising is that life expectancy is not im-

MEDICAL CARE — A GROWING MYSTERY

MEDICAL MANPOWER IS INCREASING FASTER THAN POPULATION
1955-72

U.S. population	UP 17%
Physicians in practice	UP 22%
Professional nurses in practice	UP 44%
Nonprofessional nurses*	UP 63%
X-ray technologists	UP 56%
Clinical-laboratory workers	UP 70%
Dentists	UP 13%
Dental assistants	UP 32%
Dental hygienists	UP 54%

*Practical nurses, aides, orderlies, attendants

MORE MONEY IS BEING SPENT FOR HEALTH SERVICES

Spending for Hospitalization, Physicians' and Dentists' Services

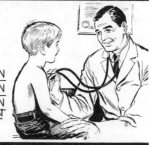

1955	$11 BILLION
1960	$17 BILLION
1965	$25 BILLION
1972	$80 BILLION

MEDICAL SERVICES HAVE EXPANDED
1955-72

Physician-directed services (all services billed to patients by private physicians, including services of medical assistants and laboratories)	UP 81%
Dentist-directed services	UP 47%
Hospital services	UP 65%

AND YET—Many American families can't find a doctor when they need one, can't get a nurse at any price, can't get an appointment to have eyes or teeth checked without waiting weeks or months. People often run into hurried and slipshod treatment in hospitals and clinics. And the situation is getting worse in many places.

Basic data: National Advisory Commission on Health Manpower
Copyright ©1972 Salem Kirban, Inc.

proving much these days. In 1900 it was 47.3 years. By 1963, it had climbed to 70. Since then, it has risen by a statistically insignificant 6 months and, for the American males, the outlook may actually be deteriorating. For them, the death rate is rising from diabetes, respiratory disease, and from some forms of cancer. And no one seems to have an explanation.

Dr. John H. Knowles, general director of Massachusetts General Hospital in Boston stated: "It's wild. Every city has health statistics that look worse than some of those of the less-developed countries."

It is apparent that there is a crisis ahead in medical care. Dollars alone can no longer buy first-class medical treatment for everybody.

In the federal government alone there are 175 federal agencies dealing with medical care. Some problems which every family has experienced has been:

(1) Long delays to see a physician for routine care
(2) Lengthy periods spent in the well named "waiting room," and then hurried and sometimes impersonal attention in a limited appointment time
(3) Difficulty in obtaining care on nights and weekends
(4) Unavailability of beds in one hospital while some beds are empty in another
(5) Reduction of hospital services because of lack of nurses
(6) Obsolete hospitals in our major cities
(7) Rising costs for treatment.

In 1965, Americans paid $25 billion for hospital care. In 1967, this soared to $47.3 billion. If the upsurge continues, as Presidential advisors predict, national spending for health will exceed $100 billion per year by 1975.

Charges for a day's hospital stay rose at the rate of 6% a year from 1960 to 1965. But with the onset of Medicare and Medicaid, costs have rocketed 16.5% in 1966 and another 15.5% in 1967 and since then have gone up and up and up!

It is predicted that hospitals may be charging $150 a day by 1975. Estimates by the American Hospital Association show that in the decade of the 1960's, the number of people using hospitals as outpatients—requiring service but not occupying a bed—will go up 80%. It is also predicted that by the year 2000 a day's care in the hospital may cost from $1000 to $1500 a day! Each year 150 million Americans pay 400 million visits to the doctor. For them, the doctors write up billions of prescriptions for a total of some 3.5 billion. And each year, 35 million Americans go into a general hospital, where they spend an average of 7 days and get a bill for $646.17, about half of which is covered by insurance.

The day of the family doctor is fast fading. In 1930, general practitioners outnumbered specialists 70 to 30. Today the ratio is more than reversed. For every 21 general practitioners there are 79 specialists. And if a doctor sat down and read the medical journals in his field as his full-time job, at the end of the year he would be three months behind in his reading.

A research specialist estimated that in the far distant future, man will have a life expectancy of possibly 200 or 300 years. He feels that the ultimate key to this is the understanding of the aging process and then slowing it down.

TO NEVER GROW OLD

It is reported that we are now in a position to add at least 20 years of health to the lives of many. One doctor at a New York Medical Center discussed a new pill which he called "youth pill." It's made from procaine. No one apparently knows why the procaine pill works but reports of its success have created a sensation in such countries as Rumania, Germany, and England. Some doctors believe that it will soon become as widely used in California as penicillin.

God's creation of man has been nothing short of miraculous. Today alone your heart will beat 103,000 times, your blood will travel 169,000 miles, you will breathe 32,000 times, inhale 438 cubic feet of air, move 750 major muscles, use 7 million brain cells, and speak an average of 4800 words.

HIGH COST OF ILLNESS

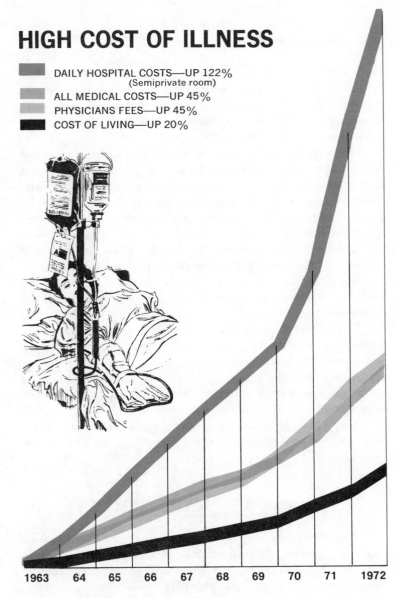

- DAILY HOSPITAL COSTS—UP 122%
  (Semiprivate room)
- ALL MEDICAL COSTS—UP 45%
- PHYSICIANS FEES—UP 45%
- COST OF LIVING—UP 20%

1963　64　65　66　67　68　69　70　71　1972

Each year 35 million Americans go into a general hospital, where they spend an average of 7 days and get a bill of $646.17.

Further . . . if you still have the energy . . . your brain has 10 billion nerve cells, receiving signals at speeds up to 300 miles per hour! It has been estimated that a computer complex to handle all the interconnections of the human nervous system would cover the earth!

And yet, there comes a time in a person's life when aging begins. It has been stated that aging is a gentle decline that begins around the 30th birthday . . . when the output of the heart and the speed of nerve impulses diminish by about the same amount between the ages of 30 and 40 as they do between 60 and 70.

A theory on aging states that nature doesn't want people to live past the age of possible reproduction and has therefore written a kind of suicide note into the inherited genes of each cell. These inborn instructions tell the body to start falling apart at a certain age.

Evidences of aging occur when people slow down, lose powers of recuperation, cuts take longer to heal, and convalescence after an illness is longer.

Arthritis is the chief crippler of older Americans. The Arthritis Foundation estimates that 17,000,000 Americans suffer from arthritis and related illnesses.

And while the normal processes of life destines everyone to death, medical science is doing everything possible to sustain life.

HARVESTING THE BODY

Two of the new innovations has been the heart transplant and the beginning of banks to hold human organs. In fact, in Houston, Texas, a central clearing house was opened recently for persons who wish to donate their bodies or organs.

The clearing house, called The Living Bank, is housed in a 43 foot trailer on the parking lot of the Medical Center National Bank. And now a Dutch scientist has also announced the start of an International Organ Exchange to salvage for transplantation kidneys, hearts, and other organs from persons dying in four northern European countries.

With heart transplants on the rise, donors of hearts are becoming more difficult to find. In the 11 medical centers in the United States where heart transplants have been performed by late 1968, there were 42 deaths of heart patients who were ready for transplants but for whom donors could not be found in time. During this same period 34 heart transplants were performed.

In October of 1968 in Philadelphia, a 41 year old woman stroke victim was flown from Philadelphia to Houston to donate her heart for transplant to one of four waiting patients. As she was wheeled down the ramp to the waiting jet, her husband looked at her for the last time alive. The woman had been taken to a local hospital in Philadelphia in a coma and had not returned to consciousness. She was kept alive at the hospital and on the plane to Houston by a resuscitator.

At the Houston Hospital, her still beating heart was removed and transplanted to a waiting patient.

At this time also began one of the biggest debates in medical history. The debate on when is a person dead?

Apparently the American Medical Association has determined that death is no longer to be declared in effect only when the heart has stopped beating. Death is now, rather, to be considered present when there is an absence of electrical activity in the brain.

At a recent AMA Convention, after one delegate asked that they include a requirement for death that the heart be no longer beating, a list of the controversial detailed evidences of death was deleted.

While this may seem a minor point to some, this decision on the part of doctors opens a new avenue for them to decide when an individual is dead and in the future it could lead to a removal of a heart because an individual is below a certain intellectual level or because the individual is a victim of a stroke or other peculiar circumstances.

Woe to the patient who for 24 hours shows no reflexes, no spontaneous breathing, no muscle activity, or no electroencephalograph response. For he may find that without his say

his heart will be removed and transplanted to another patient.

It is estimated at this time that about 81,000 persons
could be saved annually by heart transplantation.

In fact, heart transplants are no longer news.

HEAD TRANSPLANTS NEXT?

While doctors admit that brain transplants are almost
next to impossible they have found that transplants of *entire
heads and necks* is definitely possible in the near future.

This does not require the degree of major surgery that the
transplantation of the brain would require.

It is predicted that the first HEAD TRANSPLANT will be
done within the next 10 years! As long as 20 years ago the
Russians were transplanting dogs' heads . . . and there has
been much activity in this field ever since.

It is highly possible that a political leader someday will
attempt to gain immortality this way!

And sadly enough with the high cost of living, about 8,000
people will die this year because they cannot afford the
$10,000 annually that it costs for them to be hooked up to a
twice weekly machine called the artificial kidney. Perhaps
the biggest find for New York physicians was when a 57 year
old New Yorker provided surgeons with the most abundant
harvest ever reaped from a single donor in this era of organ
transplants: a heart, two kidneys, a liver, and the corneas of
both eyes.

And yet with this wealth of medical technology, we are
still living in a world where cancer will kill some 325,000
Americans this year, making it the No. 2 cause of death just
behind heart disease.

And with all these medical advances one reads tongue-
in-cheek of the Red Chinese surgical team which claims to
have cured more than 1,000 blind, deaf and paralyzed patients in two years by "relying on the invincible thought of
Mao Tse-tung."

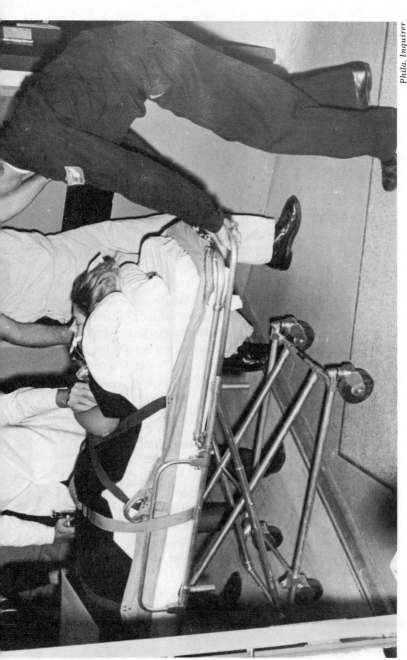

Heart donor en route to Texas where her still beating heart was removed and transplanted into another patient. Patient subsequently died. New medical guidelines for determining death create a dangerous precedent and may be another step in ushering in the reign of Antichrist.

Yes, it is a strange world which may soon find that a heart will become cheaper than a new car. In fact, artificial hearts will be readily available soon for less than the cost of a new automobile according to Dr. William J. Kolff.

Dr. Kolff, who invented the artificial kidney, has developed an artificial heart that can be placed inside a person's chest and would cost about $2000.

Thus in spite of this modern 20th century, the leaves of death keep falling.

THE DEEP FREEZE

Some would like to live forever and have actually made plans to perpetuate their life.

When Dr. James H. Bedford, a 73 year old California psychologist, died two years ago of lung cancer, the unusual method of disposing of his body drew national attention.

Newsweek reported that Bedford was packed in dry ice, his blood was drained and replaced with a bio-chemical "anti-freeze" solution and then his frozen body was shipped to Phoenix to be kept in cold storage inside a 13-foot Thermos-shaped capsule designed by an Arizona wigmaker.

This is a new program developed by Cryonics (from the Greek, *cryos* — "cold") — the Movement that freezes the dead for future reanimation, based on the somewhat unsettling prospect that science will one day revive the dead.

The theory is that the temperature of the frozen body, in years to come, will be gradually raised. Then the body will be drained of its preserving fluid, and blood will be pumped into the waiting vessels. An electric shock will start the heart beating again, and a medical team will — with the methods to be developed in the future — cure the ill that had previously "killed" the patient. Thus life will be restored, and the then developed youth-restoring inventions will add years and years of new life to a once aged and dead body!

The cryonics group's motto is, "Never Say Die," and the society now claims a membership of more than 1,000 people.

Newsweek — Tony Rollo

Curtis Henderson, chairman of New York's Cryonics Society, stands beside body of New York University student who died last year. Student is immersed in liquid nitrogen at minus 360 degrees centigrade, contained in a $4500 cryo-capsule and maintained at a $50-a-month expense. Cryonics is a movement that freezes the dead for future reanimation hoping one day science will be able to revive the dead.

Upon death, they are placed in a $4,500 cryo-capsule and maintained at a $50 a month expense. In Woodland Hills in the San Fernando Valley of California a multi-storage facility has been built at a cost of $100,000 and this will hold about 40 bodies.

THE LEAVES MUST FALL

Yes, the leaves keep falling. In fact, recently the daily Congressional Record printed the names of 31,379 youths in what appeared to be a seemingly endless column after column, covering 121 pages . . . This was the roll of the United States war dead in Vietnam.

To print these names cost approximately $83 a page and totaled more than $10,000.

But representative Paul Findley (R-Ill.), felt that it was justified, for the names "established, as no other arrangement of words can possibly do, the true dimensions of the Vietnam war in total overall terms, as well as the most intimate."

Perhaps this was the most dramatic roll call of those who have ever died.

In fact, it was amazing that General Eisenhower survived as long as he did after his many illnesses. He suffered seven heart attacks, beginning in 1955 when he was President.

Since 1956, the former President also had been stricken with ileitis, a mild stroke, and osteoarthritis, and had undergone surgery for disorders in his gall bladder and abdomen.

Shortly after the abdominal operation, he developed pneumonia. And then, the leaf of this brave warrior fell too. And all of America gathered to pay their respects to a fallen hero.

When tragedy strikes, how unusual it is that a world which turns its face away from God, suddenly recognizes God. For as the Eisenhower train reached each junction on its way back to Abilene, Kansas, it was met by groups of hymn-singing crowds.

Former President Eisenhower, himself, realizing the approaching finality of life and looking forward to an eternity in heaven specifically chose that he be buried in a simple $80 standard Army casket wearing only three of the many service medals which he deservedly won.

In another scene in a tearful White House ceremony, President Nixon conferred posthumously the highest military decoration on an 18 year old marine who died as he fired his machine gun in Vietnam while fighting off waves of Viet Cong attackers. As the President presented the Medal of Honor to the parents of this young soldier, the mother wept openly for she had tasted the bitterness of death.

When the leaves of life fall, some go out in a glorious display while others fade away unnoticed.

Then there is another scene . . . In Philadelphia, they call him "the Fox Chase boy."

It was a late afternoon on February 26, 1957 when police discovered a box in a desolate area of a section called Fox Chase, Philadelphia. He was known as "the boy in the box." No one knew where he came from but someone had placed him in a large cardboard box crossing his hands on his stomach and covering his nude body with a tattered cotton blanket.

Now, some 12 years later, he is still an unknown because no one has claimed him and in the city cemetery the only epitaph that appears on his grey marble slab, simply states, "HEAVENLY FATHER, BLESS THIS UNKNOWN BOY."

How can man turn away from God and place his hopes in a temporal world, thinking that this world will provide for him a heaven on earth?

This is our modern world . . . a world that includes a breakdown in both ethics and morals; a stockpiling of instruments of war that can wipe out not only a nation but a continent within minutes; the selfish concern of many for the luxurious things of life while others are dying of starvation; clergymen who are proclaiming a counterfeit Christ based on man-made ideas; cities whose problems are becoming more complex with air pollution, rising welfare, housing and space unavailable. Then too there is the rise of medical advances that somehow fail to meet the soaring medical problems! Can this be Heaven?

A child loved her mother dearly and it was because of this

love that she ran out to the trees and began tying all the leaves. In doing so, she thought she could stop the results of aging and the verdict of death.

She did it out of love. And yet, the leaves are still falling and will continue to fall.

You are a leaf on the tree of today's world. One of these days, the cool October night will settle on the tree and your leaf will fall into an eternity.

Will you by choice, then be ushered into an eternity in Heaven? Or will you by your lack of decision destine your life to an eternity in a real hell—as the just penalty for your sinfulness to which you choose to cling despite the pleas of a God who desires to forgive.

In the Metropolitan Museum in New York there is a monument to Edgar Allan Poe. On it are inscribed these words: "He was great in genius; unhappy in life; wretched in death; but in fame he is immortal."

As Robert C. Cunningham stated

> That is one kind of immortality. But there is a better kind; it consists not in our gift to posterity but in God's gift to us. It is not something we leave behind to be enjoyed by others; it lies ahead to be enjoyed by us.

Dr. W. B. Hinson told how his faith was tested after the doctors said he had only a few more months to live. "I walked out to where I live, five miles out of the city, and I looked across at that mountain that I love, and I looked at the river in which I rejoice, and I looked at the stately trees that are always God's poetry to my soul. Then in the evening I looked up into the great sky where God was lighting His lamps, and I said, 'I may not see you many more times, but, Mountain, I shall be alive when you are gone; and, River, I shall be alive when you cease running toward the sea; and, Stars, I shall be alive when you have fallen from your sockets in the great down-pulling of the material universe.'"

The faith of a Christian rests on a solid foundation. Christ died for our sins, was buried and arose from the dead (1 Corinthians 15:3,4). He is alive today, and because He lives we too shall live forever.

MAN REACHES THE MOON — *Will man, basking in his scientific achievements, now place more faith in self and less in God? Is this historic event another symbol of the Last Days when ". . . iniquity shall abound, the love of many shall wax cold?"* (Matthew 24:12)

The eternity of the Heavens is impossible for mere man to fathom.
He has reached the moon which is only 240,000 statute miles away
in our own galaxy. And man boasts of this accomplishment. But it
was only some 40 years ago telescopes brought to light the now
famous Andromeda Galaxy of stars that are almost TWO MILLION
LIGHT YEARS distant from the earth and containing some 100,000
million stars! How can anyone doubt the existence of God realizing
the vastness of space and the order of the universe!

A view of earth as seen from the Apollo 8 as it circled the moon. In this remarkable photograph the earth is 240,000 miles away. No wonder the Psalmist wrote in Psalms 8:3,4: "When I consider thy heavens, the work of thy fingers, the moon and the stars, which thou hast ordained; What is man, that thou art mindful of him? and the son of man, that thou visitest him?"

The sea boiled in this most amazing photograph taken November 14th, 1963 off the south coast of Iceland! From the depths of the earth lava poured out of a new crater at 500,000 tons an hour. By the end of November a new island had been formed. And in January, 1966 Surtsey (Island of the fire-god) was still erupting, an awesome witness to the forces locked up in the earth's interior!

Nimbus, the special space satellite that already provides long-range weather forecasting from outer space. Future satellites may not only predict weather but control weather, devastating an area with floods or wafting disease germs over a nation.

Tektite I, a miniature submerged city housing aquanauts. In 50 feet below the ocean surface Tektite I is designed to master the science of living in the sea.

Look at this picture carefully. It can represent the sunset of your life . . . for life is short, only a few years. But if Christ is your personal Saviour and Lord this photograph depicts the sunrise of an eternal day dwelling with Christ in a New

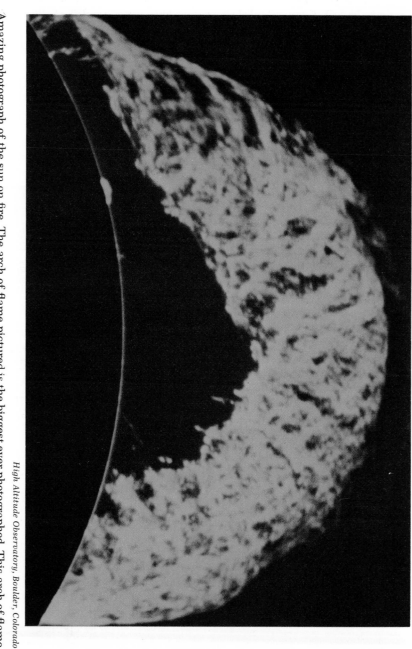

High Altitude Observatory, Boulder, Colorado

Amazing photograph of the sun on fire. The arch of flame pictured is the biggest ever photographed. This arch of flame soared over ONE MILLION MILES into the air—more than the diameter of the sun—on June 4, 1946. This will give you an idea of the intense heat and destructive power that can melt the elements of the earth at the end of the Millennium.

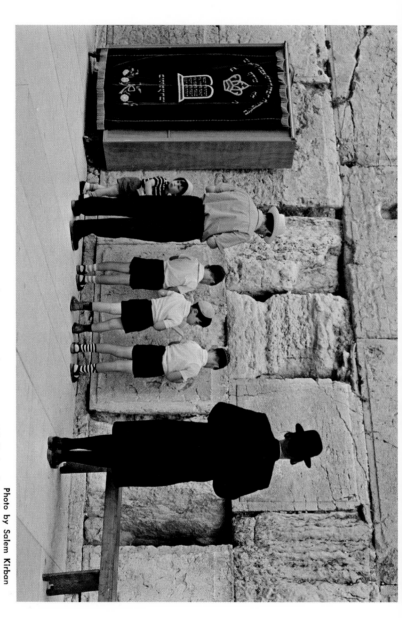

Photo by Salem Kirban

WAILING WALL.—*Most revered spot for the Jews is the Western Wall in Jerusalem, commonly known as the "Wailing Wall." In the 6 Day War of June, 1967 a brigade commander in the Israeli Army gave all battalion commanders the final objective: ". . . the Western Wall . . . For two thousand years our people have prayed for this moment . . ."*

THE STAGES OF EARTH

THIS PRESENT EARTH

ETERNITY

ORIGINAL EARTH

"In the beginning God created the heaven and the earth . . ."
(Genesis 1:1)

EARTH CURSED MAN SINS

Genesis 3

ANTEDELUVIAN
Before the Flood **AGE**
WICKEDNESS INCREASES

"And (God) spared not the old world, but saved Noah the eighth person, a preacher of righteousness, bringing in the flood upon the world of the ungodly . . ."
(II Peter 2:5)

FLOOD JUDGMENT

". . . I will cause it to rain upon the earth . . . and every living substance that I have made will I destroy from off the face of the earth."
(Genesis 7:4)

PRESENT EVIL AGE

"(Christ) Who gave Himself for our sins, that He might deliver us from this present evil world . . ."
(Galatians 1:4)

TRIBULATION PERIOD JUDGMENT

"Then shall the Lord go forth, and fight against those nations . . . and His feet shall stand . . . upon the Mount of Olives . . ."
(Zechariah 14:3,4)

1000 YEAR MILLENNIAL AGE

". . . and they shall live and reigned with Christ a thousand years."
(Revelation 20:4)

EARTH DESTROYED BY FIRE

". . . the elements shall melt with fervent heat, the earth also and the works that are therein shall be burned up."
(II Peter 3:10)

THE NEW HEAVENS AND NEW EARTH

"And I saw a new heaven and a new earth: for the first heaven and the first earth were passed away; and there was no more sea . . ."
(Revelation 21:1)

ETERNITY

One of the first nuclear explosions conveys some of the awesome destruction that is now possible by man. But as catastrophic as this is, perhaps an even greater discovery is man's ability to control the minds of others through powerful mind-influencing drugs.

As the Eisenhower family looks on representatives from each of the Armed Forces bears the casket of General Eisenhower to the National Cathedral in Washington. An entire nation mourned, singing old hymns of the church, as a beloved General was laid to rest. The highest leaders of most every nation were present to do honor. In Heaven, even the lowliest on earth will have a welcome no earthly ceremony could equal.

Seal Hunt in Canada where hunters in their zealousness to make an extra dollar club baby seals, sometimes skinning them while still alive. Here the blood from a clubbed adult seal fills the water with blood. How prophetic this is of the Tribulation Period when 1/3rd of the sea will be filled with blood at the sounding of the Second Trumpet (Revelation 8:8,9) . . . and everything in the ocean will die in a sea of blood at the pouring of the Second Vial (Revelation 16:3).

Not men from outer space but U.S. soldiers rushed to Washington, D.C. to quell disorders during a peace march on the Pentagon.

The tragedies of war are often reflected on the faces of children. This photograph was taken by the author at a jungle hospital in Vietnam.

The Taj Mahal is considered one of the most beautiful buildings in the world. It was built in Agra, India, more than 300 years ago. The emperor Shah Jehan built it as a burial place for him and his favorite wife. It stands on a marble platform that is more than 300 feet square. It has a domed roof that is more than 80 feet high. The inside of the building is decorated with mosaics of precious stones. Around the Taj Mahal is a walled garden in which there are marble walks and a pool that reflects the building. Yet this earthly structure can in no way compare to the Heavenly structures in the New Jerusalem! See Revelation 21:10-27.

Current photo of our family taken Easter, 1968 a few days after our son Dennis returned from a year's service in Vietnam. (left to right)

The author; my dear wife, Mary; Dennis and his wife, Eileen; Doreen, Diane, Duane and our youngest, Dawn.

Chapter 3
Youth's Search for Heaven

The Problems Youth Face • Great Britain • France • Spain •
West Germany • Mexico • India • Pakistan • Japan • U.S.
Student Revolts • The Crazies • Sophisticated Cheating •
Love-Making Course Popular • High Schools Catch "Protest
Fever" • Education's Growing Problem • The Bitter Harvest •
This Drugged Generation • Drug Smuggling Increasing •
Drug Addicts in Armed Service • Youthful Criminals on In-
crease • Student Survey Challenges God's Divinity • The
Growth of Cults • Counterfeit Christianity • The Search for
Life

> Our youths love luxury. They have bad manners, con-
> tempt for authority; they show disrespect for their elders,
> and love to chatter in place of exercise. Children are now
> tyrants, not the servants of their households. They no longer
> rise when their elders enter the room. They contradict their
> parents, chatter before company, gobble up their food, and
> tyrannize their teachers.

The above description sounds like a reflection of this modern age.

However, it was given by Socrates in 400 B.C.

Many people upon reading the above statement by Socrates, often comment that the problems of today's youth are
no greater than those problems were in the days of Socrates.

And they use this for an excuse to minimize the tragedy
that has struck the youth of today's world.

However, they neglect to realize that in the days of Socrates, there was no television, no automobiles, and no means

of destruction that could wipe out the entire world within a few minutes.

The world of Socrates was a world which was relatively calm. In today's world (which is even far different than the world of even 10 years ago) young people can turn on television, bring the war in Vietnam right into their living room and see tragedies occurring right before their eyes . . . tragedies that were filmed only hours before.

In the past few years, the road that Americans have chosen to follow is a road which eliminates God from the public schools and permits obscenity and pornography to run rampant throughout every state. Is it any wonder that the youth brought up in this climate are creating problems that never before have faced America.

When Cicero completed an oration, people used to say: "What a marvelous orator! What an excellent speech!" But when Demosthenes thundered his denunciation of Philip of Macedon, people leaped to their feet, shouting, "Let us march against Philip!"

The same is true today. Many leaders of campus revolts have the personality of a Demosthenes that can move students into action.

Unfortunately, misdirected leadership has come from adults and, in one sense, the adults are to blame for the misguided young people of today.

Many so-called leaders, with degrees and high education, have condoned the use of drugs, a permissive society where anything goes as far as sex is concerned, and a society which sets out to make its own god.

This chaff, which we have sown throughout America, is now bringing a harvest of students who find themselves faced with three big problems.

THE PROBLEMS YOUTH FACE

First, they feel there is a lack of purpose in what they are doing. They view some of the traditional programs that colleges are setting forth with one eye and with the other they see

A new tactic in student demonstrations reared its ugly head in April, 1969, when heavily armed Negro students marched from student center at Cornell University in Ithaca, New York. Students had barricaded themselves in protest over university policies. This new phase of armed students has since led to deaths on several campuses.

only the hypocrisy of this world. Because of this they soon involve themselves in campus revolts.

It must be remembered that today's students are far more knowledgeable than were the students of twenty or thirty years ago. They have grown up faster because of modern technological advances in education, in television, and in the other mass media.

Second, is a problem which some term the "identity crisis."

It apparently is a challenge for students these days to "find themselves." They don't want to follow the same mold and pattern that their fathers and grandfathers have followed. Faced with so much permissiveness which is condoned by many of their adult leadership, they want to reach out and be somebody different. In a sense they have a point—for many of them are fed up with the apparent goals that so many adults have always sought after—the goals of merely making money and becoming more secure.

For the students who are now better educated and more mature than the students of yesterday—the mad race for the American dollar is one which is distasteful. In this race they see not only hypocrisy, but a scramble which ends up in divorces, adultery, trickery, and man stepping on man in order to climb the ladder of success. And this life is revolting to them.

At the very least, today's rewards are not sufficient to motivate youth to desire to run in the standard adult career race. They are like a group of athletes who have discovered that the promised prize of a golden crown will only be a paper hat. Now they no longer can find the energy to train for the race . . . high school, the army, college, graduate school, struggle . . . for what?

The eighteen year old arrives at a campus with perhaps one or two friends from his high school graduating class. But out of maybe 3,000 freshmen and 8,000 upper classmen, he rarely sees them.

He is assigned to a dorm with maybe 400 or 500 other people and he doesn't know a soul. He finds himself wrapped up in a tremendous college as simply a number or an unknown name. And as he looks at the road so far ahead he grows weary and asks . . . "For what?"

And *third*, there is perhaps a guilt complex? Students have consciences just like anyone else and after delving in

Harvard Dean is forced down flight of steps in Administration Building and escorted out by students protesting Reserve Officers Training Corps program at Harvard University.

all sorts of sin, many students find themselves already in youth with a guilt complex, seeking to find the answers to the problems of this world. And all around them are false leaders with their "answers" to these problems.

Very few of them discover that 2,000 years ago, Jesus Christ came to answer the problems of this world.

But this acceptance of Christ is too simple a solution for most "thinking" students. And so they seek other avenues and try to make their heaven here on earth.

This chapter deals with these avenues. In fairness, however, to the young people of today, it must be stated here that the majority of young people are dedicated, are seeking to get a good education, and they are striving to go on in a life of accomplishment.

Unfortunately, this does not make the headlines of the newspapers. Many of today's false leaders have become well-known overnight simply because the news media find that they do make sensational news.

One way to deter these false cults which are leading young people astray would be to stop reporting them in the news and stop giving them television and radio coverage. Soon they would only become known in their own locality and they would no longer become national figures of influence.

Perhaps, however, this is one of the hypocrisies that young people just cannot understand. The purpose of the newspaper is to make money and the more dramatic and sensational the events that occur among young people – the more newspapers will be sold, and the greater income for the pockets of the publisher.

Student revolts are not limited to the United States. They are world-wide. From London to Tokyo, college campuses are hotbeds of violence and rebellion.

In the United States violence was first led by militant left-wing students seeking to generate anarchy. They wished to create an absence of any system of government and law. Confusion was their aim – and they achieved it.

Initially, the war in Vietnam and the draft were centers of attack with student power being only a secondary goal.

But since then, student power on campuses has taken a lead in the aims of college students.

Let's look at some of the student unrest in other countries.

GREAT BRITAIN

It has been stated that college students in Britain enjoy, perhaps, more personal attention than in any other country. Almost all of the students in universities and colleges receive state grants and more than half are fully subsidized by the taxpayers.

Revolt comes here from a small minority of militants and is centered mainly at the London School of Economics. This left-wing organization is trying to build up a campaign of sit-ins and demonstrations at the universities throughout Britain.

One authority gives this description of the British rebels: "These youngsters come from homes where parents embraced the new theories of permissiveness. They had to struggle for nothing. They had no idea of the sacrifices that other generations and other peoples have made to secure basic freedoms. The result is that in their lives, there is no challenge whatsoever. The excitement of the student revolt has become an end in itself."

FRANCE

In France it has been admitted that much of the student protests are based on solid grievances.

Here more than 600,000 university students compete for seats in overcrowded classrooms. Housing and recreation facilities are inadequate. Fewer than half the students manage to graduate.

SPAIN

U.S. News and World Report noted that "student rebellion has reached the point where the Franco government has declared a nationwide emergency, the first time this has happened since Franco came to power 30 years ago."

The Franco government says it has evidence that its student troubles are part of "an international strategy affecting many countries."

WEST GERMANY

Germany has had three years of revolutionary clamor and its students are more disorganized than otherwise. Their main problems stem from the Socialist Students League which has a membership of about 2,500 and is working in coalition with other leftist groups.

West Germany produced perhaps the best known student leader in Europe, called Daniel Cohn-Bendit ("Danny the Red").

MEXICO

Mexico's students revolted on a nationwide scale in the second half of 1968. Although their universities are overcrowded and their academic standards are low, the revolt was aimed primarily at the Mexican government's idea of "guided democracy." A major gun battle ensued and casualties on both sides were heavy.

INDIA

India's rebellious students can match any country in violence. Campus after campus has been closed down in recent months — but the basic aims throughout the various campuses are not the same.

Here in India student protests convey mainly their worry about the bleak economic outlook that awaits them. One university lecturer explained that they fight in this country for such things as cheaper movie tickets.

PAKISTAN

Recent student revolts in Pakistan have seen many killed, and these revolts have precipitated the sudden resignation of President Ayub Khan as the leader of that nation.

JAPAN

Japan's last year has been one of heightened rebellions that have disrupted higher education more and more. Over the last year, 117 campuses have been torn by disputes and trouble still continues at some 60 universities, while 19 more are paralyzed by student boycotts and barricades.

PREPARATION FOR LIFE WORK?

It required a police force of 8,500 to evict radical students from 24 buildings in Tokyo University in January 1969. Here in the only nation that has felt the actual fury of an atomic weapon, student unrest finds a listening ear on such subjects as politics, treaties, and nuclear disarmament.

U.S. STUDENT REVOLTS

There is student rebellion all over the world, but it is still a minority movement which occurs while the majority of students continue to attend classes.

However, it is this minority movement which gets the press coverage and which creates a false picture on the general educational program of the United States.

Let's look at some of the recent student revolts in the United States.

In the spring of 1968, student radicals closed Columbia University.

San Francisco State University has been the scene of much disorder which has continued for many, many months. This has greatly curtailed the studies of some 17,000 students who wish only to complete their education.

The tactic that most student groups follow is the tactic of "confrontation."

And their aim is that of "disruption."

Basically confrontration tactics, which are instantly escalated to nationwide attention by the mass media, bring harsh police reactions that win "The Movement" wide sympathy.

The disruptions that are caused keep thousands of students from classes. One of The Movement's aims is to disrupt the established procedures of society. And while the majority of those in The Movement are students, included with them are Marxists, housewives, black-power advocates and professional people.

To them they see this as a struggle between The Youth versus The Old. And this is their way of attacking what they

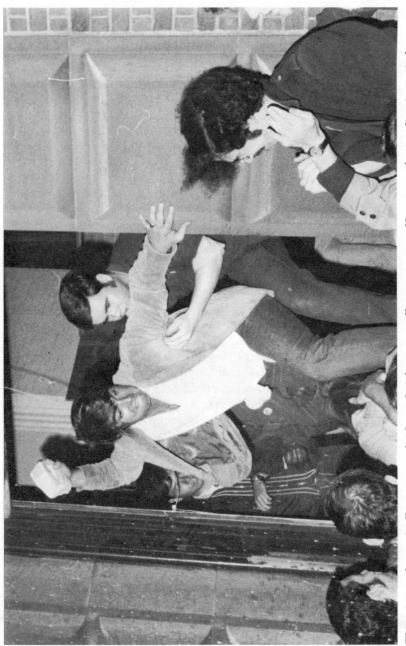

This picture dramatically captures the face of violence on college campuses. Here a youth, standing in a window, prepares to throw a brick as a group of conservatives attempt to force their way into Columbia University building.

term "an outmoded structure" in order that they may replace it with what they believe is a new set of values.

The biggest instigator of student revolts is in an organization called the Students for a Democratic Society (S.D.S.).

S.D.S. was founded in 1961 at Port Huron, Michigan, and its present membership is now estimated at 7,000. Each member pays dues of $5 per year, such participants are now located on 300 different campuses. It claims support from 35,000 other students throughout the country.

It must be kept in mind that there are 7 million college students in the United States today. And yet, a 1% S.D.S. membership can create such havoc that spreads like a cancer to affect the orderly educational procedures of 7 million college students.

From its day-to-day activities, S.D.S. is aiming at several specific targets which include: (1) groups working against the war; (2) groups concentrating on high school students, teachers and working class people; (3) a women's liberation group whose cry is "Free as women! Free as a nation!" and (4) a growing New Media project which includes a Liberation News Service which collects news for the underground press.

It is this press that reaches its tentacles into so many colleges throughout America. Its pornographic literature breaks down the morals of its readers and advocates a Godless society . . . all under the guise of freedom. They forget that with freedom also comes responsibility.

Most protest groups are simply that. Their energies are built up in protesting a society but they offer no constructive program for correcting the ills of that society.

At the University of Wisconsin in Madison, National Guardsmen were called in to restore order after a militant group disrupted classes for three days. When the rebels grew from 1,500 to 5,000, it was necessary to use tear gas and bayonets in order to maintain order.

Berkeley California has long been a hotbed for student disruptions and permissiveness.

And perhaps, it was the actions at Berkeley that encouraged students to revolt at Sir George Williams University in

Two faculty members make hasty exit from first floor window at Columbia University's Philosophy Hall after the building was seized by student radicals.

downtown Montreal. It was there that students started a major fire in a school building, demolished two computers with axes and did more than $2 million of damage. This amounted to *twice the previous record* for destruction of property, which was set by radicals at Tokyo University.

Most university administrators passively sit by allowing students to disrupt classes and to occupy student buildings under a state of siege, and then they give in to their many unreasonable demands.

However, Notre Dame's President, Reverend Theodore Hesburgh took a different approach to the problem.

His firm stand against student revolt quelled, before it started, what might have been another large student disorder. He stated, "Without stiff rules the university is a sitting duck for any small group from the outside or inside that wishes to destroy it, to incapacitate it, to terrorize it at whim. No one wants the police on campus, but if some necessitate it as a last and dismal alternative to anarchy and mob tyranny, let them shoulder the blame instead of receiving the sympathy of a community they would hold at bay!"

According to the Educational Testing Service, a mere 2% of all students are wreckers who aim to "radicalize" campuses even if some universities are destroyed in the process. In fact, such a revolt finally came even to exclusive Harvard where a small band of student rebels seized an administration building to protest university policies.

President Nathan M. Pusey had 3 alternatives. One was to send in the police, a second was to try to negotiate, and a third was to seek resolutions from faculty condemning the occupation.

President Pusey decided to use force. In a short time, a mere 25 minutes after the police made their initial charge, they had cleared the buildings. He further warned that he would shut down Harvard University if strike tactics continued. Further developments and administrative indecisiveness, however, left Harvard not much better off than other universities.

During a 4-month period from November, 1968 to February, 1969 there were 239 "serious episodes" of disorder—strikes, sit-ins, demonstrations, riots or other violence—in high schools.

In classifying 361 disruptive cases one educator noted them as follows:

Racial protests—132 incidents in 27 states.
Political protests (including Vietnam)—81 incidents in 21 states.
Protests against dress regulations—71 incidents in 25 states.
Protests against discipline—60 incidents in 28 states.
Protests for educational reforms—17 incidents in 14 states.

And government officials estimate that there are over 500 underground newspapers being published in secondary schools.

THE CRAZIES

Frankly, it takes astonishingly little to disrupt a campus today. There is a movement afoot called The Crazies. "The Crazy," says a University of Chicago radical, "is the guy no one knows or sees until the administration brings the cops on campus."

On any campus, The Crazies may number 5, 50 or 100. They are defined as being more radical than even the radicals and they believe in direct action—whether it's disrupting classes, throwing stink bombs, or kicking in doors.

One group of Crazies arrived at Harvard, and then things started to fall apart when the five—including two girls—took off their clothes to wash them in a basement laundry of Eliot House. After asking police to stand by, Harvard officials threw them out. "People seem to think that having your clothes off is something unusual," said one female Crazy. She then added, "That's an indication of the repression of our society."

At the University of Chicago, members of this Crazy organization participated in a 16 day take-over of the school's administration building—and subsequent guerrilla disruptions.

A Chicago radical commented, "I want to see the university shutdown, but I also want us to open it under our own terms. If we don't succeed, the guerrilla attacks will continue."

SOPHISTICATED CHEATING

There are more reports of college students cheating and this too is indicative of the new permissive age. A 24 year old student at a large Midwestern university quit his part-time job as a $1.65-an-hour bookstore clerk during a recent examination week. He didn't use the extra time to study, however. He quit because he had a better job lined up—taking exams for other students. In six days, he took five exams at three nearby colleges and pocketed $180.

College teachers admit that when an exam is given to almost any large group of U.S. college students, many are likely to be copying each others' answers, reading notes hidden in watches or fountain pens, listening through phony hearing aids to pocket tape recorders, or flashing signals across the room to each other.

However, outside the classroom, some students even get advanced copies of exams by breaking into offices or bribing secretaries.

In this affluent society, students are even hiring ghost-writers to do their job.

In New York, one group of recent college graduates will turn out papers ranging from a short theme on Dostoyevsky to a full thesis on Brazilian politics at fees ranging from $60 to $500.

It must be kept in mind that cheating is not new on college campuses. However, there is evidence that it is becoming increasingly common and that the attitudes toward it are changing dramatically.

It has been reported that professors increasingly are looking the other way, arguing that much cheating is a product of the educational system and some colleges are even easing their penalties for cheaters.

The American Education Council recently took a survey and found that 24% of the men and 16% of the women queried admitted cheating at least once in their college careers.

Both students and professors agree that the increase of cheating has been substantial in the last few years. Universities find themselves with very large enrollments. As an example, Ohio State has doubled its enrollment to almost 40,000 in the past 10 years. And a freshman enrolled there might attend classes with as many as 2,000 others present!

LOVE-MAKING COURSE POPULAR

Many colleges are now even changing their curriculum to meet what they term "the needs of today."

It is hard to imagine today's college students needing a course in love-making, but at the University of South Carolina some 386 college students are taking this course.

It is part of the spring semester's short courses planned entirely by students with the University of South Carolina's approval. There are no set schedules, no prescribed curriculum, and no grades. It's supposedly all for the joy of learning.

Other courses included bartending, which had an enrollment of 384 students – almost equal to that of love-making. A discussion leader stated that he hoped the class could move off campus for practical experience.

Other popular subjects were witchcraft, with 247 signed up and mysticism which had an enrollment of 104.

While in Tucson, Arizona, some students at the University of Arizona were protesting because they wanted spittoons in classrooms and chewing tobacco vending machines in their residence halls. Along with this came more lax regulations for permitting girls in boys' rooms on campuses and vice versa. In fact, on many college campuses today almost anything goes . . . and is condoned by a beclouded administration that sees in everything, no matter how immoral . . . "a degree of enrichment value in it."

HIGH SCHOOLS CATCH "PROTEST FEVER"

With such laxities occurring on college campuses it is no wonder that this letdown of authority has passed on to the high schools.

The problems in the Philadelphia schools have become so great that the Mayor has made a proposal to put public school security under Police Department control.

These problems have extended even to elementary schools in Los Angeles and throughout the rest of the country. In Washington, D.C., Senator Robert C. Byrd (Dem. of West Virginia) charged that the S.D.S. has devised "a blueprint for the destruction of the entire American educational system."

On one day in Los Angeles, 65 fires were set in city schools.

In a high school in Brooklyn, it took 40 policemen patrolling the halls to keep the school open. These Brooklyn high school students broke windows, damaged files, and staged a boycott.

A survey by a national group of school principals indicates that student protests ranging from vocal complaints to riots have occurred at nearly 60% of the nation's high schools.

So critical is the problem that a professor of sociology at the University of Michigan has been given a $187,000 Ford Foundation Grant to study the causes of crisis at seven trouble plagued high schools around the United States.

It must be kept in mind that the great majority of American youngsters are quietly and effectively working at their studies. But this does not make news. It is the vocal minority which has caused student violence and the disruption that has brought chaos into the classroom. This has caused educators to wonder about the future of public schools.

EDUCATION'S GROWING PROBLEM

Education in the United States is a big business.

45 million pupils (more than the total United States population at the time of the Civil War) attend classes in about 100,000 public schools.

Dr. Erving R. Melbo, Dean of the University of Southern California's School of Education, said,

Student disobedience in part is an expression of a fashionable behavior, just as it once was a fad to wear tennis shoes or swing a hula hoop. I don't mean to take away from their sincerity, but we see 11 year olds who think they must have a "cause" in order to be "in" and it doesn't really matter what that cause is.

One administrator in New York City's troubled schools likens the prospect there to the chaos that swept schools in Communist China when Mao Tse-tung turned loose his youthful "Red Guards" on the countryside. This educator said, "In China, professors were mocked, and led through the streets in disgrace. This leads to the destruction of education. Now the Chinese find that all the king's horses and all the king's men cannot put it together again—and this is precisely the situation being precipitated here."

In one school district of New York City, hostility on the part of students forced four successive persons to quit the post of assistant superintendent within a few months.

One top official said: "Principals have been thrown around like sacks of flour."

In fact, New York City schools last year reported 271 assaults on staff members. While students committed most of the assaults, parents and intruders often helped out.

Community concern in one high school reached a peak when the Board of Education handed down a report which stated: "The moral standards of our students cannot be protected. Acts of sexual intercourse and prostitution have occurred on campus. We are not providing a legitimate high school education. Application of even minimum standards of high school achievements would result in a failure of all but a handful of our students to graduate. Absenteeism is rampant, frequently including one-fourth to one-third of the students on a given day."

Dr. Bruno Bettelheim, Professor of Education at the University of Chicago said: "We've asked our schools to solve the problems of society, and they were not designed to do that. Heaven knows there are plenty of evils in society to be corrected, but the school is not the institution to do it without being destroyed."

THE BITTER HARVEST

In September, 1972, public schools in Philadelphia closed for nearly a month because of teacher strikes and lack of operating capital. In New York City, glass breakage in schools in 1971 alone ran $1,241,480 and damage to property, $2,050,499. Over 240 fires were set in school buildings!

Where does it all end? It is predicted that in 1973, 110,000 school-age girls will have babies born out of wedlock. And the World Health Organization states that at least 1,000 persons a day commit suicide the world over.

Last year approximately 50,000 Americans committed suicide. In the United States, suicide is the fourth most frequent cause of death. There is an alarming increase in suicide among young Americans. For college students, suicide now is the second most frequent cause of death, after accidental fatalities.

Michael L. Peck, a psychologist at the Los Angeles Suicide Prevention Center, estimates that 15,000 college students try to take their lives each year. This is the highest attempt rate of any age group.

Psychologists trace this rise among adolescents partly to the increasing frustrations and demands of today's society.

Another cause is the breakdown of effective communication in the home.

It is sad to note that at least one of an adolescent suicide's parents usually is at home when the suicide takes place, if it happens at home.

THIS DRUGGED GENERATION

Much of the problem that effects our youths is caused by drugs. Senator Harrison A. Williams (Dem., N.J.) says that the United States faces "the prospect of a coast-to-coast catastrophe — a drugged society."

With riots and protests becoming a way of life on college campuses, it is no wonder that this leadership gives ideas to the young — not only to the high school young — but to the elementary school age bracket!

In June, 1969 in Philadelphia three young brothers, 14, 13 and 12 allegedly entered an elementary school. When they walked out, they left a school "95% destroyed."

Police Lt. John Duffy said the school building was "wrecked from top to bottom." Even a basement boilerroom was damaged. All 42 classrooms were damaged. More than 100 windows were smashed, plants and flowers were uprooted from window boxes and hurled against the walls. Nearly everything upright was knocked over.

Papers were strewn around, paint from art rooms was splashed over desks, floors and blackboards. Phones were broken and their wires cut. Television sets were smashed. Office equipment was wrecked and many of the machines were thrown out of windows.

What does this mean: Can we place all the blame on the youngsters? After all, whose leadership are they following? They are the products of a permissive society which denies there is a God, promotes the breaking down of moral standards and "healthy experimentation." Such riotous living is truly an indication of the Last Days.

The drug generation is growing younger and apparently takes its lead from many adults who are condoning such activity.

In one of San Francisco's middle class Junior High schools, seventh graders trade barbiturates in homeroom— and smoke marijuana during lunch.

Newsweek magazine reports that so much marijuana has been invading Detroit recently that the sheriff's office has a marijuana-sniffing police dog that meets many flights from the west coast. The head of a Massachusetts Drug Action Committee said, "Some established families have lost everything to finance their children's drug habit. Parents would rather see the habit continue than to have their child picked up and the whole thing made public in court."

One Columbia freshman stated, "It's a whole cultural thing. It has a different vocabulary, and once you start drugs you keep different hours. You can point at yourself and the other people in it and say, 'We're into something.' "

It has become increasingly clear that the age of U.S. drug users is dropping rapidly, sometimes reaching down into elementary schools.

One educator remarked that some seventh-grade pupils in Berkeley public schools have tried LSD or its equivalent. By the twelfth grade he says 14% had at least tried LSD once. There is a massive and growing use by all segments of American youth of mind-altering drugs.

A survey of 100 Yale seniors found that 85% had smoked marijuana at least once and 20% had taken LSD.

DRUG SMUGGLING INCREASING

Last year alone 8 million 5-grain units of illicit drugs were seized at borders and ports of entry in the United States. The total weight of all drugs confiscated for the year hit 98 tons. This was well over 2½ times the amount seized the year earlier, and about 6 times as much as the Customs Service uncovered in its operation a year before that.

Relaxing with marijuana. From Vietnam down to elementary schools The Drug Generation is getting younger.

Bud Lee

When you realize that the retail value of a pound of pure heroin runs as high as $100,000 you can see that this illegal sale of narcotics is a multi-million dollar business and it is getting bigger all the time.

In New York City, it is estimated, there are at least 300,000 heroin addicts.

Dr. James L. Goddard, former Chief of the Food and Drug Administration, estimated that 35 million Americans may have already tried marijuana and that 1 million may be using it regularly.

The New York Times has estimated that 100 million Americans use some form of mind-altering drugs.

It has not been unusual for San Diego high school kids to spend $10 to $15 a week on marijuana which is easily obtainable from peddlers on the city beaches.

Then the sad fact is that when the younger people become the victims of the stronger drugs it costs them up to $100 a day to feed this serious habit. And if youths need $100 a day, they will be forced to steal, rob, or sell their bodies in order to obtain the huge amounts of money needed to buy the drugs for which their bodies crave.

Most of these drugs come from Tijuana, a town in Mexico only a few miles from San Diego, California. In fact, Tijuana is called the "most visited foreign city in the world." The United States Immigration Service figures show that 25.5 million people and 7 million vehicles entered the United States here in a 12-month period last year!

DRUG ADDICTS IN ARMED SERVICE

This drug problem has not been confined simply to the young people in the United States but is also having its effect among our fighting men in Vietnam.

One of the slogans among American soldiers in Vietnam is the one: "Dope is Hope." While there were no hard statistics on drug use in Vietnam, it was estimated that 35% of the troops used some type of drugs.

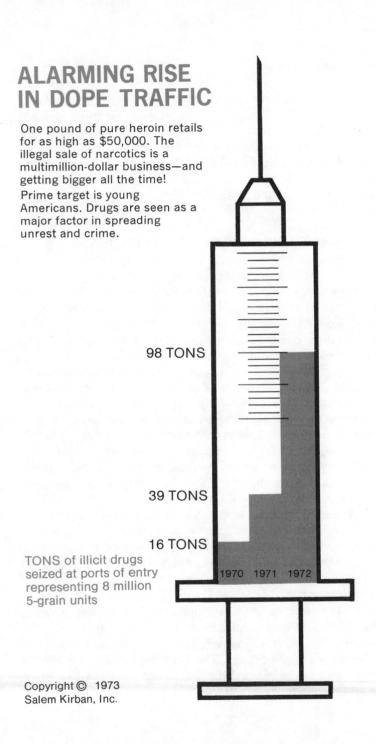

ALARMING RISE IN DOPE TRAFFIC

One pound of pure heroin retails for as high as $50,000. The illegal sale of narcotics is a multimillion-dollar business—and getting bigger all the time!

Prime target is young Americans. Drugs are seen as a major factor in spreading unrest and crime.

98 TONS

39 TONS

16 TONS

TONS of illicit drugs seized at ports of entry representing 8 million 5-grain units

1970   1971   1972

This was the result of a study conducted by an Army psychiatrist and appeared in an official Vietnam medical bulletin. Another fact that is not highly publicized is that 53,357 U.S. servicemen deserted between mid-1967 and mid-1968, or an average of one every 10 minutes. The report by the Senate Armed Service Committee said that this desertion was equal to the desertion of 13½ Divisions.

YOUTHFUL CRIMINALS ON INCREASE

With student unrest on campuses and a greater use of drugs by the younger generation...is it any wonder that the crime rate in the United States is rapidly increasing?

J. Edgar Hoover, the late Head of the Federal Bureau of Investigation, commented that criminal violence was exploding into the most serious domestic crisis facing this country.

FBI figures show an ominous surge in crimes, riots, and brutality nearly everywhere, especially among teenagers and young adults. It is particularly tragic that young people are becoming increasingly involved in crimes. A disproportionate share of national crime is committed by persons under 24 years of age. In 1972, for example, 69% of those arrested for serious crimes were below 24. And arrests of persons under 24 increased a startling 53% in 1972 over the previous rate for those under 24 in 1965.

Arrests of young people for murders increased 56% in 1972 over 1960. Violence is particularly prevalent today among young people. Vicious juvenile gangs terrorize the slum sections. It has been estimated that every 30 seconds another car is stolen. More than 950,000 cars were stolen in the United States last year.

Just recently in Philadelphia, the U.S. Customs Agents Philadelphia International Airport confiscated more than 230 switchblade knives from high school pupils returning from European Easter vacations. The Customs agent reported that the pupils tried to conceal the knives in their stockings, pockets and even in tubes of hair cream.

Such has become the conditions of today that Bob Jones University requested permission from the State of South Carolina to arm its guards with submachine guns and automatic rifles to protect its coeds against possible mob violence.

There is a general unrest among young people in America today. It is an unrest that is reflected in the violence that is sweeping across the country. It is an unrest which has come in part because the mass of this world will not receive the answers offered in the Scriptures; and it has come in part because the church has failed in its responsibility to proclaim the Bible's answers.

It has been stated that the Communists have made more converts since 1917 than Christianity has made since the days of Jesus Christ.

Perhaps one of the secrets of the Communists' success is found in their dedication. One ardent French Communist wrote:

> The Christian Gospel is much more powerful as a weapon for the renewal of society than our Marxist doctrine. All the same, we will finally beat them even though the Christians are numbered in the millions and we but few. We Communists do not play with words.
>
> Of our salaries and wages we keep only what is strictly necessary. We give the rest for the advancement of the party. To this end we also concentrate our free time and most of our holidays. Christians, however, give only a little time and hardly any money for their cause.
>
> How can anyone believe in the supreme value of Christianity if Christians themselves don't practice it? How can anyone believe in its worth if those who are supposed to believe in it sacrifice neither time nor money for it? Believe me, it is we who will win, for we believe in our communist message and we are ready to sacrifice everything for it — even our lives. Why should we be afraid of Christians who are afraid to soil their hands?

STUDENT SURVEY CHALLENGES GOD'S DIVINITY

In a recent survey taken at the University of Colorado among 410 students from 41 states and 10 foreign countries —

53% felt Christ was not divine. Here is who Christ is according to their understanding:

A great prophet
A great man
A great teacher
Not a divine being
An historical person
A philosopher
A good, kind person
"A religious myth."
"Fanatic who thought he was the son of God."
"Fairy tale of the Bible."
"He's nothing to me."
"A Jew with a messianic delusion."
"A great guy on a trip."
"Crutch for older people, maybe a farce."
"Groovy guy."
"The most significant single man in history."

What can the young people expect when adults attempt to eliminate all reference to God and religious philosophy in lectures aimed at instilling moral responsibility in its soldiers?

This is exactly what was attempted in a complaint filed by the American Civil Liberties Union against the Army, Air Force and Navy.

It objected to military Chaplains referring to God when giving the required Character Guidance talks to the troops.

The National Observer recently reported an interview with some high school students from Dayton, Ohio which revealed their personal attitudes toward the role of the churches and of religion in modern living.

A moderator asked that if teenagers were completely free to decide where to go to church, what would they do?

One youngster commented that he thought 90% of the kids would quit.

The moderator then asked: "Who gives you your strongest values—your parents, your ministers, one another?"

One of the boys answered: "I think with me it started with my parents . . . and now clergymen, I don't know—they're changing. Like last night at a party we were dancing with a nun."

Another youngster remarked: "The most effective people I've met as far as religious attitudes go are clergymen who have said forget it to the church and have resigned, and people who divorce themselves from the church. . . ."

In referring to the church, one boy commented: "The church has nothing to offer and so there's nothing to stay for."

THE GROWTH OF CULTS

And so it is that the cults are growing in the United States as well as in other parts of the world.

One cult is known as Soka Gakkai, which was originally a Japanese religion, and now claims 170,000 U.S. members. Converts to Soka Gakkai are a mixed assortment of religion seekers.

Soka Gakkai makes few demands on its converts. All a person has to do is practice Gongoyo — the morning and evening recitation of Buddhist sutras and the chanting of the Daimoku (ritual prayer) "until they feel satisfied."

There is also an "I am God" theory which is sweeping the country.

In the book by Timothy Leary titled *High Priest* he states: "I was in heaven. Illumination. Every object in the room was a radiant structure of atomic-god-particles . . . Matter did not exist. An endless variety of ecstatic experiences spiraled out around me. I had taken the God step."

While it might be hard to believe, there is even a group which calls itself WITCH. This dissenting moment is designed to destroy the illusion that women are regimented and delicate creatures.

WITCH (Women's International Terrorist Conspiracy from Hell) isn't interested in the normal trimmings of womanhood. This group which is now active on many campuses is out to destroy the idea that women should take second place in a man's world.

Members in some New York stage parties recently dressed up in pointed hats to prowl the city streets with such posters as: "Kiss me, I'm a liberal," "Thank God, I'm an atheist."

This is the face of today's youth and while many would see only a hopeless end, the Christian rejoices in an endless hope.

COUNTERFEIT CHRISTIANITY

However, what does Christianity have to offer the young person of today?

It is a sad fact that many Christian schools today have departed from their once stable evangelical foundation. Whole denominations that were once sound in the faith now deny the deity of Christ every week in their Sunday School literature, and many Christians continue to give their money to such false churches. It was not an empty warning when Jesus said:

> "Beware of false prophets, which come to you in sheep's clothing, but inwardly they are ravening wolves."
> *(Matthew 7:15 King James Version)*

Many leaders in the Christian field feel that all types of Christianity must unite in order for Christ to be heard. They wish to see those who trust in the Christ who did miracles kiss those who deny Christ's power and atoning death.

Another method of misleading our youth is that of bringing Christ down to the level of the young people instead of bringing the young people up to the level of Christ.

The Apostle Paul wisely wrote:

> I beseech you therefore, brethren, by the mercies of God, that ye present your bodies a living sacrifice, holy, acceptable unto God, which is your reasonable service.
> And be not conformed to this world: but be ye transformed. . . .
> *(Romans: 12:1,2 King James Version)*

Soka Gakkai, originally a Japanese religion, now claims 170,000 U.S. members. Converts of Soka Gakkai are a mixed assortment of religion seekers. Pictured here are U.S. converts in recitative prayer.

The impression is given to us by those who condone such action that unless we "tune in" to the present generation, they will "tune out" to Christ.

The standard phrase that they use is that, "Today's world has a new set of problems and they must be met with a new set of Christian values and Christian approaches."

We are told that what was good enough for people a generation ago or in the days of Paul can no longer work in today's "now" generation.

One well-known and once very sound Christian school has spawned such new ideas.

At this school a gospel team was formed to convey the "now" approach to reach teenagers and church members. The approach of this gospel team is to correlate worldly music to the gospel of Christ.

This group, feeling that there was a communication gap in the church, decided to close that gap by bringing the "beat of the world" into the church.

The group begins their program in a church with the singing of a secular song entitled "Sounds of Silence." This is their theme song.

And from this song, they attempt to get across a gospel message.

The song was written by Arthur Garfunkle and Paul Simon. It has nothing to do with the Christian message.

The leader of this team stated that: "We believe love is found in two spheres in the world—the secular and the Christian sphere. We believe that the idea that Christ set up, of course, applies to the Christian and is needed and groped after by the secular man. As far as I'm concerned, it is our conviction that the ideal set-up is impossible. And yet this ideal—the impossible—has become a reality in one man—the Christ—the impossible dream is real."

So with this approach, this gospel team goes on to sing another secular song titled "The Impossible Dream."

When the moderator asked how the approach of using secular music in the church went over, the leader of this group replied: "What we try to do, is by identifying a Christian message with a secular song, we find that when they hear the secular song outside the church they remember the message. It's a stimulus response kind of thing and it works!"

This is indicative of the type of pseudo-religious approach being used by many groups throughout the country. They are trying to put Christ into the groove of today's up-beat generation.

And the sad fact is not so much that Christian young people are doing this, but that many Christian adults are also condoning this as the way to reach the youth.

THE SEARCH FOR LIFE

What have we seen in the college unrest, in the unrest of the high schools, in the wide use of drugs on college campuses, in the growing crime rate among young people, and in the permissive society where young people no longer strive for standards? We have seen in these things a so-called free society that leaves youth with a heaven that is empty.

And what do these young people find to fill this empty void? Some are finding a modern man-made Christ who is nothing but an imitation of the world. This is an attempt to bring Christ down to the gutter level of this world.

Can this type of counterfeit spiritual food be any better than the drugs that students are taking on campuses throughout the country?

Many young people are seeking a heaven—a heaven here on earth. Around them, however, they see the hypocrisy of adults. Thus the void within them falls easy prey to leaders, who, with a personality like a Demosthenes, can move them into wild action.

They run in all directions, seeking an answer.

Young people present a set of demands. The demands are met and yet, they still remain unsatisfied.

The world just doesn't seem right to them. They are impatient, and yet they cannot seem to change the world or its people.

For as long as there are people, there will be men seeking to sacrifice everything to make a profit — willing to sacrifice morals, their own families, and their own lives in order to achieve personal power, glory, or gain.

The youth of today, disappointed in their race for a heaven on earth, flounder not knowing which way to turn.

For all of their wisdom, they lack the wisdom and knowledge of God.

Psalm 110:4 tells us, "The fear of the Lord is the beginning of wisdom."

How much more the responsibility lies with Christians today to point young people to Christ, and to set their feet on the solid foundation of the Lord Jesus Christ.

Young people today are not flocking to a modern counterfeit religion that merely brings Christ also down to their level. They want to reach forward and up. Many are seeking for a higher spiritual and moral plane. And that can only be achieved through their acceptance of Christ as their personal Saviour on His terms and His requirements.

> Enter ye in at the strait gate: for wide is the gate, and broad is the way, that leadeth to destruction, and many there be which go in thereat:
> Because strait is the gate, and narrow is the way, which leadeth unto life, and few there be that find it.
> *(Matthew 7:13,14 King James Version)*

When they reach up and accept these terms set forth in God's Word, they will find their long night is over. And the youth's search for Heaven will not be the heaven that this world has to offer but the eternal Heaven which Christ has promised to all who will believe.

> Come unto me, all ye that labour and are heavy laden, and I will give you rest.
> Take my yoke upon you, and learn of me; for I am meek and lowly in heart: and ye shall find rest unto your souls.
> For my yoke is easy, and my burden is light.
> *(Matthew 11:28-30 King James Version)*

Chapter 4

The Businessman's Paradise

Awaiting the Population Explosion • America's Automobile
Heaven • Heaven on Earth Heavily Mortgaged • A Galaxy
of Gadgets • The Sex Approach to Fashion • Basking in
Wealth • New York City . . . Profits and Pains • More Business
and Less God • The Race for Money • High Priests of Finance
Meet Secretly • Soaring Salaries • Those Terrible Taxes •
Mammoth Mergers • The Vapor That Vanishes • Tomorrow's
World

"I've finally become rich enough," a Ford Motor Company
executive observed not long ago, "that I can afford to pay
somebody else to cut my grass. But now I can't find anybody
willing to cut it."

This is the kind of lament heard throughout the United
States.

The rising standards of society tend to reduce the supply
of some services.

And businessmen who have strived for years to build up
a private fortune finally find at the end of the line that the goal
they were seeking leaves nothing but a hollow shell.

The businessman's paradise is made up of big profits,
quick sales, a continuing income, a nest egg in the bank, and
a healthy portfolio of stocks and bonds.

And so it is that many businessmen strive to make earth their paradise. To this idol, they sacrifice everything—many times their own marriages and the happiness of their children to reach what they feel is the pinnacle of success.

But in reaching their prize they find out too late that their goal is corrupt and means nothing in an endless eternity. Perhaps, some of them are laboring under the assumption that they will live forever? Alfred Lord Tennyson observed that there would be bigger business to be conducted in Heaven.

His well-known poem in part reads:

> For I dipt into the future, as far as human eye could see,
> Saw the Vision of the world, and all the wonder that would be;
> Saw the heavens filled with commerce, argosies of magic sails,
> Pilots of the purple twilight dropping down with costly bales;
> Heard the heavens fill with shouting and there rain'd a ghastly dew.
> From the nations' airy navies grappling in the central blue.

AWAITING THE POPULATION EXPLOSION

Actually many businessmen have been worried because the population of the United States has *not* been exploding at a rate they would like.

While the births in 1957 hit almost 4½ million, they dropped by a million in 1966 to approximately 3.6 million.

Many businessmen are anxiously waiting for the year 1975 when it is expected that the births will increase to approximately 5.4 million births in the United States.

This will be a heyday for a sizable number of businessmen who have been waiting restlessly for the new wave of marriages and births to power the economy in the mid 1970's.

If for some reason births do not zoom to this new level, some businessmen are going to be greatly disappointed, particularly those dealing in diaper services, bicycles, linens, milk, toys, baby furniture, children's clothing, baby food, and soft drinks.

One startling thing that has already come to the attention of many (and this is often an unreported detail) is the recent trend of births in the United States which are illegitimate.

For while total births have been falling, illegitimate births have been rising—over 600,000 in 1970, as an example, which is about 400,000 more per year than 10 years ago.

It has been estimated by studies made at the University of Michigan that aside from the 600,000-odd women who are not married when they bear children, another 550,000 or so, it appears, become pregnant before they have husbands—and then get married.

This is a sad commentary on the state of America today and reflects the new theory of permissiveness where "anything goes."

However, these shot-gun marriages help to boost the national economy and make a paradise for those men who are merely seeking more profits to bolster their business operations.

AMERICA'S AUTOMOBILE HAVEN

One of the best measures of the economy is the apparent unquenched appetite for Americans to buy cars, cars, and more cars. It is estimated that in 1973, approximately 9,500,000 new cars (including imports) will be sold.

This market in 1975 will amount to 11,500,000 new cars.

Despite the outcries against the automobile—for fouling the air, killing so many people, and laying waste cities and countryside—the United States remains an automobile-loving society.

Sociologists tried to explain this phenomenon by telling us that a car removes a man from real life, seals him up in luxury, and responds unquestioningly to his commands.

Fortune magazine, in its special report titled "Markets of the Seventies" reports that since 1960 the number of families with two or more cars has risen from nearly 10,000,000 to nearly 14,800,000. In fact, one household in four now owns two or more cars!

The big three car manufacturers in Detroit are now preparing campaigns to educate people to become *three-car families.*

In 1969 Ford showed the best gain over 1968 sales at 26%...while General Motors gain was only 8%.

It was the imports that brought a remarkable surge to one million car sales in the United States or a remarkable 31% over 1970 sales. And it was this amazing fact that caused Ford Motor Company to come out with a competitive car in order to stop this trend.

For in spite of the millions of cars sold by U.S. car makers, there is still a desire for more profits and more sales.

A competitive system in the United States is an excellent system and no one decries this. However, as is often the case, man in his selfishness and greed is never satisfied and seeks to make more and more profits and build a bigger and bigger mansion for himself here on earth—losing sight of the fact that striving simply for material gain is vain and foolish and these temporal riches will soon pass away.

Fierce competition often leads to ruthlessness and a misdirected sense of values—this is the nature of man.

HEAVEN ON EARTH HEAVILY MORTGAGED

It is also interesting to observe how many people are concerned about their home here on earth, and at the same time they spend little time preparing for their home in eternity.

During the first half of the 1960's the number of households increased by an average of just under 900,000 a year. And this increase is expected to jump to 1,250,000 during the first half of the 1970's.

But the amazing thing is that *Fortune* magazine's estimate of the number of second homes increased by at least 100,000 a year in the early sixties.

Based on this fact, *Fortune* projects a potential second-home market of 200,000 a year in the early seventies.

So just as a second-car family is becoming a common place thing—in the near future a second-home family will likewise become common. The personal income of Americans has been rising steadily. The total annual personal income of everyone in the United States is now $2000 billion and is increasing at the rate of approximately $5 billion per month.

Can earth be heaven when such inequalities exist? On one hand, a majority in the United States are so affluent that many own two and three cars and have a second home. Yet in other parts of the world, 10,000 people a day are dying of starvation and have no place to call home. Two million human beings died in the Nigeria-Biafra conflict alone!

How can anyone say that earth is Heaven and that conditions will get better? Anyone who has made a study of current and past history will realize that as nations become more sophisticated and more wealthy, conditions only become worse.

A GALAXY OF GADGETS

Let's look at the home-goods with which America is blessed.

Over the next five years, home-goods expenditures will probably increase about as fast as disposable income. This means a rise in sales from $30 billion in 1966 to about $37 billion in 1971.

Sales hopes for 1973 come to about 7.7 million black and white TV sets. Last year, 1,500,000 TV sets were imported from Japan and for the mid seventies businessmen are striving for $7 billion in color TV sales.

It is not uncommon for Americans to have two, three and four television sets at home.

And the race is on to saturate America with all types of appliances. In 1966 retail sales of appliances came to $6.8 billion. Sales of clothes dryers almost doubled. Dishwashers doubled in sales. In 1966, sales of blenders quadrupled to about 2 million.

Is it no wonder, businessmen are somewhat happy ... but never quite satisfied. For in every company there is a striving for greater sales and a better balance sheet.

THE SEX APPROACH TO FASHION

Perhaps, one of the biggest markets for the businessman is in the market of fashion.

One manufacturer and designer of high-style women's shoes, recently summed up his industry's extraordinary success in the last four years by stating: "Fashion is the ingredient that sells things."

And as *Fortune* magazine reported, "Fashion has indeed been selling a lot recently: shoes and boots, colorful coats and vivid dresses, miniskirts and 'fun furs,' patterned stockings, pop jewelry, bows and belts; and men's colognes and tattersall slacks and turtleneck sweaters."

Indeed fashion has come up with a new sex appeal. Today, for fashion, consumers are expected to spend over $45 billion and their spending for footwear will run to an additional $7 billion.

Fashion goods for 1972 accounted for more than $60 billion in consumer outlays, making this market second only to food among all consumer markets.

Americans spend at least 10% of their personal disposable income on apparel and other fashion goods.

One dress manufacturer noted, "In fashion there is no such thing as an old woman ... The whole look is young, from head to toe, because today we are all young."

This has been termed in the fashion market as the "youth quake."

How significant it is in this day and age when Americans can have practically anything they want, they are still striving for one thing which is really impossible for them to secure — and that is youth.

And so they spend their money with a sense of religious dedication in order to achieve the youthful look. But God tells us that the emphasis on a woman's achieving true beauty should be placed on the inner woman rather than merely upon the outer. Thus Peter says of women:

> Whose adorning let it not be that outward adorning of plaiting the hair, and of wearing of gold, or of putting on of apparel:
> But let it be the hidden man of the heart, in that which is not corruptible, even the ornament of a meek and quiet spirit, which is in the sight of God of great price.
> For after this manner in the old time the holy women also, who trusted in God, adorned themselves, being in subjection unto their own husbands. . . .
> *(I Peter 3:3-5 King James Version)*

For, you see, beauty and youth do not remain with us for long on this earth, and Christ's words apply here too when He says:

> Lay not up for yourselves treasures upon earth, where moth and rust doth corrupt, and where thieves break through and steal:
> But lay up for yourselves treasures in Heaven, where neither moth nor rust doth corrupt, and where thieves do not break through nor steal.
> For where your treasure is, there will your heart be also.
> *(Matthew 6:19-21 King James Version)*

When sales in the fashion industry are lagging, designers come up with new ideas in order to boost sales and keep their profit margin at an all-time high. This was true when they introduced fancy stockings—brightly colored, patterned, glittery—stockings that are giving a lift to the sagging market. Women may not wear them daily, but they do wear them on special occasions and even at $10 or $15 a pair.

With the new theme of "everything goes" the miniskirts have accentuated what might be called the "peeping garter" problem and have created a boomy new market for panty hose. Hanes Hosiery (*Fortune Reports*) revealed that even after doubling production of panty hose in the summer of 1967, it was still some two months behind in deliveries.

With the short skirt, there was also a demand for a different shoe and this helped, of course, to boost the market of the shoe industry.

The high-heeled, pointed-toe shoe didn't go with the new dresses. Accordingly, there arose a large new market for low-heeled, broad-toed shoes. And with this women became sold also on boots which became fashionable in high, low, leather, plastic, and colored versions.

Because the fashion theme then became the "Total Look," sales of jewelry also increased by more than a third between 1969 and 1972 to nearly $4.2 billion.

But the "Total Look" didn't stop there, for there was more profits to be made. And to this look there was added the list of "necessary" cosmetics with new items in the field of eye-shadow, eyeliner, eyelashers, blushers, shaders, and brushes.

Special lipsticks were created to go with special clothes.

One individual remarked, "It just takes a lot more thought to get dressed in the morning these days."

Perhaps, that was what caused one individual to comment on the high divorce rate by stating that, "In the old days, marriages were more permanent because when the wife got up in the morning and washed her face, she was still the same girl that the husband had married the day before!"

BASKING IN WEALTH

At no time in history have the American people been so wealthy and American businessmen so prosperous.

In fact, the United States is entering the era of the mass *high*-income market. By 1975, *Fortune* projects that the average family income after federal taxes will be around $12,000.

Surprisingly enough, of the 30 million families who now have incomes of $10,000 or better, about 11 million have a second earner in their family.

Herman Kahn and Anthony J. Wiener of the Hudson Institute, in their recent book, *The Year 2000*, contemplate the possibility of a "leisure-oriented" work pattern, with a seven-and-a-half-hour day, and a four-day week, thirteen weeks a year off, and ten legal holidays.

We are truly entering into an era that the businessman would term as paradise. At any rate, those businesses involved in supplying consumer goods and services can look forward to a very big stream of income to fish in.

And as the nation becomes more wealthy it relies less and less upon God, as it strives to build its own heaven here on earth. For many, big business profits are heaven!

Even Russia is beginning to feel the effects of America's affluence.

Russia's population is 249 million. Its autos-to-people ratio is less than one car for each 235 persons, the U.S. ratio is one car for every 2 persons.

But the Kremlin now aims to put Russia on wheels, and by 1974, it hopes to have an auto output of over a million cars a year. This, of course, would bring Russia's auto-production to the level that the U.S. had reached in 1916.

It may be surprising for some to realize that even in Moscow, a city of over 7 million people, there are only about 25 gas stations and drivers pulling into any one of them almost invariably have to wait in long lines of cars and trucks to reach the pumps.

Even today, it takes three days to find a repair shop that will change one of your sparkplugs in Moscow.

NEW YORK CITY . . . PROFITS AND PAINS

Most everyone will agree that the business capital of the world is New York City. And the rapid population growth which brings with it a rapid business growth, has created many ills which give rise to doubts about New York City's future.

For a family of four to maintain even a moderate existence in New York it takes an income now of $10,195.

New York has the second highest crime rate in the nation. In addition, about six people out of every hundred thousand residents in New York die each year from emphysema caused by air pollution.

The noise ratio in New York has reached a dangerous level so that it is a fact that New Yorkers now talk louder than most people simply because of the increased noise that comes with progress.

Yet even in this densely populated city the Human Resources Commissioners of New York say that the city is short 200,000 low-skilled jobs.

Airline pilots always know when they are approaching New York without any flight map. Because New York City throws into the air 3,200 tons of sulphur dioxide, 280 tons of dirt and 4,200 tons of carbon monoxide *daily*.

New York City is a city where 2000 cars a week are stolen and where robberies increased 50% in 1972 over 1971. Murder increased by 21.3%; 58 murders alone in one week in July, 1972!

New York is a city where 350 million gallons of raw waste still pour everyday into the surrounding rivers and oceans.

Can this be Heaven?

MORE BUSINESS AND LESS GOD

More and more there is a turning away from God as income rises and a nation becomes more affluent.

Just in the last year, housing costs have gone up 24.5%. The income of individuals has risen since 1971 to an increase of 6.4%.

With the new space projects centered around the Apollo program, new jobs have been created and big business has grown even bigger.

It takes 350,000 people to put 3 men on the moon. For this is the number of managers, engineers, technicians, and safety experts employed by more than 20,000 companies throughout

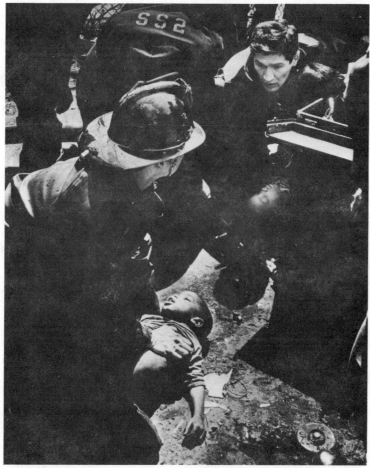

Chicago Daily News photo by Perry Riddle

Firemen attempt to restore the breath of life to rescued fire victims in Chicago during the disorders after Martin Luther King's death.

the United States who are working on this specific project. An Apollo spaceship has 91 engines and some 6,100,000 parts!

The businessman's interest goes beyond that of space

projects, but is aimed at many world-wide activities that are geared to make today his paradise.

As an example, U.S. companies now have an investment of more than $10 billion in Latin America. This is substantially larger than the United States' investment of $8 billion in Europe's Common Market nations. And of course, it is also substantially more profitable.

U.S. companies have long learned that in Europe they can only make on an average of 6.7% on their investment, while in Latin America, they can earn a handsome 11.8% a year.

American businessmen in seeking their paradise here on earth, are investing their dollars in Latin America for many things from bananas to banks and from coffee to chemicals.

While there are many responsible businesses — it is becoming increasingly evident — as we have discussed in the New York City problem, that many businesses are more interested in profits than in making a better world. Pollutions, both in the air and in rivers, continue to make the United States a mass dumping ground.

In Midland, Pennsylvania, pipes from a steel company's titanium plant pour a bright green poisonous waste fluid into the river.

In Steubenville, Ohio, iron oxide from a steel company blast furnace stains the river a reddish brown; while in Wheeling, West Virginia, an oil company plant pours a bluish-black goo down the banks into the water.

Over the years, private industry and government alike have tended to regard the Ohio River basin and its tributaries not as something to conserve, but as a huge waste disposal system.

THE RACE FOR MONEY

This nation is a nation of unrest. While businessmen are frantically seeking more ways to make more dollars and more profits, some soon discover that earth is not Heaven. With the increase of technology and population growth come insurmountable problems.

There seems to be an intense desire among businesses to want to continue to grow and grow and grow. Businessmen expect this year to spend $73 billion, 14% more than last year to expand their factories.

And the nation is heading towards more and more complex problems in its attempt to curb an inflation which one day may explode and cause a nation to turn once again to God.

The credit squeeze in the United States is getting so tight that American businesses are going across the ocean to borrow funds in order to continue their businesses. As an example, U.S. banks have borrowed $9.8 billion Eurodollars (dollars owned by people or companies outside the United States) to lend in America. In one week, they borrowed $335 million for this purpose.

This withdrawal of funds, of course, leaves that much less money for Europeans to borrow. So now European banks and governments are taking steps to keep their money at home.

This international scramble for funds has helped push interest rates on both sides of the Atlantic to what one Swiss banker calls the highest general level in 50 years.

Wall Street Journal reported that American banks are now borrowing dollars in Europe at an annual interest cost of 8½%, up from 6½% a year ago — and then lending the Eurodollars to their best customers in America at an effective annual rate of about 9%.

This greater reliance of United States businessmen on money from other areas of the world, brings about a very interesting factor of which many people are unaware.

This is the beginning of a trend which could very well usher in Antichrist and a One World type of government.

One can easily see how the stage is being set for the Federated States of Europe, which may include the United States, and in which there would be a unified money system and a unified dictatorship.

Concerning the Antichrist's future domination over the world business system we read:

> And he causeth all, both small and great, rich and poor, free and bond, to receive a mark in their right hand, or in their foreheads:
> And that no man might buy or sell, save he that had the mark, or the name of the beast, or the number of his name.
> *(Revelation 13:16,17 King James Version)*

Newsweek reports that there already has been developed an unusual machine which provides quick identification.

In the coming "cashless society," it will be absolutely essential that the dispensers of goods and services be able to quickly and positively identify those who offer credit cards and checks in payment. Sibany Manufacturing Corp. of Riverside, Conn., has developed an electronic machine that, unattended and automatically, performs verification with what is described as scientific accuracy.

Identity of the prospective purchaser or check-casher is established by the geometry of a person's hand. A person granted a credit card, check-cashing ID card, security pass, etc., puts his right hand into the Identimat device (photo) that mechanically measures the geometry of the hand and reduces these unique measurements to an electronic code (magnetic or optical markings) which are placed in the individual's credit or ID card.

When the card bearer goes shopping, he establishes his credit by placing both his card and right hand into the Identimat which electronically compares the two and lights up an "accept" button, signifying the person is who the card says he is. The machine will lease for about $15 a month.

One can see how such a machine could be used by Antichrist in the Tribulation Period.

Many businessmen have privately stated such a course of unifying world finance would be more than welcome! More and more they see the problems of running their business, and they see the cities becoming so complex that it will take a dictatorship-type of unified government to keep things simply on an even keel.

HIGH PRIESTS OF FINANCE MEET SECRETLY

There already exists, in Basel, Switzerland, a once a month meeting of men who hold the purse strings of the Western World.

They have been termed the high priests of international finance and they gather in this small Swiss city for the most secret of financial conclaves.

The casual visitor to Basel would never even suspect that anything unusual was happening. But on the second Sunday of each month, he might notice a few soberly suited men in the big hotels around the Station Square. But he would not recognize them for their faces seldom appear on television screens or in the press.

There is only one clue, and that clue is offered by the building where they gather. For on this building there is a little plaque beside the door saying simply "Bank for International Settlements." This appears in English, French and German.

These high priests of world money affairs veil their rites in strictest secrecy. Less is known about the workings of this so-called "Basel Club" than about any other aspect of international financial cooperation.

Actually the men who come here every month under cover of secrecy are the central bank governors from the world's major industrial nations.

The sole purpose of their conclave is to keep the wheels of international finance greased and turning. For they are the guardians of their national currencies, protected by law from interference by politicians and civil servants.

A representative is sent from Britain, from Italy, from Germany, from France, from the United States as well as from Canada and Japan.

This group of central bankers shun publicity and have done everything in their power to resist the growing interest the press has begun to take in their activities in recent months.

But it is this tiny band of men who gather monthly that rule the international finance of these countries and determine what will and what will not be done.

And it is organizations of this type, as well as desperate times, that will make softer the ushering in of Antichrist to control the Federated States of Europe.

Sin has a way of instilling an insatiable appetite for profits among many businessmen.

Their striving to make more and more money gives them a drive that nothing else apparently can.

SOARING SALARIES

Whether it is the insensible clubbing of baby seals in Canada or the producing of inferior merchandise in order to keep the profit margin high, there appears to be a desire for rapid increase of wealth.

But the sad fact is that when this status of wealth is achieved, it leaves nothing but a hollowness — an emptiness.

This is a day and age when a basketball player is offered a 40,000-acre ranch stocked with 3500 head of cattle in addition to $1 million if he will play pro-basketball on a certain team.

This is a day and age when a golfer can make a $1 million in a year. Or when a ski champion can secure $2 million by endorsing several products.

Despite the government's anti-inflation campaign — everybody seems to be earning more and more these days. Even

Congress doubled the U.S. President's salary to $200,000 while boosting the pay of its own members from $30,000 to $42,500.

Barbra Streisand, in early 1969 signed a contract with a Las Vegas hotel giving her an estimated $500,000 (plus stock in the hotel) for four weeks' work a year.

Harvard Business School graduates now begin their working lives at an average $15,000 a year.

Americans are undoubtedly the world's highest paid people. Many truck drivers last year earned more than $25.000.

Pilots are now earning as high as $75,000 a year with the jumbo jets in service.

Even some clergymen are realizing richer worldly rewards. *Time* magazine reported, "While Catholic priests in New York have to get by on a maximum of $2,400 a year plus free room and board, the starting salary of an Episcopal minister in California is $8,000 plus housing. Rabbis are the best off, perhaps because Jews do not hold such firm beliefs as do Christians about the rewards of the hereafter. A Reform rabbi receives up to $15,000 in his first congregation and can look forward later to $30,000, and in some cases $50,000."

One college football hero who turned his business arrangements over to a businessman finds such an agreement very profitable.

The businessman claims that he will make the football hero a millionaire before his first season is over and a multimillionaire within a few years.

A businessman who finds that he is making too much profit and wants to circumvent paying taxes, many times buys cattle. He then takes the generous deductions permitted to farmers—even part-time farmers—writing them off against non-farm income that otherwise would be taxed at rates of up to 70%.

While other manufacturers, not satisfied to keep even the hot dog the way it is, strive to make a greater profit by seeking to put 15% chicken meat in hot dogs without stating so on the label.

The dedication of many businessmen is amazing, that is, when it comes to making a dollar.

One sales executive logged 3800 miles on six separate commercial flights in one week and visited 17 regional sales managers, distributors, manufacturers, agents or customers. During this trek he downed 25 hard liquor drinks — all this so he could earn an income each year of $20,000 to $40,000 a year.

He is keeping up this pace because he feels his job offers the surest route to top corporate management.

But even this dedicated businessman realizes that his job has its drawbacks. His hair is already a solid gray and he is aging tremendously. His marriage failed last year. These are the penalties that many businessmen will absorb in order to secure a questionable security in life.

The *Wall Street Journal* recently reported concerning another businessman,

> Aristotle Onassis has a 325-foot yacht with gold-plated faucets in the bathroom, a 500-acre island in the Ionian Sea, a shipping fleet of about 100 vessels (larger than that of most nations) and a personal fortune estimated at about $300 million.

THOSE TERRIBLE TAXES

Reports coming from Washington have shown that there are about 500 rich or super-rich Americans, who even though they had an income in excess of $100,000, paid not one penny in federal income tax last April.

Actually, 27 of them had incomes of more than $1 million in 1971 and paid no income tax. And in 1966, four Americans with incomes in excess of $5 million paid no income tax. In fact, in just 12 years taxlessness among those with incomes of more than $1 million has increased five-fold. These were some of the facts disclosed to Congress. And yet, on the other side, there are 25.5 million who live below the official "poverty line" who must pay taxes.

The subject of taxes has been a sore point among Americans for many years and is now reaching a climax.

More and more Americans are becoming disturbed about the high rate of taxes and the misuse of money in areas which are questionable.

Even if a single factory worker who gets $5,000 a year receives a pay raise of $300 — out of this $300 increase, $245 will go towards paying taxes! This leaves him a net increase of $55!

And a single junior executive with a pay of $15,000 a year, receiving an increase of $900 will pay $873 of that additional $900 in taxes! Thus out of a $900 raise he will net exactly $27.

The cost of living is going up approximately 3.3% each year. A new car is priced about $100 more than a year ago. Increases of 15% or more on auto insurance rates are not unusual. If a worker rides a bus, he will find the fare a nickel higher than last year.

A pair of work shoes that cost $10 two years ago is now priced at close to $12. Two years ago, $1,000 would have bought goods worth $54 more than it does today.

Not only are federal taxes rising but so are state and local taxes.

While it must be conceded that Americans surrender less of their income to the tax collector than do citizens of many other industrial countries, nevertheless, *their total tax burden has reached the highest point in U.S. history!*

May 7 may go unnoticed by many but it should be celebrated. On this date the average person, for the first time this year, starts earning money for himself. The United States Chamber of Commerce estimates that for the preceding 127 days he will be working to make enough money to pay his federal, state and local taxes.

Former Secretary of Treasury, Joseph W. Barr commented to Congress, "We now face the possibility of a taxpayer revolt if we do not soon make major reforms in our income taxes."

To avoid taxes there is a rising growth in tax-free private

foundations. In 1964 there were 15,000 tax-free foundations. In 1968, this grew to 22,000 and it is still growing.

In 1960, foundations controlled $11.5 billion of the nation's wealth. But in 1968, this rose to $20.5 billion. While many of these foundations are created for very worthy causes, others are being used to channel funds into questionable areas which have as their goal an increasing of materialism. This further contributes to the breaking down of the *spiritual* foundations upon which this country was founded.

MAMMOTH MERGERS

Many businesses, finding that they can not make as great a profit as they desire as an individual company, have joined the trend of what is now called the "Conglomerates."

The word "conglomerate" means: "Made up of miscellaneous materials gathered from various sources."

When groups of businesses merge together under one controlling head, it is often impossible for small businesses to compete — this is especially the case if the merged businesses are sufficiently interrelated so as to provide each of the merged companies with new strong business advantages.

Eventually, during the reign of Antichrist, there will be a conglomerate of nations which may be called the Federated States of Europe. It will be headed by one individual — Antichrist.

Business is adapting a similar technique. Thus with only a few people directing the major businesses in the United States, if this be the case, it will be much easier for Antichrist to take over for he may only have to persuade a few conglomerate heads to his way of thinking.

A decade ago, Ling-Temco-Vought, Inc. did not even exist, but in 1967 this conglomerate was number 38 in Fortune's Corporate listing of the 500 biggest corporations in the United States. Up until recently it was among the 15 largest companies in the United States. Ling-Temco-Vought, Inc. was the public-owned parent company of 10 individual subsidiaries — each of which was listed on the major stock exchanges.

SO YOU GET A PAY BOOST—WHAT WILL BE LEFT?

Examples: Three families, each with four members, getting pay raises of 6 per cent in 1972. Figures show that a raise of this size is almost wiped out by higher federal taxes, including the proposed income surtax, an increase in the Social Security tax base, and a rise of 3.3 per cent in yearly living costs, as officially forecast.

No. 1 Factory worker receiving $5,000 a year
Pay raise: **$300**

Federal income tax on $300 raise	$ 48
Proposed increase in income tax	$ 34
Higher Social Security tax	$ 13
Higher cost of living	$150
Total offset to pay raise	$245

LEAVING, OUT OF A $300 RAISE: $55

No. 2 Construction worker earning $8,000 a year
Pay raise: **$480**

Federal income tax on $480 raise	$ 82
Proposed increase in income tax	$ 85
Higher Social Security tax	$ 53
Higher cost of living	$230
Total offset to pay raise	$450

LEAVING, OUT OF A $480 RAISE: $30

No. 3 Junior executive with pay of $15,000 a year
Pay raise: **$900**

Federal income tax on $900 raise	$178
Proposed increase in income tax	$224
Higher Social Security tax	$ 53
Higher cost of living	$418
Total offset to pay raise	$873

LEAVING, OUT OF A $900 RAISE: $27

Note: State and local taxes, on the rise all over the U.S., will eat even deeper into any pay raises for millions of wage earners. Many workers, as a result, will find that wage boosts lag behind the increases in living costs and taxes.

This is just one example of the many conglomerates that are spreading like wild-fire throughout America and have the United States government worried about the future of individual American businesses. Whether or not the Justice Department's 1969 anti-conglomerate anti-trust suits will alter the picture is yet to be seen.

It seems odd that the cost of producing U.S. paper currency is less than one cent a note and yet for the purchasing power that this currency will buy, many businesses will sacrifice integrity and sensibility in order to construct out of this currency a paradise here on earth.

THE VAPOR THAT VANISHES

One very well-known cowboy singer superstar rose from nothing to a millionaire. He then realized that at the end of this rainbow there was only an imitation glitter that left him with no foundation for an eternal life.

Brought up on a little farm in Arkansas where he picked 350 pounds of cotton a day he rose to a point where he is now annually grossing nearly $2 million. This was quite a rise to the pinnacle of business fame.

Most successful businessmen will tell you the reason for their success is because they worked 25 hours a day. This fast pace in 1961 caused this popular singer to turn to a stimulant, Dexedrene, to keep up with the pace. Then to relax, he needed a tranquilizer.

He found himself soon locked into the cruel cycle of "nice" drugs.

In 1965, he was arrested returning from Mexico with 1,143 pills. By 1967, he had run through his first marriage. He estimates that he used up to 100 stimulants, plus tranquilizers to get through a day. And all this for what?

> . . . ye know not what shall be on the morrow. For what is your life? It is even a vapour, that appeareth for a little time, and then vanisheth away.
> (*James 4:14 King James Version*)

TOMORROW'S WORLD

This is the day of many new inventions.

Our civilization is already giddy with gadgets. By the year 2000, more than 5,000,000 patents will have been issued by the U.S. Patent Office.

By the year 2000, many experts predict that many Americans will be flying around in aerodynamic autos powered by fuel cells, batteries or atoms.

Micro-electronics will yet produce an electron beam — a super beam that can crumble a mountain of granite in a few minutes!

Miniaturization will enable the businessman of the future to carry equipment in his briefcase which today fills an entire room: video camera, electric typewriter, computer terminal, picture-phone and a tiny TV screen.

Bio-engineers say that by the manipulation of DNA, the chemical substance important in genetics, they will be able to "engineer" physical and emotional makeup *before* birth.

Think of the impact this could have when if at the whim of some leader, certain chemical substances could be injected into women to determine what type of children will be produced — morons, geniuses, or automatons that will follow instructions without questioning, etc.!

Climate-controlled cities will be covered by domes two miles in diameter.

Knowledge and memory pills may be administered to make people instantly more conversant with any subject . . . or to make them instantly forget the past.

We will be able to travel from Chicago to Tokyo in $\frac{1}{2}$ hour.

Undersea ranches may be operated by men able to breathe like fish, thanks to artificial plastic gills attached to their lungs.

Icebergs will be floated to the shores of arid nations as a source of fresh water.

A laser light beam directed from the ceiling towards a dinner plate will broil your steak in an instant.

Pinhead-size microcircuit radios in stereo, may be planted in our ears.

These are some of the inventions that Dr. Peter Goldmark, an inventor, predicts our future will have.

However, after examining these and many more, his consensus of opinion is that *none of these*, singly or in combination, will increase man's happiness or peace of mind by one iota.

In a recent comment he noted:

> I say we already have inventions enough – now we must catch up with the inventions we already have. Our bathrooms are more luxurious than those of ancient Rome. We jet around the world faster than Caesar could march from Pompeii to Rome. If we could have push-buttoned our way to happiness, we would already have reached nirvana (the Buddhist idea of heavenly peace).

It was Lord Ritchie-Calder, a professor at the University of Edinburgh, who stated: "The greatest tragedy of science today is that we've got a great stockpile of knowledge and no philosophy."

Basically, we have stockpiles of knowledge, of wealth and of luxury. But we have turned away from the God that made all of this possible. We have turned away from the Scriptures and put our total reliance on man. On human wisdom the Apostle Paul well observed:

> For it is written, I will destroy the wisdom of the wise, and will bring to nothing the understanding of the prudent.
>
> Where is the wise? where is the scribe? where is the disputer of this world? hath not God made foolish the wisdom of this world?
>
> For after that in the wisdom of God the world by wisdom knew not God, it pleased God by the foolishness of preaching to save them that believe.
>
> For the Jews require a sign, and the Greeks (Gentiles) seek after wisdom:
>
> But we preach Christ crucified, unto the Jews a stumbling block, and unto the Greeks foolishness;
>
> But unto them which are called, both Jews and Greeks, Christ the power of God, and the wisdom of God.
>
> Because the foolishness of God is wiser than men; and the weakness of God is stronger than men.
>
> *(I Corinthians 1:19-25 King James Version)*

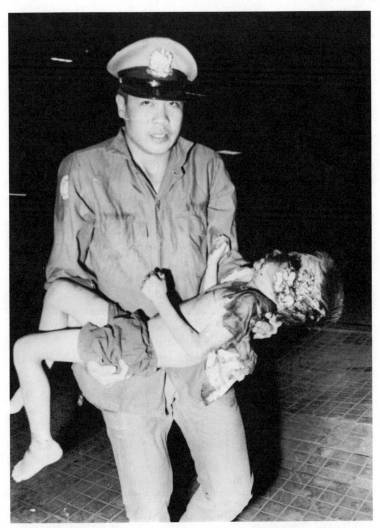

A South Vietnamese soldier carries a wounded child to a waiting ambulance in Saigon after his house was hit by a Communist rocket. The child's mother was killed. In man's cruelty to man, children often become the victims.

Further on human wisdom: It has been stated that scientists have developed ways to communicate with astronauts working on the moon—but what we need is a better way to communicate person to person right here on earth.

Dr. Goldmark, the inventor, further observed that:

> We need parents whose example does not fill sons and daughters with the attitude that money, flashier cars and bigger houses are the only goals of life; who, instead of abdicating their responsibilities, are not afraid to set moral standards. . . .

Dr. Goldmark summed up his remarks by stating: "It is not hardware, gadgetry or beautiful labor-saving devices that will give man the peace of mind he craves."

How prophetic this is from a man who has devoted a lifetime to creating inventions.

In the past 100 years the world population has almost tripled and the amount of knowledge that we have been accumulating has jumped 100-fold.

And 90% of all scientists of all time are now living in this present era! Man has devised machines that can now mathematically compute a problem in 2 seconds that would take man 38 years to compute . . . and yet man is unable to solve the problems of war, hunger and disease!

It might be well for every businessman to read Ecclesiastes:

> What profit hath a man of all his labour which he taketh under the sun?
> One generation passeth away and another generation cometh: but the earth abideth for ever.
> I have seen all the works that are done under the sun; and, behold, all is vanity . . .
> For in much wisdom is much grief: and he that increaseth knowledge increaseth sorrow.
> (*Ecclesiastes 1:3,4,14,18 King James Version*)

It was a dedicated Christian who wrote back in the 16th Century:

> Teach us, Good Lord, to serve Thee, as Thou deserveth;
> to give and not to count the cost;
> to fight and not to heed the wounds;
> to toil and not to seek for rest;
> to labor and not ask for any reward.
> Save that of knowing that we do Thy will.

How important this message is in today's highly sophisticated world.

There is nothing wrong with the desire of man to make a profit. This is right in the sight of the Lord.

American business to succeed must make its fair share of profits and must continue to improve its general productivity to keep up with the demand.

The sin is not in the making of the profit.

The sin is in a total dedication toward building a materialistic world at the expense of duty to God and to one's neighbor. The sin results in the sinner's losing his own soul and often helping to destroy the souls of others.

It was Martin Luther who wrote: "For where God built a church, there the devil would also build a chapel."

And more and more, the businessmen of today's world, unknowingly are helping the devil to build that chapel, thinking that they are building their own paradise here on earth.

On this subject Christ's words challenge every man or woman who makes money his idol. Christ said,

> For what shall it profit a man, if he shall gain the whole world, and lose his own soul?
> *(Mark 8:36 King James Version)*

> No man can serve two masters: for either he will hate the one, and love the other; or else he will hold to the one, and despise the other. Ye cannot serve God and mammon [the god of riches, money, possessions].
> *(Matthew 6:24 King James Version)*

Chapter 5
Living Till I Die
PART 1

The Perils of Wealth • Basking in the Lap of Luxury • The Day Everything Stops • Air Traffic Jams • How to Get Rich • Mansions on Earth • Nobody Wants You When You're Down and Out • The Underground Bank • The Rise in Counterfeiting • What Happened to Ice Cream? • Freeze Your Age • The Thrill Seekers

In 1914 an American worker had to work 6 hours and 44 minutes to earn enough to buy a shirt. Today he earns a better shirt in 1 hour and 49 minutes.

In 1914 he worked an hour and 37 minutes for a pound of butter; today he does it in 19 minutes. In 1914 he labored 1 hour 14 minutes for a pound of bacon; today 22 minutes. In 1914, it took 12 hours 52 minutes to earn a good pair of men's shoes; today 6 hours 54 minutes. If you listed everything you eat, wear, and use—you will find that the story is much the same.

It has been said that the modern American is a person who drives a bank-financed car over a bond-financed highway on credit card gas to open a charge account at a department store so he can fill his savings-and-loan-financed home with installment-purchased furniture.

Many husbands probably believe that women have a passion for arithmetic; they divide their age by two, double

126

AMERICA'S PROGRESS COMPARED

	IN 1914	In 1914 an American worker had to work 6 hours and 44 minutes to earn enough to buy a shirt.
	TODAY	Today he earns a better shirt in 1 hour and 49 minutes.
	IN 1914	In 1914 he worked 1 hour 37 minutes for a pound of butter.
	TODAY	Today, 19 minutes.
	IN 1914	In 1914 1 hour 14 minutes for a pound of bacon.
	TODAY	Today, 22 minutes.
	IN 1914	In 1914 12 hours 52 minutes for a good pair of men's shoes.
	TODAY	Today, 6 hours 54 minutes.

the price of their dress, triple their husband's salary and add five years to a best friend's age.

It was Carlyle who wrote

> One life; a little gleam of time between two eternities;
> no second chance for us forever more.

The American way of living is geared to a fast pace of pleasure and a struggle for security.

Through the years men seek to build up an income that will provide security for their future. Yet at the same time many strive to drink in all the pleasures this world has to offer because they realize that one day it will be too late.

It was Bret Harte who wrote:

> Of all the words of tongue and pen,
> The saddest are, "It might have been,"
> More sad are these we daily see
> "It is, but it hadn't ought to be!"

THE PERILS OF WEALTH

Although the Scriptures recognize that poverty may bring sorrow, it also emphasizes that wealth has its dangers. Jesus condemned the man whose main interest was in building larger barns. See Luke 12:16-21.

Wealth also may imperil one's salvation.

> Then said Jesus unto his disciples, Verily I say unto you, That a rich man shall hardly enter into the kingdom of heaven.
>
> *(Matthew 19:23 King James Version)*

In reading the Scriptures one will find many warnings directed to the rich.

> Charge them that are rich in this world, that they be not highminded, nor trust in uncertain riches, but in the living God, who giveth us richly all things to enjoy.
>
> *(I Timothy 6:17 King James Version)*

> Go to now, ye rich men, weep and howl for your miseries that shall come upon you.
> Your riches are corrupted, and your garments are moth-eaten.
> Your gold and silver is cankered; and the rust of them shall be a witness against you, and shall eat your flesh as it were fire. Ye have heaped treasure together for the last days.
>
> *(James 5:1-3 King James Version)*

One of the great dangers of wealth—and the Scriptures make this clear—is that the wealthy are especially easy prey to certain specific sins. The Scriptures point out that wealth may result in one's trusting too much in self:

> The rich man's wealth is his strong city, and as an high wall in his own conceit.
>
> *(Proverbs 18:11 King James Version)*

> The rich man is wise in his own conceit; but the poor that hath understanding searcheth him out.
>
> *(Proverbs 28:11 King James Version)*

It may also result in high mindedness (people thinking that they are self-sufficient, and too good to be associated with others):

> Charge them that are rich in this world, that they be not highminded, nor trust in uncertain riches, but in the living God who giveth us richly all things to enjoy.
>
> *(I Timothy 6:17 King James Version)*

And selfishness:

> And one of the company said unto Him, Master, speak to my brother, that he divide the inheritance with me.
> And he said unto him, Man who made me a judge or a divider over you?
> And he said unto them, Take heed, and beware of covetousness: for a man's life consisteth not in the abundance of the things which he possesseth.
>
> *(Luke 12:13-15 King James Version)*

Jesus made it abundantly clear that all would be held accountable for the use made of their riches.

There are many who have accepted Christ and are blessed with material gains who are misdirecting their income for selfish reasons and much sadder will be their day when the leaves fall.

So Bret Harte's four-line poem has deep significance to each of us because when the leaves of our life fall, the saddest words we might utter are "It might have been."

Those who know not Christ as personal Savior and Lord . . . find themselves on an endless treadmill trying to find a peace and happiness through money. But they will find that when they reach their pinnacle of success it leaves a hollow echoing ring. In the end, no amount of money whether it be thousands of dollars or millions can extend their life one additional second. Thus of the rich man who had treasure stored up for years to come Christ said:

And He spake a parable unto them, saying, The ground of a certain rich man brought forth plentifully:

And he thought within himself, saying, What shall I do, because I have no room where to bestow my fruits?

And he said, This will I do: I will pull down my barns, and build greater; and there will I bestow all my fruits and my goods.

And I will say to my soul, Soul, thou hast much goods laid up for many years; take thine ease, eat, drink, and be merry.

But God said unto him. Thou fool, this night thy soul shall be required of thee: then whose shall those things be, which thou hast provided?

So is he that layeth up treasure for himself, and is not rich toward God.

(Luke 12:16-21 King James Version)

Yes, rich men soon discover the frailty of money and all its purchasing power is of no avail when it comes time for them to meet their Master and their Judge.

In light of this how tragic are the lines:

Of all the words of tongue and pen,
The saddest are, "It might have been."

BASKING IN THE LAP OF LUXURY

Once the tentacles of greed for more money and the desire for more leisure grab hold of you it is difficult to push them away. America is actually closing a very dramatic period. In the last 36 years the United States has been involved in 3 foreign wars and the United States government has been financially in the red for 30 of those 36 years. It was a period that changed a nation's entire way of life. The curtain is now opening on a new phase — a phase which will bring higher incomes, more money for luxuries, and more leisure time. Such an inheritance will open the doors for an even greater neglect of God and His Word.

If you value the dollar at 100 cents when the Democrats took over in 1933, it is now worth only a little more than 39 cents in terms of buying power.

SIGNS OF THE TIMES

A California Assemblywoman breaks a porcelain toilet with a sledge hammer on the steps of the Capitol in Sacramento. She was protesting pay toilets in public places.

During lunch hour in Philadelphia at a busy downtown intersection a belly dancer performs, bringing traffic to a slowdown.

In 1933 it took $20.67 to buy an ounce of gold. Today it takes $35 and private citizens are denied the right to own gold even at that price.

In 1933 the population of the United States was 125 million. It is now above 210 million and where 39 million then had jobs, now over 80 million are working. *U.S. News & World Report* reveals that the Federal Government's debt in these 36 years has risen over 21 fold—from 19.5 billion dollars to 429 billion—and it is still rising. And here is an interesting fact! All the debt in the nation including mortgaged debt, installment debt, business debt, government debt of all kinds totalled less than 175 billion dollars in 1933. Today that debt total is 1.5 trillion dollars (8½ times the 1933 total debt figure!) and is zooming upward rapidly.

However in spite of this it is important to note that the per capita income today buys three times what is could back in the depression days of 1933.

We are now living in an entirely new era with a new way of life.

There has even been a era of revolution in household aids. We now have electric washers, electric dryers, electric dishwashers, automatic garbage disposal units, air conditioners, and many other electric gadgets.

We have power mowers. Gas, oil, or electricity now heats our homes. There is no more coal to shovel. And complete meals can be bought pre-cooked ready to heat and serve. Automobiles have taken the place of the trolley car and airplanes in many cases have replaced passenger trains. To the older generation it may be hard to realize that 6 out of 10 persons in today's population were born after Franklin Roosevelt first took office and half of the American people have no personal recollection of the Great Depression.

In fact *U.S. News & World Report* points out that 1 person out of 2 in the nation has been born since the start of World War II and has no recollection of this period. Almost 1 out of 3 has been born since the Korean War. After World War II, the United States rose to a position of undisputed eminence in the world—becoming the most powerful single nation on earth. And in this period Americans poured out more than 100 billions in aid to other people. There were more people on the farm in 1933 — actually 1 U.S. worker in 4 was on the farm. Today only 1 worker in 20 is still on the country's farms. The average weekly pay in 1933 of a factory worker amounted to $16.89. At that time there was no withholding tax. Now the pay level is $122, with deductions made for income tax, payroll tax and various forms of insurance.

The purchasing of gadgets of various kinds accounts for twice as much spending as it did a generation ago, and medical care accounts for 50% more in the family's budget.

This is an affluent age . . . for 2 out of 3 of today's families own or are buying a house. It was only 1 out of 2 when the present era began.

Where in 1933 fewer than half of the American families earned as much as $5,000 (43% earned less than $1,000) — today we find that 86% earn more than $5,000 a year and over 50% earn more than $10,000.

Colleges that then turned out 122,000 graduates, now graduate 740,000. Yes this is a changing America! It is an America, where its people are finding themselves with more money than ever before and where there is more gadgetry to make living easier and free time greater.

There seems to be a fanatic rush to live every minute of every day to the hilt.

THE DAY EVERYTHING STOPS

With the growing population and its attendant problems, one national magazine recently asked the question, "Are we nearing the day everything stops?"

For while we have advanced tremendously in some directions . . . in others we have made no progress.

The Saturday Evening Post in one of its last articles reported:

> Americans like to think of themselves as people on the move, jetting across the country for a business conference, driving hundreds of miles for a vacation, generally on the go. It comes as a bit of a surprise, then, to learn that a rush

hour trip from downtown New York to downtown Chicago is no faster today than 20 years ago, that an automobile driver requires just as much time to make the circuit of Manhattan Island as a horseman required half a century ago. That some commuter railroads provide slower service than they did during World War I.

The highway system is having problems keeping up with a growing America. The 41,000 mile Federal Interstate Highway System, almost completed and likely to cost more than 60 billion by the mid-1970's, will link 90% of our cities with populations of 50,000 or more.

It has been termed the greatest public works undertaking of all time – more ambitious than the TVA, the pyramids, or the Great Wall of China.

It has been further estimated that there are some 100 million motor vehicles of all kinds currently being operated in the United States. It may surprise some to realize that California alone has more cars – some 9 million – than either England or France. Los Angeles has 700 miles of freeways and plans 622 more.

Federal, state and local governments have built 3,700,000 miles of roads, enough to provide a 15-lane expressway from here to the moon! And some $32,000 a minute is still being spent on this network of roads.

Since the end of World War II alone the number of automobiles on the road has more than tripled.

In fact *U.S. News & World Report* in a recent survey stated that 3-car families are becoming as common as 2-car families used to be a few years back.

Recent surveys show that almost 14 million U.S. families own 2 cars and an additional 2 million own 3 or more ... and the trend is accelerating. The President of Chrysler recently stated that in 1970 54 per cent of all new car sales were made to families who already have 2 or more cars.

AIR TRAFFIC JAMS

Along with the impossible traffic on the ground, warnings of disastrous traffic jams in the air are starting to come.

There are so many planes in the air over the United States that our system of controlling air traffic is approaching total collapse. There are 200 near-collisions a month. This is because planes are getting bigger and faster and almost nothing is being done about it.

Such are the growing complex problems of people living in the United States. America is a country on the move! People are hurrying from one destination to another to keep the wheels of business moving, to keep profits going up, and to seek additional leisure. Yet in spite of all this they end up still more restless than those who lived in the relatively calm and quiet 1930's.

HOW TO GET RICH

There are times when one wonders how anyone can accumulate a fortune with the high rate of taxes.

Someone once said, "The art of taxation consists in so plucking the goose as to obtain the largest amount of feathers with the least possible amount of hissing."

The story is told of a country retail merchant who retired with a fortune of $100,000 dollars. He termed this success. His ability to retire with $100,000 after 40 years, was due to hard work, strict attention to duty, absolute honesty, economical living, and to the death of his uncle who left him $98,500.

Many of today's youth will find themselves wealthy without working due to the high level of income their parents are earning today.

When this occurs, tomorrow's generation will be even more geared to one aim . . . that of absorbing every pleasure the world has to offer.

Fortune recently estimated that there are 153 Americans who are now worth $100 million and 66 are worth $150 million or more.

In fact, two people in the United States are estimated to have a net worth of $1 billion or more—J. Paul Getty of the Getty Oil Company and Howard Hughes of the Hughes Aircraft Company.

MANSIONS ON EARTH

So wealthy is our nation today, that big mansions are coming back into vogue again. One lavish abode even sports a dining room that floats atop a pool. In Washington, one person's ideal dream house is a snug little 43-roomer. This includes 11 bathrooms, 3 art galleries, a swimming pool big enough to float a destroyer, a music room, an indoor garden, a built-in waterfall, and a servants' quarters that rival Buckingham Palace's. The cost for this "little" home was $1.9 million.

One 40-year old attorney constructed a $1 million home in the Bahamas so that he could entertain friends in the proper style. Another wealthy homeowner, not content with one dream house, also built another on a faraway island. This second one is said to have cost more than $2.5 million.

It's amazing how many people invest so much of their income and devote so much of their time in building mansions for themselves here on earth. And yet, some spend little time, if any, preparing their heart and souls for a mansion in the Kingdom that Christ promises us in glory.

> In my Father's house are many mansions: if it were not so, I would have told you. I go to prepare a place for you.
> And if I go and prepare a place for you, I will come again, and receive you unto myself; that where I am, there ye may be also.
> *(John 14:2,3 King James Version)*

There is a wild scramble these days for higher priced homes in the $40,000 to $60,000 price range.

Previews Inc., a national real estate clearing house says that the $100,000 house is now commonplace in high-income areas. For a home to be considered highly expensive these days they report, a residence must be priced at $250,000 or more. A Chicago businessman not long ago bought a winter home in Arizona at a cost of $120,000 — without even looking at it — just from a brochure.

And one real estate broker told the story of a Pasadena,

California couple that looked at a home in a heavy December fog.

They couldn't see much behind the swimming pool although a brochure promised a view stretching for miles when the sun was shining. Rather than risk losing the property— which was priced at $165,000—the couple bought it.

A Chicago real estate firm stated, "Its a fast market; a sellers' market. We've got plenty of buyers. We are short of listings."

One Stamford, Connecticut, real estate expert said that one house that sold four years ago for $54,000 dollars now is up for sale at $176,000.

In this mad dash for an earthly home it becomes more amazing to see the amount of money people will invest while the world around them is starving and in need of a Savior.

It was the millionaire, Amir of Kuwait, who recently left Washington in an outraged protest against the high price of medicines. Taken ill during a visit here his medicine cost him $70. In Kuwait, medicine is free.

But Kuwait is a place where the average annual income per family is $30,000. And of course the Amir's income is many many thousands of dollars higher.

NOBODY WANTS YOU WHEN YOU'RE DOWN AND OUT

There is hardly a day goes by that one does not read of someone who reached the top of their financial heaven only to find the world collapsing around them.

Wall Street Journal recently reported that, "In 1957 Charlie Steen and his wife, Minnie Lee, threw a party for 8,800 friends, complete with barbecue dinner, drinks, dance bands and acts imported from Las Vegas."

But now Steen, once a free spender with millions, can hardly afford to buy new shirts.

At one time he was the undisputed king of the uranium prospectors.

His enterprises numbered more than 30.

With a flowing income he and his wife were able to travel 3 and 4 months a year, many times aboard a plush 69-foot yacht, the Minnie Lee, which was converted from a British Navy vessel for $250,000.

It is reported that up until the last two years his income was over a million dollars a year.

In the early 1960's they built their $1 million dream house with more than 30 rooms, 5 pagoda-peaked copper roofs, indoor sunken gardens, and a heated indoor pool.

His wife estimates that in one 18-month period, there were only five nights in which they didn't have house guests. Open to all was a liquor cabinet which was continually stocked with $5,000 worth of liquor. Poor investments and problems with the Internal Revenue Service reversed this trend, and as *Wall Street Journal* reported, brought him from "riches to rags."

THE UNDERGROUND BANK

It was the *National Observer* that reported on an unusual home owned by "Silver Dollar" Jim West.

He was a wealthy Texas oilman. It is reported at the time of his death that an underground vault in his home held 80,000 silver dollars. A huge frozen food locker beneath his house was stocked with pounds and pounds of his own butter which he carried with him no matter who was his host. His garage was home to part of a fleet of 9 Cadillacs and 21 other cars. He had a massive underground system in which one room was a fur-storage vault. He possessed his own electrical system, built after a quarrel with the power company, and his own water system which was built after another quarrel with the water company.

One important fact that many people do not seem to realize—or if they do realize it, they will not accept it—is the fact that when the leaves of death fall riches cannot be taken along on this final journey.

Wilburn Dowell Cobb holds the Pearl of Allah, a 14 pound gem he sold for $3.5 million. For more than two decades he kept it in bank vaults and museums.

Wilburn D. Cobb realized this before it was too late when he sold the world's largest pearl for what was considered a bargain price at $3.5 million.

At a news conference Cobb said "I'm pressed for time.

I'm 65 years old. I want to go back to the Philippines and buy a plantation for some of my old friends who are needy."

This pearl was found in 1934 by natives on an island near the Philippines. Cobb related that a boy drowned when his arm was caught in the shell of a giant clam, which was brought up and later found to contain the pearl, which weighs 14 pounds, 1 ounce.

The pearl was given to him as a gift when he cured the chief's son of malaria.

Here was a chief so filled with gratitude because the life of his son was spared that he turned over to Cobb a pearl which Cobb later sold for 3½ million dollars.

Cobb had given the boy atabrine . . . then a new drug . . . that cost just a few cents. His kind act brought him a reward of 3½ million dollars!

This chief valued his boy's life above every earthly treasure. This is how we should value Heaven and eternal life. On this Christ well said,

> . . . the kingdom of Heaven is like unto a merchant man, seeking goodly pearls:
> Who, when he had found one pearl of great price, went and sold all that he had, and bought it.
> *(Matthew 13:45,46 King James Version)*

THE RISE IN COUNTERFEITING

While most Americans are content to earn their wealth through legal means there are others who are so hungry for money they will use any means.

The rise of counterfeiting has reached staggering proportions.

In the past year, the loss to citizens totaled $2.9 million, up nearly 75 per cent from the year earlier and 11 times the loss of 1960.

With money changing hands so frequently at such a fast pace, one Secret Service agent assigned to track down counterfeiters stated "Nobody looks at his money anymore."

WHAT HAPPENED TO ICE CREAM?

In fact, manufacturers eager to make a greater dollar find that hardly anyone looks at the contents of what goes into a food package or can on the supermarket shelves.

Most shoppers do not know it, but the bulk of the low-priced ice cream they pluck from food store freezers contains as much air as it does ice cream.

It is also artificially flavored, laced with seaweeds, psyllium seed husks, cellulose, and laboratory-concocted salts made from antifreeze chemicals. It comes as close to being completely synthetic as it legally can — so reported *National Observer* in a recent article titled, AND THAT'S WHAT ICE CREAM'S MADE OF.

Ice cream is sold by volume and pumping air into ice cream increases its volume. It is possible to make a relatively small amount of mix fill a lot of half gallon or gallon cartons.

And within the next generation, synthetics may replace natural fruits and vegetables in the human diet, says Dr. Philip L. White, secretary of the American Medical Association's council on foods and nutrition.

FREEZE YOUR AGE

With the overflow of money reaching the pockets of almost everyone in the country, there is a greater and greater emphasis on reducing diets brought about by overstuffed Americans.

And with industry predicting that in 1973 sales of color TV sets will reach over 7 million, we find another step to encourage lack of exercise and inactivity on the part of the United States public.

Is it any wonder that one book publisher is having tremendous sales for a $5.98 book on Yoga?

The book promises to freeze your age for the next 30 years.

Yoga defines middle-age as the period between 40 and 80

and the publisher states that "middle-age is the last great crossroad of every human life."

The publisher of this Yoga book encourages you to make the decision that will, "Either propel you onward to sickness and old age or turn your physical clock backward in health and strength and appearance to what can only be called a second youth."

Even this book realizes that:

> If you leave your body alone after 40, the aging processes pick up a disastrous speed. A chronic tiredness begins to haunt you every day. You put on weight you can't take off. The skin on your face begins to crumble faster and faster — because your heart just can't pump up enough nourishing blood to keep it young any longer.

It goes on to relate:

> It becomes difficult to walk, almost impossible to run, a terror to climb stairs. Until your entire body becomes a battle field of aches and pains. Until you find your self cutting out half the real FUN in life — because suddenly, tragically, you're just TOO OLD!

The book promises that every page is filled with priceless health secrets including a method by which the body can continue to repair its own cells, right up until 90.

Of course it doesn't tell you what happens after 90.

And this desire for an eternal youth is one which each of us has.

FitzGerald's translation of Omar Khayyam's Rubaiyat well declares,

> The Moving Finger writes; and, having writ,
> Moves on: nor all your Piety nor Wit
> Shall lure it back to cancel half a Line,
> Nor all your Tears wash out a Word of it.

Perhaps it is because so many people realize that this is true that they race forward at a breakneck speed to pack all of life's thrills within their lifetime, hoping that their life will be different than others — that their life will go on forever.

But without Christ, your life will suddenly end one day and then where will you spend eternity?

THE THRILL SEEKERS

One of the new themes of this current rich and luxury filled generation is the idea of the playboy.

A magazine by the same name comes out with a philosophy which by its content, in the opinion of the author, is leading people directly down the road to destruction and damnation.

Jesus said, concerning such philosophies,

> Ye have heard that it was said by them of old time, Thou shalt not commit adultery:
> But I say unto you, That whosoever looketh on a woman to lust after her hath committed adultery with her already in his heart.
> And if thy right eye offend thee, pluck it out, and cast it from thee: for it is profitable for thee that one of thy members should perish, and not that thy whole body should be cast into hell.
> *(Matthew 5:27-29 King James Version)*

Time magazine recently reported that the owner of *Playboy*, so dedicated to his work, would labor as long as 72 hours at a stretch eating practically nothing, drinking about 25 Pepsi Colas a day and "popping bennies."

Time reported that he allegedly said "I've developed a tremendous tolerance for amphetamines which dropped my weight from 175 pounds to 135 pounds. It was a way of living not well calculated to be either lengthy or pleasant. I finally woke up to the fact that I had the world by the tail and if I wanted to enjoy it, I'd better start taking care of myself." *Time* magazine reports that his wardrobe includes $15,000 worth of Edwardian suits.

He is now having built for himself a $5 million dollar version of the DC-9 jet which is painted black.

The *Playbody* publisher calls it, "My big black mother in the sky."

While most DC-9 jet liners can carry 115 passengers, this one will probably seat 50 and sleep 15.

It is reported that the publisher's private compartment on the plane will boast a stereo console, a movie screen, and a step-down Roman bath.

Playboy magazine is in terms of worldly endeavors—a smashing success. The magazine sells 7,500,000 copies a month. A recent issue sold almost $4.5 million in advertising.

At this present writing, there are 17 Playboy clubs throughout the world and more are planned in Puerto Rico, Hawaii, Mexico and Spain.

It has been reported that the Playboy publisher's empire earned him and his fellow stock holders $6,868,165 last year, after taxes.

But apparently all of this wealth and business has drawbacks. Hugh Hefner is reported to have said, "When a man is in his forties, he realizes there are only so many years in which to do certain things. I have decided that putting my philosophy in book form can wait until I'm 60." He further stated "Everyone should have the right to go to Heaven or hell in his own way."

Time magazine ends its report by this comment

> Hefner himself is trying for Heaven. What is more, the mass producer of plastic-wrapped sex, the purveyor of pop hedonism (the doctrine in which happiness or pleasure is the highest good), the great anti-Puritan who is out to make every square feel that he too can be a swinger, is looking for a Heaven less in the style of Playboy than the Saturday Evening Post. "You know," says Hef wistfully, "in the next ten years I would rather meet a girl and fall in love and have her fall in love with me than make another hundred million dollars." He really means it, or thinks he does.

Christians and concerned Americans have thus far at least in a small way revolted against this preoccupation with sex but their efforts are fruitless.

Already the major television networks are scheduling X-rated motion pictures for their viewers. And late night talk shows are filled with guests whose discussions usually center on sex.

And when "In the beginning God" was removed from the Apollo space stamp, efforts under the initial leadership of Dr. Carl McIntire and the support of other Christians which arose brought enough pressure on the United States Government to reinsert these words into the commemorative postage stamp.

These, however, are only small needles of protest buried in a haystack of people in America whose morals and ideals are, sadly enough, becoming more corrupt daily.

Chapter 5
LIVING TILL I DIE
PART 2

Tranquilized America • Gambling Tours Flourish • Sex and Self Indulgence • The Seal Pup Slaughter • Gazing at the Stars • Growing Old Young • Money Can't Buy Happiness!

TRANQUILIZED AMERICA

The National Council on Alcoholism has termed alcohol the Number ONE disrupter of human satisfaction.

It has been stated that 50% of those first submitted to mental hospitals suffer from alcoholism.

Likewise, 50% of delinquent drivers involved in fatal auto accidents are alcoholics. Plus 49% of all police arrests are for alcohol-related offenses, and 63% of those involved are alcoholics.

With the tragedy of alcohol now comes a possibly greater sister tragedy — the growing misuse of mood-changing drugs. Fast living in today's world with its added pressures is apparently catching up with millions of Americans. And they are turning to drugs in order to get away from it all. Dr. James P. Louria, a Cornell University medical professor and President of the New York State Council on Drug Addiction, says that if present trends continue, by the year 2000,

We may have a completely drug-controlled society, where a wife slips an anti-grouch pill into her husband's coffee in the morning and the pharmaceutical equivalent of the liquor store sells chemicals to produce any mood from euphoria to mystic contemplation.

Last year some 200 million prescriptions, or about 20% of all those written, were for tranquilizers, amphetamines, barbiturates or related psychotropic drugs.

In 1972 alone, Americans spent over $2 billion to have over 150 million prescriptions for tranquilizers filled.

Recent surveys show that people whose annual income is $10,000 or more are more likely to be in the drug taking category. A senior psychiatrist in Bellevue Hospital in New York, Dr. Edwin Roberts, states:

People have been given the crazy idea that they should live a tension-free life. They are told that there is some kind of pill that will handle any sort of life situation—like an Excedrin headache. It's tough for doctors to deal realistically with people who have such ideas.

Hence we have this growing and widespread desire to escape from this present world. How sad it is that more people do not realize that by escaping to Christ they will find the only true release from sin's chains and life's problems.

The untimely death of Judy Garland reveals the real tragedy behind Hollywood's glitter. Her successes on screen and stage were overshadowed by the pathos of her personal life, which often seemed a fruitless search for the happiness promised in "Over the Rainbow."

When she was 18 she was seeing a psychiatrist. She wrote about the experience years later: "No wonder I was strange. Imagine whipping out of bed, dashing over to the doctor's office, lying down on a torn leather couch, telling my troubles to an old man who couldn't hear . . . and then dashing to the movie set."

It was during this period that she also began taking stimulants and depressants. "They'd give us pep pills," she wrote, "Then they'd take us to the studio hospital and knock us cold with sleeping pills. ... After four hours they'd wake us up and give us the pep pills again. ... That's the way we got mixed up. And that's the way we lost contact."

We are living in a day and age when there is a pill for every problem. Parents get the same drugs legally that children get illegally.

Drugs are a big business. Americans spend over $7 billion each year on legal drugs — $3 billion of it for over-the-counter preparation — headache pills, cold remedies, tonics. Some $4 billion is spent for drug prescriptions.

In one California county, 37% of the adults received at least one prescription for a mood drug during the course of one year.

In 1972, the reported legal production of amphetamines (pep pills or speed) had risen over 12 billion tablets per year. That is enough for each American adult and child to take one tablet a day for a month! Far less than 1% of these were medically indicated.

Jesus, concerning true freedom and release from anxiety, said:
... Whosoever committeth sin is the servant of sin.
And the servant abideth not in the house for ever: but the Son abideth ever.
If the Son therefore shall make you free, ye shall be free indeed.
(John 8:34-36)

Come unto me, all ye that labour and are heavy laden, and I will give you rest.
Take my yoke upon you, and learn of me; for I am meek and lowly in heart: and ye shall find rest unto your souls.
For my yoke is easy, and my burden is light.
(Matthew 11:28-30)

Therefore take no thought, saying, What shall we eat? or What shall we drink? or Wherewithal shall we be clothed?
(For after all these things do the Gentiles seek:) for your heavenly Father knoweth that ye have need of all these things.
But seek ye first the Kingdom of God, and His righteousness; and all these things shall be added unto you.
(Matthew 6:31-33)
(All above King James Version)

Many people use hobbies as an escape technique. In California there is a group called the California Barb Wire Collectors Association.

Only a few months ago it held its first barbed-wire show in Paso Robles, California. The secretary of the organization stated that thousands of people collect barbed wire.

We are told that collectors mount short pieces of wire on peg boards or plywood and frequently pay $20 to $45 for single pieces. Others have more sophisticated hobbies such as gambling.

GAMBLING TOURS FLOURISH

It is believed that the Mafia and its several affiliates, having exhausted their gambling paradise in the United States, are now shifting to the Continent.

The Mob feels that it can get away with more in England, at least for a while, than it can in the United States – and this is true.

So strong is the desire for gamblers to gamble that El Al Airlines has taken to providing chartered flights to London, which is 3500 miles away, so that Americans can gamble their excess income.

On one recent weekend, 130 passengers went on such a pleasure spree.

Each man on the plane had paid $1,000 for himself and $300 for his wife or girl friend if he brought one along. In return he was promised not only a round trip to London but accommodations at a new hotel for a week plus a free dinner every night in the restaurant. He was also promised his full $1,000 back in chips to gamble with at the casino.

One reporter who went along on the trip asked the head of the casino how successful he was in making money on this group of 130 passengers.

He was quoted as saying, "We don't know exactly yet, but it should be about $350,000."

Perhaps the ravages of sin are no more clearly seen than in the dedicated mobster whose life is controlled by Satan and whose every breath is invested in perpetuating the numbers game, protection shake-downs, smuggling, narcotics, or prostitution . . . as well as an assorted variety of killings and outright undercover operations which defy description.

Such a mobster's brief time on earth is spent in sowing seeds of corruption that will deal him a life in eternity of constant torment. Yet he will not be alone, for even the so-called righteous man who spends his entire life doing seemingly good things, helping the poor, aiding the sick, and living a moral and upright life, is destined to the same destination—unless he accepts Christ as his personal Saviour and Lord. This is true because,

> As it is written, There is none righteous, no, not one.
> For all have sinned, and come short of the glory of God.
> *(Romans 3:10,23 King James Version)*

Both the gambler and the do-gooder are destined for judgment and doom, unless they accept Christ's free gift of eternal Life . . .

> For the wages of sin is death; but the gift of God is eternal life through Jesus Christ our Lord.
> *(Romans 6:23 King James Version)*

There is so much misdirected energy in this world today, both in time and in man's quest for money, that many a Christian wonders how God can be patient much longer before the Rapture of the Saints occurs and the judgment of those left on earth begins (I Thessalonians 5:1,2,9).

SEX AND SELF INDULGENCE

Just the hay and grain bill for *pleasure* horses was estimated at more than $500 million last year.

Health products for pets including drugs and cosmetics accounted for close to $100 million of purchases last year.

And it has been predicted that by 1985 families will be able to select TV channels on the basis of their area of special interest, much as they buy magazines. The cable antenna system will create 2000 TV stations which will be available on every TV set in the country and in Europe. Think of the possible added tensions that may develop because people will have difficulty in making a decision as to which of the 2000 channels they are going to watch!

With our fast pace of living and today's preoccupation with worldly pleasures, is it any wonder that the number of divorces is rising? In the year 1972, 800,000 divorces and annulments were granted in the United States, compared with 494,000 in 1966. Americans are living a life which makes the night spots more crowded and more and more attractive to the non-Christian.

A person can now look over an elaborate dinner menu that offers a $28 bottle of liquor at a club which charges an initial entrance fee of $500 with annual dues of $350.

One 1000 member club which recently opened had no trouble filling its rolls with people who were glad to pay $500 a clip in order to be among the numbered few.

Newsweek reported that one club is called, "Salvation Too." It is reported to be a psychedelic discothéque in a posh Central Park South penthouse. To get into Salvation Too "one must pass the bouncer in the lobby, submit to a close circuit TV camera monitored by the manager upstairs and then wait for a phone call from the top for an o.k."

In another night club a "participant" enters a long, all-white room with 14 carpeted platforms raised 2 feet above the floor. His guide helps him into a transparent white sheet and urges him to take off as many clothes as he wishes. The creator of the night club states "When you take your clothes off you can be anything you want, there are no signs of the outside world. . . ."

This desire to be "free" has perhaps had its sexual innovation among the theater arts. In its first week in a small theater, "I am Curious" broke all records for an "art" film in New York City by grossing almost $80,000.

It was not unusual to pass 57th Street in the heart of New York City at ten o'clock in the morning and see a long line of well dressed people waiting to get tickets.

(Continued)

These ads convey the climate of many of the people of our Nation in their obsession with sex. The daily newspapers contain scores of such movie ads which promise to "outshock" the "shockers." It is such moral decline and permissiveness that Christ warns will usher in the Tribulation Period.

Now you've got a date with *Inga*

From
Sweden...
the
classic
female
concept

Inga
is so graphic, I could have
sworn the screen was smoking."
—*N.Y. Daily Column*

"If I were to describe in detail what
goes on in 'Inga', I'd get arrested."
—*Robert Salmaggi, WINS Radio*

Starring
MARIE
LILJEDAHL
A CANNON Production

A CINEMATION
INDUSTRIES
Release

JERRY GROSS and
NICHOLAS DEMETROULES
PRESENT
Inga

X | NO ONE ADMITTED UNDER AGE 18

SEATS NOT RESERVED
COME ANYTIME • Continuous
Performances • Regular Prices

BOYD
19th & CHESTNUT • LO 4-3751

DOORS OPEN 10:45 AM
Feat. at 11:20 AM - 1:00 PM
2:40-4:20-5:55-7:35-9:20-11:00

The co-owner of the theater stated, "The only complaint we have had so far is that people can't get in."

Meanwhile in Texas the vice president of a 17-theater chain was dickering for the rights to exhibit "I am Curious" in his area.

He stated, "I know how much money I can make with this picture in Texas . . . about $2 million." *Newsweek* magazine, in reporting this, commented that

> The flood gates have opened one by one, and the inundation is now a matter of fact in the hinterlands as well as the big cities. The flood is multifarious and includes hard-core pornographic books and magazines showing full genital exposure, movies of sexual intercourse and homosexual publications.

Newsweek goes on to report that

> It is a fact of recent culture history that both the legal definitions of and the accepted standards for obscenity, pornography and their like are in a state of total confusion . . . recent Supreme Court decisions have made it difficult to erect legal barriers against pornography. Not the least of the difficulties is the basic one—what, legally, is pornography?

Our nation is pursuing wildly after the same decay that weakened and eventually destroyed the ancient Greco-Roman empires. The Apostle Paul, writing at about 56 A.D., when he tells of the corruption of the surrounding nations of his day, speaks also of our own nation:

> Because that, when they knew God, they glorified Him not as God, neither were thankful; but became vain in their own imaginations, and their foolish heart was darkened.
> Wherefore God also gave them up to uncleanness through the lusts of their own hearts, to dishonour their own bodies between themselves:
> Who changed the truth of God into a lie and worshipped and served the creature more than the Creator, who is blessed for ever. Amen.
> For this cause God gave them up unto vile affections: for even their women did change the natural use into that which is against nature:
> And likewise also the men leaving the natural use of

the woman, burned in their lust one toward another; men with men working that which is unseemly, and receiving in themselves that recompence of their error which was meet [their fitting retribution].

And even as they did not like to retain God in their knowledge, God gave them over to a reprobate mind, to do those things which are not convenient;

Who knowing the judgment of God, that they which commit such things are worthy of death, not only do the same, but have pleasure in them that do them.

(*Romans 1:21,24-28,32 King James Version*)

Newsweek in its special article devoted to sex and the arts went on to comment that,

Rudi Grenreich, the first American designer to raise skirts above the knees, has concentrated on "freeing" the female body with see-through blouses . . . He commented, "We have greater and greater freedom now . . . the skirt as we know it, is on the way out. The whole concept of masculinity and femininity is being destroyed. More and more girls wear pants, men will continue to wear long hair, enormous sleeves, and see-through shirts. I definitely see something called unisex coming, and it has nothing to do with masculinity or femininity."

Fashion designers in keeping up with the new leisure world filled with sin state that the old ways are dead and at the rate of moral decline in the United States this statement is probably true. *Newsweek* in culminating this article stated in part,

More than ever we need direction from mature leaders. . . . The luxuries of yesterday seem like a small toyland compared to the sinful lusts of today.

THE SEAL PUP SLAUGHTER

When some people get tired of the glittering night clubs they turn to other areas of diversion. In the area of the Gulf of St. Lawrence in Canada approximately 250,000 harp-seal pups are born each year but nearly one-quarter of them die at the hands of their natural enemy—man.

The reason for this is that their white coats have long been prized for boot and glove trimmings and for fur jackets. In this desire for a fast dollar hordes of hunters invade the ice floes on foot, by boat, on ski-equipped planes and in recent years by helicopter. With their stout oak clubs they move systematically through the herds beating the seal pups to death with raps on the skull.

This bloody slaughter generally nets for each hunter $600 to $1,000. *Time* magazine reported,

> The hunter, his face smeared with seal blood to cut down ice glare and to prevent chapping, grabs a 60 lb. pup by a hind flipper, whacks it on its soft skull, spins the pup over, punctures the throat and then neatly skins away pelt, flippers and blubber with swift strokes of a razor-sharp knife.
>
> Some hunters so desirous to work at a faster rate in order to make their dollar quicker have been known to skin these animals alive because the stout oak club did not deal a deadly blow.

GAZING AT THE STARS

Some people with time and money on their hands and concerned about the future invest quite a bit of their wealth in astrology. This is becoming quite a popular fad in these closing days before Christ's Second Coming.

The number of Americans who have found astrology fascinating has been so great that it has turned this fad into a phenomenon.

America's best known astrologer has a byline that is carried by 306 newspapers each weekday in to some 30 million homes. He is only one of about 10,000 full-time and 175,000 part-time astrologers in the United States.

One American describes a recent visit to the presidential palace of President Thieu in Vietnam.

While waiting in an ante-room, he became involved in a conversation on fortune telling with an aid to Mr. Thieu. "What happens if a fortune-teller makes a prophecy that turns out to be untrue?" the American asked. The Presidential aide, mingling faith and pragmatism responded, "It just means you have the wrong fortune-teller."

It is amazing how many people in the United States put great stock in astrology and other seers such as Jeane Dixon.

GROWING OLD YOUNG

In a recent essay in *Time* magazine it was pointed out that we are living in a sad state of contradictions.

We are living in an era where Madalyn Murray O'Hare, spouting the Constitution as Scripture, forced the Supreme Court to ban public school prayers, yet when the ex-President and five star General of the United States, Dwight D. Eisenhower died, an entire nation turned to an old familiar hymn of the church.

Yes, only the Bible has a satisfying comfort in times of death (I Thessalonians 4:18). Nevertheless the theme song of Americans today appears to be "I'm going to keep on living, living, living, until I die."

This new fast age is taking its toll in health disabilities. One-third of those who are unable to work between the age of 35 and 65 are unemployable because of stroke disability. The estimated cost of care for this is $3 billion, not counting the cost of care during hospitalization.

Now it must certainly be realized that not every victim of illness is ill because of some sin he committed; *the Bible makes this absolutely clear* (John 9:1-3; 11:3,4). God has called on Christians who are ill to glorify His name by means even of their illness (Romans 8:28).

Nevertheless, we cannot help noticing the statistical trends which are beginning to come to light in today's fast-living fast-paced TV-tranquilizer-sex obsessed-tension ridden society.

And from recent post mortem studies of U.S. casualties in Vietnam it appears that this is exactly what is happening.

For these studies have shown a higher incidence of potential heart trouble than was found in similar studies during the Korean conflict.

An Air Force flight surgeon in a report issued to his superiors revealed that significant signs of hardening of the arteries, a potential prelude to coronary heart attacks, is apparently higher among the troops in the 18 to 23 year age groups now than it was in the early 1950's.

Colonel Kenneth H. Cooper, attributed the situation to "lack of sufficient exercise, plus high-fat diets and cigarette smoking."

For in this age of refined luxurious living many in the nation are dedicated only to living a life full of pleasure and irresponsibility. And this may bring them an inheritance of an early death.

Christian Times recently observed that:

> In 1969, while 97 percent of Americans attest to some belief in God, Americans will spend more than $30 billion on gambling, $20 billion on crime, $9 billion on liquor, $5 billion on tobacco and four times more on comic books than on all public libraries. In the same 12 months American Christians will give less than $135 million to support the church's worldwide missionary program.

Someone once said:

> Money is that which, having not, we want;
> having, want more;
> having more want more still;
> and the more we get
> the less contented we are.

It was Dr. Bob Jones, Sr., who said, "Jesus never taught men how to make a living, he taught men how to live."

How important it is to let God have your life. He can do more with it than you can. Thus Christ said to His followers, "I am the vine, ye are the branches . . . without me ye can do nothing."

ALL THE TREASURES OF EARTH
CANNOT BRING BACK ONE LOST MOMENT!

It was a flight from Dallas to Chicago. Next to me was a man having trouble deciding what drink he would have.

THIS FLEETING LIFE

It was Heraclitus in 513 B.C. who remarked: "There is nothing permanent except change." Christ reminds us: ". . . He that heareth my Word, and believeth on Him that sent me, hath everlasting life . . ." (John 5:24).

On one page of today's newspaper appeared the following reports which reveal the temporariness of one's life on earth.

ion"
force
"nati
catio
nam;
on "j
   Ma
whos
cy pl
eral
met 1
dentia
U. S
Bunk
depu
Abra
+roc

DYING ON THE DOORSTEP of his mother-in-law's home near Bryan, Tex., is Robert S. Dent, an ex-convict, who held a state trooper captive during a 300-mile chase through southwest Texas. Dent was shot by a sheriff waiting at the house. His weeping wife, Ila Faye, is in the background.   AP Wirephoto

Toms River Man Killed in Crash on Eve of Wedding

Toms River, N. J. — The minister who was to have married Thomas E. Greenwood, Jr., 23, of 305 Morrell drive, will officiate at his funeral services on Monday.

Greenwood was killed at 1.35 A. M. yesterday when his car overturned on Brick blvd. in nearby Brick Township as he was returning from a bachelor dinner prior to his wedding today.

He will be buried in the dark suit he purchased two weeks ago to wea

Man Is Still Living; Gets $40,000 Damages

Los Angeles—(AP)—Three and a half years ago, Donald J. Correll was told he would die within 12 months. He didn't.

A Superior Court jury yesterday awarded the 49-year-old bus driver $40,000 in damages from the doctor who made the fatal diagnosis.

Correll had testified that the doctor's warinng had prompted him to quit his job, losing 18 years of seniority and pension rights.

Noticing that I declined the cocktails offered me . . . a conversation began.

It was one I will never forget!

President of a college . . . he was despondent . . . at times confused. Two tragedies had occurred within a span of a few months. Both he and his wife were teachers. He had always traveled with her to conventions.

But now . . . suddenly . . . she was gone. She had entered the hospital for a few tests on a Wednesday. By Friday she had died. Now he admitted to me quite frankly that sometimes "I can still hear her voice."

And just a short time after this tragedy his house burned down.

What was I to tell him. I knew he would give *everything he had* to recapture those fleeting moments of some 28 years which he and his wife had spent together. But now they were gone. And life seemed to have lost its purpose.

And I remembered an old Indian Proverb . . . "I will not complain about my fellow brother until I have walked in his moccasins two moons."

And while I could offer words of encouragement to him from God's Word . . . I found that I could not experience the same depth of sorrow that he was experiencing. Only he could fathom this tremendous sorrow. And in that plane I silently prayed. As we neared Chicago the conversation turned to my new book, GUIDE TO SURVIVAL, and I told him of God's plan for each of us and promised to send him a copy. As he left the plane he told me that now there would be a new purpose in his life . . . material gains were insignificant . . . spiritual gains were far more important.

And then I remembered last summer.

And I was glad for the beginning of an experience I had seldom before undertaken.

Running my own advertising agency . . . and insisting on giving personalized service to each client . . . I seldom had time for anything else.

Last summer, I decided that my wife Mary and our children, Doreen, Diane, Duane and Dawn would go on a vacation together (Our other son, Dennis, was already married).

It was a leisurely drive to upstate New York which would finally take us to Niagara Falls.

My wife's doctor had recently made what I felt was a most unusual and satisfying decision.

He had a very large practice in Philadelphia and was literally on the go day and night. But around him he watched as slowly his associates in the field of medicine were dropping off the scene . . . victims of heart attacks . . . and all in their late 40's or 50's.

It was then he decided that material gains are not the ultimate in fulfilled joy. And last spring he purchased a two-story home in a small town in upstate New York, and coincidentally, it was just one house away from where he was born.

We stopped there. It was a quiet summer day. The wide streets of the small cozy town were shaded by big overhanging trees. Stately homes were nestled on wide expanses of lawn. And while the world was worried about Dow Jones averages, missed deliveries of merchandise, maneuverings to secure that big order . . . these empty sounds of man were outblasted by the heavenly sounds of birds singing, an occasional dog barking and the quiet warm wind rustling through the trees.

This doctor had not only been able to purchase an adequate home in a small town, but also a cabin by the side of a lake a few miles away. And I have never seen a more contented man and wife.

Our family was very impressed with this as we continued toward Niagara Falls. And I am sure you can imagine the joy or our youngsters as they finally saw the sight they had so often read about.

All of them had cameras and each is keeping their separate albums not only of this memorable vacation but of all the other happy experiences of their childhood.

For my wife Mary and I, these are our treasures and their value is without price.

I have met many men who in their desire for financial

gain and prestige have sacrificed the growing up years of their most precious jewels . . . their children . . . only to realize too late that

> . . . all the treasures of earth
> cannot bring back one lost moment . . .

What about you?

MONEY CAN'T BUY HAPPINESS!

A couple of weeks ago I raked and fertilized a small plot of ground near our patio and gave each of 4 of our children a section to plant their own vegetables and flowers. Dawn (8), Duane (10), Diane (12) and Doreen (15) each chose their own seed packets and started planting. Diane planted cucumbers, radishes, pansies and parsley, Doreen planted tomatoes and everyone planted radishes. The next day they were out bright and early to see what came up!

In my travels I have had occasion to meet many well-to-do people. Some millionaires and most were so busy thinking up ways of making money . . . that they had lost sight of the real values in life. Money can't buy happiness. In fact, often, money is a hindrance to happiness. The world seems to be getting more and more complex and everyone wants to specialize. This reminds me of an incident that supposedly happened when I was in College.

It seemed that a water pipe had burst in the cafeteria during lunch time. The students quickly called for a plumber. Down he came with wrench in hand—touched the spouting water—then quickly left saying to the flabbergasted group . . . "That's hot water . . . I'm a cold water plumber."

Someone once said . . . since life is so short, lets make it broader. And that's what our family is trying to do. Life is not a cup to be drained, but a measure to be filled. Happiness is in the heart, not in the circumstances. For the last 3 or 4 days we have had nothing but rain . . . and it does seem to change personalities. But I always tell myself . . . that above the clouds THE SUN IS SHINING. How many times I have taken off from an airport in cloudy weather . . . and in just a few minutes the plane had broken through the clouds and I felt the warmth of a bright shining sun. Life is that way too!

But too many people are on an Express Train through life . . . when they should be taking the Local. Our lives are becoming computerized and programmed for every minute of the day. I have watched many businessmen wrapped up in nervous energy . . . working day and night to increase profits, create new ideas, and make more money at the expense of their family . . . they are simply too busy to share time with their children, their wife . . .

and

for

what?

So they increase their profits . . . so they get more business . . . so they grow bigger and bigger . . . and soon these years of ceaseless energy take their toll . . . and then it's too late.

My wife, Mary, as busy as she is with her family, has in the past devoted many hours as a Volunteer Aid in a local cancer hospital. In her own way . . . she brought happiness to those patients and invariably came home in the evening with a thankful heart herself.

Forgive me if I'm preaching . . . but too often in the business world I have seen God's Garden of People trampled by ambitious individuals who will ruin lives in order to build their own castle of gold. And I have witnessed others so inflexible in their day to day routine of making money . . . that they fail to take inventory of their purpose in life.

Money can't buy happiness. It won't even cover a down payment. Digging a little garden for your son or daughter . . . taking your wife out to dinner . . . going out of your way to make someone else happy . . . these are the investments that make happiness grow.

For us . . . it's radishes and roses. For you it may be playing baseball with your son or grandson. I challenge you—right now—ask yourself the question, "What castle of Happiness did I build this week that did not involve making money?"

". . . AS A LITTLE CHILD . . ."

It's been just about two years ago since I made my independent world-wide reporting trip . . . searching for avenues of peace.

I flew to San Francisco, then Japan, then Hong Kong, Vietnam, Bangkok, Lebanon, Jordan, Cypress and Israel. Of all the areas around the world the two areas that impressed me most were Vietnam and a refugee camp near Amman, Jordan.

For it was there I found CHILDREN . . . in like circumstances . . . children who had every reason to be confused, dismayed and discouraged. And yet in spite of their suffering, I found them courageous and resilient.

The photo in the center color section of this book I took near Nha Trang, Vietnam (where my son was stationed). It was on hospital grounds for Vietnamese civilians. The hospital does not feed their patients. Relatives stay by the hospital, cooking on little burners by the hospital wall. Please look at the photo—for more than a moment! It is a scene I cannot forget. The older child—really only a child herself—taking the adult responsibility of watching over her brother. She wove a little bird from a sugar cane leaf and to ease her hunger started nibbling at the shredded tail. As I knelt down to take the photo the little boy opened his arms as though he was seeking assurance and love.

It was then that the verse in Isaiah came to me . . . "The wolf also shall dwell with the lamb, and the leopard shall lie down with the kid; and the calf and the young lion and the fatling together; and a little child shall lead them" (Isaiah 11:6).

And I thought to myself . . . what a difficult verse for sophisticated man to believe. Who could ever dream of a little child leading a lion, a leopard and a wolf peaceably with a lamb, a kid and a calf!

Perhaps that's why that verse in Mark 10:15 states . . . "Whosoever shall not receive the kingdom of God as a little child, he shall not enter therein."

Can we learn something from little children? Or are we too proud as "mature" adults to realize that perhaps in our process of growing up we have lost by the wayside some of the true values of life . . . that make life worth living? Let's examine this a moment!

I have heard many times political orators say in their flowing speeches that Americans have made their greatest technological, industrial, and social accomplishments in the last 20 years.

In a sense this is true. But in another sense it is not!

Look back at the photo again. As I looked at these little children one word seemed to be shouting at me. That word was "WHY?"

And it was but a few days later that in tears I was asking myself that same word — WHY?

I can remember as if it were yesterday arriving at Tan San Nuit Air Base just outside Saigon. I can remember seeing the Medical Evacuation jets loading the wounded. I can remember talking to the wounded as they told me how their buddies "didn't make it."

And then I can remember seeing their buddies "who didn't make it." I remember the bloodied, muddied canvas stretchers stacked outside a plain, low building. I can remember the still forms under still white sheets. I can remember the hum of the fans that seemed to drone the tragic melody of war. I can remember seeing the aluminum carriers stacked at one door. I can remember reading the name tags on each container. I can remember crying!

And then I remembered the hollow echo of a troubled world of mature adults.

I remember them saying everything was rosy and bright.

I remember them saying "God is Dead."

I remember them saying God does not belong in our public schools.

I remember them saying "We must search and destroy."

I remember them saying "We will meet for peace talks every Wednesday."

Whether you believe the Vietnam war is right or wrong is

a decision you must personally make . . . and it is not the thrust of my comments.

I do remember when I saw that country as a war correspondent that American casualties at that time were 15,000 dead. Since then a total of 50,000 died. My heart goes out to the parents who must bear this sorrow.

And to me . . . what perhaps is an even greater sorrow . . . is that when the country was in the throes of anguish over the assassination of Senator Kennedy . . . the President merely appointed a Committee to determine the causes for violence in the United States.

How much more effective if the President had urged America to get back to God and get on its knees in prayer. And then placed billboards throughout America reminding them of that promise in II Chronicles 7:14 which reads,

> If my people, which are called by my name, shall humble themselves, and pray, and seek my face, and turn from their wicked ways; then will I hear from heaven, and will forgive their sin, and will heal their land.

But then I think to myself . . . "How can a sophisticated America ever accept the Bible as a true and literal message from God?" We can bask under God's sunlight, sleep under God's starry sky and then, when tragedy strikes throw God's flowers on a grave and in anguish ask ourselves "WHY?" We are so wrapped in careful diplomacy and artificial barriers that it's time we become as little children—honest, sincere, forgiving and loving.

> Whosoever shall not receive the Kingdom of God as a little child. . . .
> *(Mark 10:15 King James Version)*

Yes, the United States and the world is on a treadmill of life that is continuing at a faster and faster pace with many people more preoccupied with this present world and dedicated only to the religion that they will keep on living till they die.

What about you? In the din of today's riotous living are you able to hear the still small voice of Christ which says,

> ... I am come that they might have life, and that they might have it more abundantly.
>
> *(John 10:10 King James Version)*

Chapter 6

The United States and Heaven

"Prisoner" in the White House • Economy Booms • Social
Welfare Rising • Crime Perils Our Nation • Too Big . . . Too
Powerful • The High Cost of Preparedness • Anti-Missile
Protection • Caretaker of the World

It was Donald Marquis who wrote, "For a territory the
size of the United States, 5 millions of people would be about
right . . . The human population of the entire world should be
kept well under 100 million . . . If the world were not so full of
people, and most of them did not have to work so hard, there
would be more time for them to get out and lie on the grass,
and there would be more grass to lie on."

The United States now has a population of 210 million.

It was reported that Lincoln said, "You can please all of
the people some of the time, some of the people all of the time,
but you cannot please all of the people all of the time."

And any President, regardless of how dedicated he is,
finds the task of the Presidency an impossible one.

For the United States is the most powerful country in the
world and upon the shoulders of the President, rests the most
awesome decisions. One mistake on the part of the President
could result in a catastrophe in which millions of lives would
be lost.

It was President Nixon, who in August of 1968 at the GOP
National Convention, sharply criticized President Lyndon B.

Johnson for letting "a fourth-rate military power like Korea" seize the U.S. intelligence ship, Pueblo.

But just eight months later, when the government of North Korea shot down a U.S. reconnaissance plane said to be over international waters, he was faced with the problem of how to deal with a similar act—but not an identical one.

Mr. Nixon had stated in his acceptance speech at Miami that the Pueblo showed the need for "new leadership to restore respect for the United States of America . . . It is time we start to act like a great nation around the world."

There were many in both incidents who advocated declaring war on Korea and using military might.

It was Robert Leavitt who said, "People don't ask for facts in making up their minds. They would rather have one good, soul-satisfying emotion than a dozen facts."

And perhaps it is because when one assumes the Presidency of the United States, and has before him a set of facts that are almost unbelievable, that political promises must often yield to common sense.

For President Nixon realizes that an unwise move by the United States in Korea or any other part of the world could start the avalanche rolling for a world holocaust . . . a holocaust that would mean the death of millions of Americans as well as others. And all this could be started over what initially was a small incident, such as the capture of an intelligence ship or the shooting down of one plane.

What the President of the United States has to weigh is this: Is saving face worth the possible sacrifice of millions of American lives?

It was this same predicament that President Eisenhower was faced with when overnight the Berlin Wall was erected.

Should we send our troops in and destroy the wall or should we give Russia a diplomatic slap.

Since the Berlin Wall affair, rather than risk the involvement of war, the United States generally has preferred to go through diplomatic channels and simply issue protests.

This happened in Berlin, it happened with the Pueblo situation, and it happened with the Korean incident of the

U.S. Navy reconnaissance plane where 31 crewmen lost their lives.

When one realizes this, then he can appreciate the fact that this same type of diplomatic approach will possibly be taken by the Federated States of Europe when Russia someday sweeps down to invade Israel and take Jerusalem during the Tribulation Period (Ezekiel 38:1-39:16).

The United States and the European nations, fearful of causing another world war, will allow Russia to invade Israel and simply protest such action through normal diplomatic channels.

With the advent of nerve gas, germ warfare, and the possibility of controlling the world through spy satellites in outer space . . . it becomes increasingly more difficult for the President of the United States to commit his nation to war.

It is the hope of every President—before assuming office—to promise the people that he will strive to make the United States a "heaven on earth."

And certainly, the leadership of the United States for the most part, is dedicated to improving living conditions and to striving to make this country a heaven on earth.

But what many people fail to realize is that man in his own abilities will not achieve a Heavenly Kingdom here in the United States or in England or in any other part of the world.

In Daniel 2:34,35,44,45, through a vision, the Millennial 1000 year Kingdom of God is shown entering the world scene and vanquishing the governments of the end-times by a stone "cut without hands." What does this stone "cut without hands" signify? Answer: It signifies that no man-made agency will bring in the promised Kingdom, but rather it will be brought in by a divine agent—a stone "cut without hands" (Compare I Corinthians 10:4).

On the contrary, as the United States progresses, as the population grows, as people become better fed and richer; the problems of the United States will become increasingly insolvable. There will be a growing disrespect for our country—a disrespect which even now can be evidenced, not only

In its ever growing role as "policeman of the world" the U.S. must bear the brunt of soaring costs and increasing casualties. Here a paratrooper wounded during an assault against 3000 foot Dong Ap Bia (the mountain dubbed Hamburger Hill by GIs), grimaces in pain as he awaits evacuation. In this particular assault in Vietnam, 46 Americans lost their lives before the mountain was taken, the first time. Since then it has been the scene of recurring battles.

among young people, but among many adults whom many young people are idolizing and following.

"PRISONER" IN THE WHITE HOUSE

Let us look at some of the problems which face the United States right now in its attempt to make this country a heaven on earth.

First it must be realized that the President of the United States is the world's most guarded person.

Here we are living in a land of democracy and yet it becomes necessary for our President to protect himself against possible assassination by riding in a new armored limousine which is almost as impenetrable as a military tank.

The President has hundreds of guards who are assigned to protect him on a 24-hour basis.

The White House in which the President lives, is equipped with outward facing floodlights and electronically operated gates that can be opened only from the inside.

Can this be the land of the free when the President must be constantly on guard to protect his life and the leadership of this country?

How odd it is that the official residence of the Prime Minister of England is guarded only by 2 unarmed policemen outside. And his official car has no extra equipment except a telephone.

King Hussein also has the same freedom of travel and, in fact, if a military skirmish occurs at the border, he shows up at the battlefront. He even pilots his own plane.

Nowhere – not even in Communist police states – do security arrangements appear to be as elaborate and as technically intricate as those now being provided for American Presidents.

Then in 1973 came the revelation that President Nixon secretly taped all conversations in several of his offices. This plus the Watergate episode and charges made against Vice-President Spiro Agnew resulted in the general public losing confidence in those in high office. And on October 10, 1973 came the dramatic announcement that Vice-President Spiro Agnew had resigned! Yet these were the leaders who were committed to bring a "heaven on earth" with a lasting peace for the world!

ECONOMY BOOMS

And while the security network tightens around our President, the economy of the United States still hums along at almost full throttle in terms of labor force utilization.

Buying power, in the form of wages and salaries, now pours into American pockets at an annual rate of some $685 billion. That's $23 billion above the level of just a year ago.

In the last quarter of 1968, the grand total of all government (Federal, state, local) spendings for goods and services soared to an annual rate above $200 billion for the first time in history.

The following table, in BILLIONS of dollars and broken down between defense and non-defense, shows how this money flow has jumped since 1965.

	(In Billions of Dollars)		
CATEGORY	*1965*	*1972*	*% UP*
All Government Spending	$137	$256	88
Defense Spending	50	77	54
Non-defense Spending	87	179	106

With the growing economy, the government is naturally concerned about the statistics that describe its population.

In 1970 another census was taken and this has caused additional problems for the United States government.

One man in Texas wrote his Congressman that he would go to jail before answering all those "nosy" questions. He added grimly, "If I'm sent to jail, I think I will refuse to eat until I am released or die."

As the nation grows, it takes more and more taxes to support that growth. People are starting to rebel against this tax bite.

All over the United States, taxpayers are showing signs of revolt. In 1957 the total tax collections were $28.8 billion. By 1972, just 15 years later, the total tax collections soared to $221 billion.

One of the problems in attempting to make the United

States a heaven on earth is the problem of living within one's budget.

According to the Treasury Bulletin for December 1972, *interest* on the Federal debt is now costing approximately $20 billion annually.

The interest cost on state and local debts, on approximately $115 billion and assuming an average rate of 4.6%, would amount to $5.3 billion.

In fact, the government is trying to continue to work on its "tight" 1972 budget of $256 billion.

Howard E. Kershner, who is the editor of a wonderful publication titled *Christian Economics* stated recently in an article titled *The Cost of Foreign Aid:*

> How much does foreign aid cost? Most informed Americans would probably answer $3 to $5 billion annually. The actual figure is much higher. For 22 years it has averaged $7.78 billion per year.

He goes on to report,

> This is all very tragic and all in accordance with Lenin's plan for debauching American finances. We were formerly so strong and would be yet had we not listened to the siren song of "foreign aid." Somebody in Washington, probably many of them, assisted by a large clique throughout our country, have cleverly deceived the American people into supporting this disastrous program far beyond their ability to finance without destroying the strength of our country.
>
> The bankruptcy of the United States is probably the number one objective of World Communism. Those who have sold "foreign aid" to the American people have done exactly what the Communists wanted them to do. As of December 31, 1967, the public debt of the United States Government was $345,947,345,000. On the same date the debt of all other nations of the world was $302,128,345,000. Thus our country actually owes $43,819,000,000 more than all the rest of the world combined. Here again, this does not include Social Security, obligations to veterans, Civil Service workers, guaranteed loans and many other items adding up to far more than the so-called National debt stated above. The sad fact is that total public and private debt exceeds the total wealth of our country by about one-third.

Perhaps partially because of the problem of foreign aid,

we find that there are millions of Americans who don't even have sufficient food to eat right here at home.

Right now there are 50 million Americans who get at least some free food.

This is so because about 50 million Americans—mostly children—share in the Federal Government's food program. The cost of this food is $2 billion per year.

SOCIAL WELFARE RISING

One of the big problems is the problem of social welfare here in the United States.

In order to make the United States a heaven on earth, the President finds himself caught up on the horns of a dilemma.

U.S. News & World Report observed that, "In the past

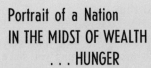

Portrait of a Nation
IN THE MIDST OF WEALTH
... HUNGER

Right now . . .
50 MILLION AMERICANS GET SOME FREE FOOD!

Cost of this FREE FOOD: $2 BILLION dollars

FREE LUNCHES IN SCHOOL	15.5 million children
SUBSIDIZED LUNCHES in School	8.5 million children
FREE MILK	15 million children
SURPLUS FOOD PACKAGES	9 million people
FOOD DONATIONS TO SUMMER CAMPS	2 million people

eight years, Federal spending for education, old-age pensions, health, hand outs to the poor and all other 'social welfare' has jumped to $70 billions a year. Add to this the more than $55 billion spent by State and local governments for similar programs and the bill exceeds $125 billions a year."

Looking at these figures, one can realize that this represents a *doubling* of welfare outlays in the eight years from 1964 to 1972. And it is 40% more than the United States spends annually for defense *including the war in Vietnam!*

On the basis of the current trend, in 1975 the United States' cash outlay for social services may total $245 billion a year...nearly double the present spending and about eight times as much as the nation spent for social aids in 1950.

Where will it all stop?

No one knows. In fact, the government is already testing even a negative income tax that will provide additional monies to individuals who do not come up to a specified level of income.

With everyone looking to the Federal government for money...it should be remembered that:

> Any government that is big enough to give you everything you want is big enough to take everything you have.

In 1955 there were 6 million people on relief. But look at this! In spite of the economic growth of this country, in spite of the added luxuries and new inventions...just 17 years later in 1972, there are 13-1/2 million people on relief.

In 1955, $2.7 billion was spent for relief costs. In 1972 this has risen to $14.8 billion.

In the first three months of 1969 the state of Pennsylvania added nearly 50,000 persons to their relief rolls.

This 3 month total exceeds the *entire* new public assistance caseload for all of 1968!

This means that one out of every 24 Pennsylvanians is now receiving public assistance!

People of the United States are familiar with the so-called "crash" programs that will solve all the ills.

In fact, it was Daniel Patrick Moynihan, the chief advisor to President Nixon on the Council of Urban Affairs who stated, "The social history of the 1960's is already littered

THE ALARMING TREND OF WELFARE IN THE UNITED STATES

Recent U.S. studies indicate that in the 1970s more than 1/5th of the U.S. entire output will go to social-welfare causes.

Year Ended June 30	Federal, State and Local-Government Programs	Private Welfare Outlays	Total	Share of All U.S. Output of Goods and Services
1950	$23.5 bil.	$11.9 bil.	$35.4 bil.	13.5%
1960	$52.3 bil.	$26.9 bil.	$79.2 bil.	16%
1968	$112.4 bil.	$50.7 bil.	$163.1 bil.	19.8%
1975 (est.)	$208.0 bil	$84.0 bil.	$292.0 bil.	22.5%

In 1975 social outlays will nearly DOUBLE our present spending and will be 8 times as much as the United States spent for social aids in 1950!

These projected estimates for 1975 do not even take into consideration the massive new programs advocated by some members of Congress. (Guaranteed income known as Negative Income Tax and Medicare for all.)

with the wreckage of crash programs that were going to change everything and in fact changed nothing."

CRIME PERILS OUR NATION

On top of this problem of relief, the President of the United States finds himself faced with a crime problem that is becoming impossible to handle. Much of this is due to an attitude of permissiveness that is becoming more and more evident in our society. This is leading to a progressive relaxing and discarding of all forms of restraint and discipline.

The sad fact is this attitude has been fostered and promoted by many educators and clergymen as well as public officials and parents.

No thinking American would decry legitimate dissent.

But much of this dissent gives way to lawlessness and a lack of respect for all law and authority.

Much today is being done to discredit law enforcement agencies. Certainly, most people would agree that there is room for improvement in police personnel and their operations.

Too few Americans, however, are willing to pay a fair price so that more people will be called to this civil service.

The communications media and for the most part, newspapers and television, exert a strong influence upon the national tastes of the nation.

The obsession with sex and sadism in criminal acts too often have their effect on the viewer.

The average American child watches television from 3 to 5 hours a day. By the time he reaches adolescence, he has been exposed for about 20,000 hours to whatever influence TV may exert on his attitudes and behavior.

Child psychiatrist Fredric Wertham blames television for much of the current disorders. He contends the medium has produced a "generation of violence worshippers."

Dr. Ralph Garry (a Boston University education professor who served on a committee for the Congressional investigation of violence on TV), stated:

It was my conclusion that children are of no concern to network officials, except to the degree that they have money to spend. And then they are only a commodity to be exploited.

Ben H. Bagdikian, former *Saturday Evening Post* editor who is a respected critic of communications media, notes that the television industry earns $2.5 billion a year from advertisers for its power to make viewers "buy Brand A instead of Brand B."

How, he asks, can the same medium deny its power to influence the behavior of children who watch violence, crime and gun shooting as high as 59% of viewing time!

Motion pictures also contribute to this cesspool of crime which our nation has inherited. And it is a fact all too obvious that the morality depicted by the movie industry in recent. years has decayed from bad to worse.

Our needs only to scan the lurid advertisements of current or coming film attractions to see how far our nation has sunk as far as moral stature is concerned.

The late J. Edgar Hoover, head of the F.B.I. recently reported that 12 serious crimes are committed each minute and one murder is committed each 30 minutes.

Of the 17,800 murders reported in the United States in 1967, over 12,600 were committed with firearms.

While in the last 10 years the population has increased 10%, crime has increased 88%.

The serious crime rate in the United States for 1972 reached 2740 victims per hundred thousand population. This is more than triple the 1940 rate.

One-fifth of our 20 Presidents since Abraham Lincoln's time have been murdered in office!

In his more than five years in office, Lyndon B. Johnson had some 6000 written threats against his life.

Before you finish reading the next two pages of this book, five Americans will have been murdered, raped, robbed or assaulted.

And a particularly tragic facet of the crime and violence problem in this country is the increasing involvement of young people.

In 1972 for example, 77% of those arrested for serious crimes were under 25 years of age.

The late J. Edgar Hoover commented in a report, "The enormous cost in money and ruined lives, which the statistics of American crime represent, touches almost every citizen in some manner. The cost in dollars and cents is staggering—estimated at over 27 billion dollars a year."

The Internal Revenue Service estimates that the underworld collects more than $600,000 *an hour* in untaxed profits from illegal bets alone. It is estimated that more than $20 billion is wagered with the underworld every year in this country by so-called upstanding American citizens. Of this, an untaxed $7 billion goes into the pockets of racket bosses.

In his own back yard, the President of the United States finds crime running rampant.

In 1972, there were about 52,000 serious crimes committed in Washington, D.C. This necessitated the adding of 1760 more sodium-vapor lights on streets to thwart criminals.

Recently Sherman Banks, president of the Los Angeles chapter of the Black Panthers, is reported to have said: "The only power we have is the power of destruction. America has given us no alternative but to relate to that."

How prophetically J. Edgar Hoover concluded his report on crime by stating, "There is no way, of course, that crime and violence can be completely eliminated. We will continue to have crime and violence in this country and throughout the world, because, unfortunately, criminal and violent behavior is the nature of some men."

Thus the President of the United States finds himself straddled with another insurmountable problem—crime—a problem that will make it impossible for him to build a heaven here in the United States.

TOO BIG . . . TOO POWERFUL

And as the nation gets bigger, the government gets bigger.

Running the government of the United States means running the biggest business in the world.

CRIME WAVE HITS NEW HIGH

YEAR-BY-YEAR RISE IN CRIMES AGAINST PEOPLE AND PROPERTY

	1960	1961	1962	1963	1964	1965	1966	1967	1970
	2,014,600	2,082,400	2,213,600	2,435,900	2,755,000	2,930,200	3,264,200	3,802,300	5,568,200

SERIOUS CRIMES IN U. S.

	1960	1961	1962	1963	1964	1965	1966	1967	1970
MURDERS	9,000	8,600	8,400	8,500	9,300	9,900	10,900	12,100	15,800
FORCIBLE RAPES	16,900	16,900	17,200	17,300	21,000	23,000	25,300	27,100	37,270
ROBBERIES	107,400	106,200	110,400	116,000	129,800	138,100	157,300	202,100	348,380
AGGRAVATED ASSAULTS	152,000	154,400	162,100	171,600	200,000	212,100	231,800	253,300	329,940
BURGLARIES	897,400	934,200	978,200	1,068,800	1,193,600	1,261,800	1,387,200	1,605,700	2,169,300
LARCENIES OF $50 OR OVER	506,200	528,500	573,100	648,500	732,000	792,300	894,600	1,047,100	1,746,100
AUTO THEFTS	325,700	333,500	364,100	405,200	469,300	493,100	557,000	654,900	927,500

Source: Federal Bureau of Investigation

Along with the President are needed 2500 appointive officials who direct 3 million individuals—including 1.3 million civilians in the Defense Department.

This Federal bureaucracy has offices in more than 421,000 buildings in the United States and most of the countries in the world. Along with this, one must add the military establishment with approximately 3.5 million personnel in uniform, operating from hundreds of installations in the United States and about 450 abroad.

It has been estimated that this immense and cumbersome Government operation takes in and spends funds approaching 260 billion dollars each year.

One Senator recently warned the nation that the United States was well along the road toward "an elective dictatorship."

He stated:

> If the nation continues its role of involvement and unilateral military action overseas, then the future can hold nothing for us except endless foreign exertions, chronic warfare, growing expense and the proliferation of an already formidable military-industrial-labor-academic complex—in short the militarization of American life.

What a prophetic description of the nations under the rule of Antichrist in the Tribulation Period!

One person estimated that Government employees use more than 1,000,000,000,000 (1 trillion) pieces of ordinary writing paper a year in the course of their duties.

The Government spends about $500,000 a minute and this is continually rising. This amounts to $5 billion a week and $260 billion a year.

U.S. News & World Report observed, "Federal spending on education and employment assistance to help the poor has increased to $14.8 billion dollars a year."

THE HIGH COST OF PREPAREDNESS

It was Joseph Berger who in a letter to the editor of *Newsweek* commented concerning the recent Vietnam peace talks,

THE UNITED STATES GOVERNMENT
Is it getting too BIG?

The BIGGEST Organization on Earth:

EMPLOYS 6.4 million people and pays them 39 BILLION dollars a year!

1 out of every 13 Americans works for the U.S. Government!

OWNS 760 million acres of land or 1/3rd of the Nation

PLUS
422,000 BUILDINGS valued at 103 BILLION dollars!

PLUS
about 200 BILLION dollars in EQUIPMENT including 381,000 vehicles, 47,000 airplanes and almost 1000 ships.

SPENDS $500,000 a MINUTE and this is increasing! That makes 5 BILLION DOLLARS A WEEK!

and all this contributes to a **DEBT** of $494 BILLION DOLLARS with Congress about to authorize a new "ceiling" of over half a TRILLION!

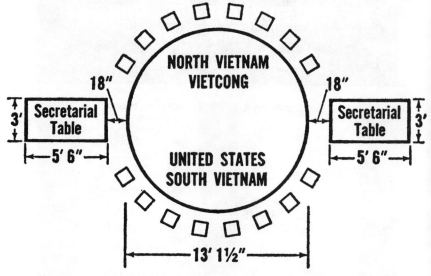

How can anyone believe that man himself can achieve a Heaven here on earth when it took 8 months of argument just to settle the shape of the peace table in Paris . . . during the course of which some 8000 more U.S. soldiers lost their lives in Vietnam.

saying: "It is a sad bit of irony that man is able to construct a vehicle that can convey him safely on a 500,000-mile trip through space, but unable to design a table that will accommodate him so that he might embark upon a journey to peace."

This further points out the complexities which face the nation today in its effort to be all things to all people.

When nations have a difficult time agreeing on even the shape of a table for a peace conference in order for them to sit down and discuss the problems that confront them, can it be possible to assume that nations will ever learn to live in peace?

Perhaps it is this desire to be militarily ready that makes the Defense Department spend $4 million a year on a lobbying force of 339—more than 1 for every 2 members of Congress—to keep the Congressmen informed and to make sure they pass legislation in favor of the military.

THE PRICE FOR WORLD LEADERSHIP RUNS HIGH FOR THE UNITED STATES	
Aircraft carrier in World War II	$55 million
Carrier Nimitz, now being built	$545 million
Destroyer in World War II	$8.7 million
Latest destroyer	$200 million
Submarine in World War II	$4.7 million
Latest nuclear submarine	$200 million
Bomber in World War II	$218 thousand
B-52 bomber built in 1961	$7.9 million
Fighter plane in World War II	$54 thousand
F-111 fighter plane	$6.8 million
M-1 rifle made in 1946	$31
M-16 rifle used in Vietnam	$150

To protect America, the military is always seeking new and more efficient ways to carry out its missions.

In 1970, as an example, a new helicopter called the Cheyenne made its appearance in Vietnam. It is able to fly 2,500 to 3,000 miles nonstop and carry a 30-mm. high-speed cannon that can fire 425 times a minute at a range of 3,000 meters (about 2 miles).

And the U.S. Navy has asked Congress for more than $2.7 billion to begin modernizing its fleet.

Perhaps, the biggest problem that faces the President of the United States is the problem of attempting to preserve the peace.

Right now, the United States is dropping more tons of bombs in Vietnam, than it did before the halt in the bombing of North Vietnam was ordered on November 1, 1968.

Some bombing strikes have cost the U.S. at least $15 million per day!

The Vietnam war has been the perplexing problem for many Presidents and is the new type of war which seems to find no answer for a permanent peace.

Up to the present time the total war cost equals $800 for every man, woman and child in both North and South Vietnam.

$6 billion has been spent for ground ammunition alone. 5 tons is fired by each soldier per year. This totals $12,000 worth of ammunition shot by each soldier.

Just 1/10th of the total amount of money spent in the Vietnam war could build South Vietnam into a paradise.

More is budgeted for chemical and biological weapons than is to be spent for vocational education.

Less is proposed for elementary and secondary education than it costs to assemble an attack carrier force of which the United States has 15.

More will be spent on the ABM (antiballistic missile), taking the military estimate at face value, than will be invested in higher education.

Five times as much will be spent on a nuclear carrier as will be provided for libraries and other community services.

Six times as much is budgeted for the Air Force's Manned Orbiting Laboratory as is slated for education of the handicapped.

This has made the United States overly cautious in becoming involved in any other war throughout the world, and yet, it finds that a necessary evil is the evil of being prepared against possible attacks against missiles from hostile countries.

ANTI-MISSILE PROTECTION

The Nixon Administration's decision to build a Safeguard anti-ballastic-missile system in the United States has brought up a storm of protests as well as approvals. It has once again drawn the attention of the citizens to the perplexing problems that confront the President.

Between 1962 and 1967 the U.S. Air Force stored 1,000 Minutemen and 54 Titan-II intercontinental ballistic missiles beneath the productive soil of eight states west of the Mississippi River.

These missiles are covered with an 80-ton concrete lid which covers the missile in its 80-foot-deep reinforced silo. At the bottom of this elevator shaft is an enormous 8-ton blast proof door which leads to a small tunnel where the missile is housed.

In this day and age when the President must make a split second decision on whether or not to release anti-ballistic missiles, it is evident that a cloud of despair pervades the country.

While some may go merrily along . . . they perhaps are unaware or do not wish to recognize the fact that death in the tens of millions could occur within a matter of seconds . . . with whole cities being carbonized and entire nations being reduced to a state of barbaric anarchy.

Because the cost of a complex defense system is so high, the President finally decided on a compromise believing that the nation must proceed with at least a limited or "thin" system. This is a system that will not protect the cities of the nation, but will protect the retaliatory missile bases in the United States so they can launch their deadly nuclear holocaust in Russia or other striking countries.

This Safeguard system will cost about $7 billion.

It was Defense Secretary, Melvin R. Laird, who brought the awesomeness of the precarious position of the United States to the forefront.

In a recent interview he stated, "We assessed our intelligence information on what the Soviets are doing with their missile deployment and because of the increased Soviet missile deployment that has been going on over the last 24 months, we became increasingly concerned."

The Soviet Union has what is called the SS-9, which is the largest intercontinental ballistic missile in its inventory. It has a capability of carrying a warhead of up to 25 megatons (25 MILLION TONS).

This missile is much more powerful than anything we have here in the United States.

The Russians have about 200 of these SS-9 missiles and these 200 could destroy 55% of the population of this country.

Oddly enough, it is the Russians who have been able to supply about 80% of the war materials used by the Communists in Vietnam at a total annual cost of around $2 billion a year!

While at the same time it was taking the United States $30 billion a year to maintain the war in Vietnam!

Thus annually we had in Vietnam: A $2 billion investment by Russia and a $30 billion investment by the United States.

This is why the Russians have much more money to put into missiles that can spell doom for an unprepared United States.

That is why there are some difficulties in believing a recent statement made by Secretary of State, William P. Rogers. When asked whether the Soviet Union would be foolish enough to strike at the United States with a missile he replied, "It is hard to believe because any leader or leaders of sound mind would know that it probably would result in the destruction of mankind."

Perhaps Mr. Rogers should examine more closely the Chinese Defense Minister's political report to the Ninth Congress of the Chinese Communist Party, April 24, 1969 when he said:

> ". . . the days of U.S. imperialism and Soviet revisionism are numbered. We should make adequate preparations, be prepared for their all-out war effort . . . and also be prepared for nuclear war with them."

The Nuclear Non-proliferation Treaty as signed by the representatives of the United States, Britain and Russia. Purpose of the Treaty is to prevent other countries from using nuclear power for weaponry. But while Russia, under this Treaty has the right to inspect other nations . . . Russia, as usual, has refused to accept such inspection herself. Will this become another worthless piece of paper that will give Russia a head start in domination over freedom-loving countries?

The Soviets have a history of truce-breaking and no one can predict what nuclear actions the Chinese might suddenly generate. While it may be "hard to believe" that any country might unleash nuclear bombs against the United States . . . nevertheless it is most possible right now!

At this point, perhaps, some of our readers can appreciate the tremendous burdens that face the President of the United States in his trying to alleviate the living conditions at home and, at the same time, protect its people in case of nuclear attack.

It is expected that in the 70's, Red China will be capable of launching a nuclear attack and at this time it should have about 30 intercontinental missiles.

With our protective network missile system, it is estimated that Red China would only be able through its nuclear attack to kill 1 million Americans and that our defense system would be able to destroy the other missiles before they arrived in the United States.

However, if Russia attacked, 20 million lives might be saved by our missile system, but casualties would be in the tens of millions. Any President facing today's world hopes that the years immediately ahead will be a time of negotiation and not confrontation.

And yet while hoping for negotiation, the President must at all times have his country prepared.

The year 1972 was an historic one for President Nixon. On Sunday, February 20, Richard Milhous Nixon became the first president in history to visit China. He arrived in Peking as the Chinese band played the "Star Spangled Banner." He met with Chinese Communist Party Chairman Mao Tse-tung and Premier Chou En-lai in what he termed a "...journey for peace."

Then, on Monday, May 22nd, President Nixon flew to Moscow and met with President Nikolai Podgorny and Communist Party Secretary Leonid I. Brezhnev. Together they signed a pact of "peaceful coexistence."

Yet, out of 25 summit agreements, Russia has already broken 24 of them!

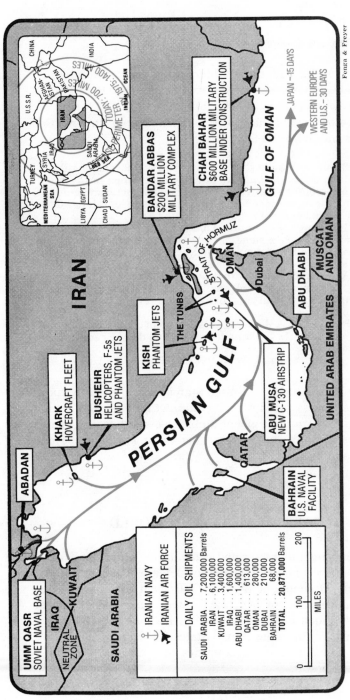

Fenza & Freyer

The Persian Gulf: One of the few places that is genuinely vital to everyone's national interest

The most important 25 miles in the world can be said to be the Strait of Hormuz in the Persian Gulf. For through here must pass the oil on which Asia depends for 90% of her needs and Russia, U.S. and Europe rely for 55% of their need. This area is basically controlled by one man...The SHAH OF IRAN! The route through the Straits is so precarious that it can be interrupted by a few mines thrown over the side of a fishing boat. Such an interruption could wreak havoc...perhaps even setting the U.S., Asia and Russia against each other in a bitter war.

One of the sad facts which Americans still have not learned is that we know from experience that the Communists do not respect treaty obligations.

On agreements made with known wicked nations, God through Isaiah declared:

> Because ye have said, We have made a covenant with death, and with hell are we at agreement; when the overflowing scourge shall pass through, it shall not come unto us: for we have made lies our refuge, and under falsehood have we hid ourselves:
>
> Therefore thus saith the Lord God, Behold I lay in Zion for a foundation a stone, a tried stone, a precious corner stone, a sure foundation: he that believeth shall not make haste.
>
> And your covenant with death shall be disannulled, and your agreement with hell shall not stand; when the overflowing scourge shall pass through, then ye shall be trodden down by it.
>
> For the bed is shorter than that a man can stretch himself on it: and the covering narrower than that he can wrap himself in it.
>
> *(Isaiah 28:15,16,18,20 King James Version)*

The President of the United States finds himself in a position where he is faced with Communist nations who are not about to give up their global ambitions, and because of this he bears a staggering defense load that is almost beyond understanding.

CARETAKER OF THE WORLD

To maintain its power and place in this world, the United States wants $84 billion annually for defense. This expenditure represents 92 cents out of every $10 spent for all purposes, public and private. In fact, the United States spends almost 3 times as much for defense as all of its Allies together.

Along with this, the United States Government must continually give aid to other countries in order to maintain a balance of power.

In World War II we gave our Allies enormous help in outright financial gifts which included over $11 billion of Lend-Lease to the U.S.S.R.

We also, however, paid over $50 billion in interest on the money we had to borrow to carry out these foreign aid programs.

From 1945 through 1966 in foreign aid we gave the following sum to countries all over the world: $122,358,500,000.

Perhaps in this one aspect other nations have found that the United States is their heaven here on earth.

But along with the many problems at home facing our President and the problems of war, comes the necessity for venturing into outer space in order to keep abreast of our enemies.

It is estimated that it will cost $100 billion to put men on Mars. Plans for such adventures are necessary because some authorities are convinced that the Soviet Union is now preparing to assemble a huge earth-orbiting laboratory from which a smaller space craft could carry a crew to the moon and control much of the world.

In the past decade, the United States has invested $57 billion in outer space programs.

Through this investment, the United States has taken the lead in the number of spacecrafts launched. At this writing, the U.S. record is 818; Russia's total is 530.

Some scientists believe it will require a yearly spending of $6 billion on the civilian space program alone to keep the U.S. ahead of the Soviet Union.

The cost of one Apollo space flight mission is estimated at $40 million. And while much of our attention has turned to space . . . we find that our country is becoming more and more engulfed in garbage.

Recent reports indicate that Americans are already spending $4,500,000,000 a year for refuse collection and disposal services.

And such garbage, sadly enough, can also be seen in America's moral decline. Outsiders, coming to the United States, now see a country they have often termed as heaven on earth,

(Continued)

Why We Have a Shrinking Dollar and Adverse Balance of Trade

We print below a list of countries and the amounts they have received from the American taxpayers from 1945 through 1966. These sums do not include the enormous help we gave to our Allies. during World War II including about $11 billion of Lend-Lease to the U.S.S.R. Nor do they include over $50 billion paid out in interest on the money we borrowed to carry on the foreign aid program.

Many of these countries such as Albania, Czechoslovakia, East Germany, Hungary, Poland, U.S.S.R., Yugoslavia, Laos, Afghanistan, United Arab Republic (Egypt), Cuba, Algeria, Congo (Brazzaville), Congo Kinshasa, Tanzania, Zambia and probably others, are certainly numbered among our enemies—some of them our worst enemies.

Albania $20,400,000
Austria 1,198,000,000
Belgium-Luxembourg 2,004,900,000
Czechoslovakia 193,000,000
Denmark 920,500,000
East Germany 800,000
Finland 134,400,000
France 9,409,600,000
Germany (Federal Republic) 4,997,400,000
Berlin 131,900,000
Hungary 31,500,000
Iceland 84,000,000
Ireland 146,500,000
Italy 6,092,900,000
Malta 6,100,000
Netherlands 2,470,400,000
Norway 1,236,000,000
Poland 554,500,000
Portugal 519,100,000
Spain 2,004,300,000
Sweden 109,000,000
United Kingdom 9,044,900,000
U.S.S.R. 186,400,000
Yugoslavia 2,863,900,000
Europe Regional 2,735,000,000

Australia 275,300,000
New Zealand 27,700,000
Trust Territories of the Pacific Islands 125,400,000
British Solomon Islands 400,000
Tonga Island 300,000

Canada 36,300,000
Vietnam 4,590,100,000
Burma 100,600,000
Cambodia 341,100,000
China (Republic of) 4,899,500,000
Hong Kong 41,900,000
Indochina, Undistributed 1,535,200,000
Indonesia 834,600,000
Japan 3,972,900,000
Korea 6,676,700,000

Laos 473,400,000
Malaysia 47,500,000
Philippines 1,925,000,000
Ryukyu Islands 340,600,000

Thailand 1,089,200,000
East Asia Regional 731,800,000
Afghanistan 346,400,000
Ceylon 101,500,000
Cyprus 19,300,000
Greece 3,749,400,000
India 6,769,200,000
Iran 1,752,000,000
Iraq 102,700,000
Israel 1,104,500,000
Jordan 572,800,000
Lebanon 87,900,000
Nepal 97,800,000
Pakistan 3,079,800,000
Saudi Arabia 209,100,000
Syrian Arab Republic 73,300,000
Turkey 5,039,800,000
United Arab Republic (Egypt) 1,133,300,000
Yemen 41,800,000
Central Treaty Organization 52,800,000
Near East and South Asia Regional 1,082,300,000

Argentina 758,600,000
Bolivia 460,600,000
Brazil 3,185,700,000
British Honduras 4,400,000
Chile 1,242,200,000
Colombia 834,800,000
Costa Rica 149,000,000
Cuba 52,100,000
Dominican Republic 320,100,000
Ecuador 279,600,000
El Salvador 108,100,000
Guatemala 209,200,000
Guyana 24,400,000
Haiti 108,800,000
Honduras 88,500,000

Jamaica 44,300,000
Mexico 1,068,200,000
Nicaragua 133,100,000
Panama 173,000,000
Paraguay 106,200,000

Peru 678,900,000
Surinam 10,100,000
Trinidad and Tobago 52,200,000
Uruguay 119,400,000
Venezuela 392,200,000
Other West Indies 3,700,000
Regional 83,100,000
Latin America Regional 997,600,000

Algeria 179,400,000
Botswana 7,400,000
Burundi 6,700,000
Cameroon 27,200,000
Central African Republic 3,500,000
Chad 5,500,000
Congo (Brazzaville) 2,200,000
Congo (Kinshasa) 351,000,000
Dahomey 9,700,000
Ethiopia 317,500,000
Gabon 5,800,000
Gambia 600,000
Ghana 174,800,000
Guinea 75,700,000
Ivory Coast 28,800,000
Kenya 57,200,000

Lesotho 1,100,000
Liberia 241,600,000
Libya 220,000,000
Malagasy Republic 9,600,000
Malawi 11,800,000
Mali, Republic of 18,700,000
Mauritania 3,000,000
Morocco 584,100,000
Niger 10,600,000
Nigeria 190,300,000
Rwanda 5,500,000
Senegal 21,500,000
Sierra Leone 32,500,000
Somali Republic 52,200,000
*South Africa, Republic of 150,600,000
Southern Rhodesia 7,000,000
Sudan 108,400,000
Tanzania 50,000,000
Togo 12,000,000
Tunisia 487,900,000
Uganda 21,000,000
Upper Volta 6,800,000
Zambia 36,100,000
East Africa Regional 18,400,000
Regional USAID/Africa 1,300,000
Africa Regional 76,000,000
Non-Regional

Total 6,462,800,000

Total, all countries $122,358,500,000

*(Source: Agency for International
Development)*
Subsequently repaid with interest

Only one country in the above list has repaid with interest the sums loaned to it during this period. That country is the Republic of South Africa.

These sums reach the gigantic total of $122,358,500,000. This is the main reason for our adverse balance in world trade. It is one of the main causes for our disastrous inflation, the shrinking value of the dollar and the fact that we have balanced the Federal budget only seven times in the past 37 years. Here we find the reason for the loss of more than half of our gold.

The past cannot be reversed. The money is gone and will never return. Surely, America has now learned its lesson and will stop bankrupting itself to aid its enemies as well as its friends. The road to recovery from this long debauch of foolish wastefulness will be long and hard. The sooner we stop the waste and begin the hard, thankless task of practicing thrift and economy while working hard to restore our dissipated fortunes, the brighter will be our hope for the future.

Howard E. Kershner in CHRISTIAN ECONOMICS, January 21, 1969

marked by riots, strikes, racial tensions, obscenity, sexual license, and spiritual deadness.

It is estimated that by 1975 a full 10% of our babies will be born out of wedlock.

And the sad fact is that many clergymen are encouraging this "freedom" even in the pages of such publications as Playboy.

This is a country that watches prostitutes and homosexuals parade their profession openly through interviews on TV.

This is a country where more than 5 million Americans are alcoholics. And where Hollywood and back-alley film producers have stooped to new moral lows in film production.

Books and magazines of the worst sort are peddled above and under the counter all over the land.

Christianity Today reported that "within two blocks of the White House are found some of Washington's most obnoxious pornographic outlets. People wallow in this cesspool of putrescence legally, because recent Supreme Court decisions serve to protect those whose pockets are filled with the filthy lucre of this abominable trade."

Christianity Today goes on to report that, "The moral foundations of America are not crumbling; they have crumbled. And the churches have contributed to the disaster."

The average age of the world's great civilizations is 200 years. These nations progressed through this sequence:

> From bondage to spiritual faith
> From spiritual faith to great courage
> From great courage to liberty
> From liberty to abundance
> From abundance to complacency
> From complacency to apathy
> From apathy to dependency
> From dependency back again into bondage.

In three years the United States will be 200 years old. This cycle is not inevitable. It depends upon us!

It was Shakespeare who made Marc Antony say at Caesar's funeral, "If you have tears, prepare to shed them now."

For dedicated or not, the President of the United States will find it is impossible to make this country or any other country a heaven on earth. What better time than now for the people of the United States to fall down on their knees and repent and seek the face of the Lord.

For,

> Be not deceived, God is not mocked, for whatever a man [or nation] soweth, that shall he also reap.
>
> *(Galatians 6:7 King James Version)*

Every American ought to hang upon his wall a copy of that blessed promise of God which states,

> If my people, which are called by my name, shall humble themselves, and pray, and seek my face, and turn from their wicked ways; then will I hear from Heaven, and will forgive their sin, and will heal their land.
>
> *(II Chronicles 7:14 King James Version)*

Chapter 7
This Gathering Storm

Too Many People • Harvesting the Sea • Towards One World Government • The Pattern for One World Government Has Already Been Set • Internationalizing Money • After the Moon—What? • The U.S. and Its "Sky Spies" • Policeman for the World • U.S. and the Mideast Crises • The U.S. Reservoir of Destruction • Dump Poison Gas Into Sea • Russia's Heaven on Earth • The Mideast Tinderbox • Israel . . . Its Changing Face! • Arab Guerrilla Warfare • Pawns in a Bitter Struggle • No Siesta in South America • India's Growing Pains • The Threat of Red China • Africa • Destiny Disaster • Scattered Observations

The world is in a terrible mess. And like Humpty-Dumpty, none of the King's horses or none of the King's men will be able to put the world back together again.

While some nations strive diligently to make this world a heaven on earth—others strive just as diligently to create chaos, confusion, and tragedy.

Because man was born in sin, man cannot be expected to live a sinless life. The condition of today's world is the product of sinful man.

It was Shakespeare who said, "All the world's a stage, and all the men and women merely players."

And perhaps Moore put the condition of the world precisely in his poem which reads:

> This world is all a fleeting show,
> For man's illusion given;
> The smiles of joy, the tear of woe,
> Deceitful shine, deceitful flow—
> There's nothing true but Heaven.

The greatest country in the world, the United States has taken the lead in striving for peace but it has found that peace is an elusive dream. For history has shown that there have been more wars within the last decade than in any other previous decade.

It was Petrarch who said, "Five great enemies to peace inhabit with us: avarice, ambition, envy, anger, and pride. If those enemies were to be banished, we should infallibly enjoy perpetual peace."

Unfortunately, most of the people in the world think that the above statement is true, but it is not. For even if these enemies were banished, there would still not be peace on earth. Peace will not come until the people of the world recognize Christ as personal Saviour and Lord and dedicate their lives and their hearts to Him.

Men simply cannot build a world of peace without God. Men cannot guard the peace without God. On this the Bible rightly declares:

> "Except the Lord build the house, they labour in vain that build it: except the Lord keep the city, the watchman waketh but in vain."
>
> *(Psalm 127:1 King James Version)*

One day peace will come on earth. We will discuss that Day in future chapters. It is a day that will not occur until many great tragedies strike the peoples of the earth and multiple millions are killed.

Let us, however, first look at some of the problems which now face the world and which are deterrents to peace.

TOO MANY PEOPLE

Perhaps the world's number one worry is that there are too many people.

Today's world contains about 3.8 billion people.

And by the year 2000, the United Nations predicts that the world's population will be about 6 billion.

This means that in the next 27 years, the world will acquire 2.2 billion additional people — an increase of more people than all those who existed on this earth in 1938!

The world is already having problems trying to cope with the 3.8 billion people. You can imagine the increased problems which will occur with 6 billion people in the world in the year 2000.

There will not only be a much greater increase in famine, but there will be more violence, more riots, more revolutions, and more wars.

For the more crowded the living conditions on earth, the greater grows the likelihood of violence and potential upheaval.

It is important to note that much of the huge population growth is going to occur in those parts of the world that are already overcrowded—those parts of the world which are even at present the poorest and least able to feed and support any additional people.

And these are the same areas where unrest is the greatest today . . . where the pressures of an expanding population contribute to revolution.

It is estimated that about 2.5 billion people or 70% of the world's *present* population live in such underdeveloped regions as Asia, Africa and Latin America. And by the year 2000, 77% (or 4.7 billion) of the world's population will be centered in these critical regions.

China alone, which already has 740 million people, will have more than 1 billion. India, which is already hungry with its 600 million today, is expected to have a billion people by the turn of the century. Asia's population increases by over one million every week! And it is anticipated that Africa will

Too Many People Too Fast Spells Disaster in Year 2000

Billions of People

0 1 2 3 4 5 6

2000
6.1 billion
people

NOW
3.8 billion
people

1939
World War II
2.2 billion
people

1914
World War I
1.7 billion
people

1848
California
Gold Rush
1.1 billion
people

1776
Declaration of
Independence
850 million
people

1492
Columbus
Discovers
America
400 million
people

1215
Magna Carta
350 million
people

476
Fall of Roman
Empire
290 million
people

Birth of Christ
250 million
people

more than double its present population and by the year 2000, she too will have 768 million people.

Latin America, which now cannot even support 280 million, will by the year 2000 have about 638 million people.

In contrast, the United States, where some 209 million people live in the highest income brackets, there will be a total of 318 million by the year 2000.

Soviet Russia's present population of 245 million is expected to reach 353 million people.

Though there are efforts worldwide at birth control, it is not working effectively enough to dramatically change any population explosion which should occur about the year 2000.

10,000 people a day starving to death in this *present* age! Can you imagine the starvation that will occur when there are 2½ billion more mouths to feed in the year 2000?

Is it no wonder that leading scientists are warning the United States and other nations that they must look to the seas for food, water, fuel, and metals to prevent starvation and keep industry going in the 21st Century.

The problem that the United States finds itself confronted with is that it must spend some $24 billion to land men on the moon and about another $20 billion in the next 10 years to tap the riches of the sea—while trying all the while to satisfy the other needs of the people right here on earth.

HARVESTING THE SEA

The Federal Government is now spending about half a billion dollars a year to explore the seas and to develop the resources in and under them.

It has been estimated that ocean fisheries today supply about 3% of the protein consumed by people around the world.

This is estimated at approximately 50 million tons per year.

Ocean scientists estimate that if additional efforts are put into the harvests of the seas, this could be raised to 500 million tons.

Drought-stricken Chileans pray for rain at a farming settlement near Santiago, Chile. Chile faced its worst drought in history in March, 1969. There appears to be an increase of droughts, famines and earthquakes in these end-times.

At present, there are more than 12,000 oil wells off the U.S. coast and the number is increasing at the rate of 1400 a year.

There are 22 nations now that are either producing oil or drilling for it offshore.

In fact, even diamonds are being brought up in deposits of gravel off the west coast of Africa. And coal is mined by the British in tunnels running out from land and under the North Sea.

Sea water itself contains huge amounts of minerals.

It has been estimated that equipment, which will be built to extract fresh water from sea water, could also be expected annually to produce as by-products: 100 tons of salt, 8 million tons of magnesium, 2 million tons of potash, 250,000 tons of bromine, and 50,000 tons of strontium and 6 pounds of gold.

One of the problems that will arise as more people tap the sea's riches is the question: "Who owns the ocean's treasures?"

The problem of solving this question could strike off many new wars as the world sees its land resources rapidly vanishing as we approach the year 2000.

Dr. Julius A. Stratton, a former President of the Massachusetts Institute of Technology, said recently: "We have enough water, enough resources to last us until the year 2000."

But what happens after that could set off the world's greatest catastrophe! Christ said of the end-times:

> And ye shall hear of wars and rumours of wars: see that ye be not troubled: for all these things must come to pass but the end is not yet.
> For nation shall rise against nation, and kingdom against kingdom: and there shall be famines, and pestilences, and earthquakes, in divers places.
> All these are the beginning of sorrows.
> *(Matthew 24:6-8 King James Version)*

TOWARDS ONE WORLD GOVERNMENT

With problems becoming more complex, more nations will favor a "one-world" concept of government.

Bible prophecy makes this very clear (Revelation 17:12-13; 13:8). Even today, there exists 16 bureaus — everyone of them designed to tie the nations of the world together — Christian to pagan, believer to atheist, democracy to totalitarianism.

THE PATTERN FOR ONE WORLD GOVERNMENT HAS ALREADY BEEN SET

Here are 16 international agencies already under the control of the United Nations.

1. **International Atomic Energy Agency (IAEA).** The published aim of this agency is to promote peaceful use of atomic energy. The inevitable result will be to disseminate among foreign enemy nations vital information on atomic resources.

2. **International Labor Organization (ILO).** The purpose of this arm of the one-world government is to coordinate labor demands throughout the world. It provides an ideal vehicle for promotion of the one-world philosophy.

3. **Food and Agricultural Organization (FAO).** This organization is set up to standardize food qualities and the levels of nutrition internationally. It is the model instrument for implementing the Antichrist law in Revelation 13:17.

4. **International Bank for Reconstruction and Development (World Bank).** This international bureaucracy is designed to internationalize money standards. Ultimately, it will place all the money power of the world in one giant agency. Already there is talk of issuing international currency under the direction of United Nations.

5. **International Development Association (IDA).** This one-world financing organization aims to set up international control of natural resources.

6. **United Nations Educational Scientific and Cultural Organization (UNESCO).** This agency is set up to promote collaboration among nations through education, science, and culture.

7. **World Health Organization (WHO).** To internationalize medicine, surgery, and all treatments of diseases. This serves a political advantage to a world dictator. . . .

8. **International Finance Corporation (IFC).** A plan to take over the "poorly developed" areas of the world. To bring the smaller nations of the world into subjection to a one-world government.

9. **International Monetary Fund (IMF).** To promote and expand international trade, to standardize commerce and industry, which will make it a very simple matter for the Antichrist to issue his decree that those who refuse his mark cannot buy or sell (Revelation 13:17).

10. **International Civil Aviation Organization (ICAO).** To standardize aviation laws, procedures, patterns and practices throughout the world.

11. **Universal Postal Union (UPU).** This agency is designed to promote uniformity of postal services and development of international collaboration. Openly to promote reciprocal exchange of mail. This is the first step toward the international control of communications and censorship.

12. **International Telecommunications Union (ITU).** To provide international regulations for radio, telegraph and telephone services, thereby making worldwide preaching of the Gospel of Jesus Christ by means of radio and television a practical impossibility.

13. **World Meteorological Organization (WMO).** The aim of this agency is to standardize and co-ordinate all meteorological work—weather information and forecasts—of the world. Weather control and modification of climates is a sinister possibility.

14. **Intergovernmental Maritime Consultive Organization (IMCO).** To promote co-ordination of international shipping and to remove all discrimination by governments and all restrictive practices by shippers. Thus international transportation will be under the control of another giant bureau which can dictate who and what can and cannot be served.

15. **International Trade Organization (ITO).** To tighten terms of commerce and to promote free flow of goods from

Atlanta, Georgia area police officials watch a demonstration of a "smoke breathing" armored personnel carrier. This machine is designed for use during riots and is equipped with 15-man cab and emergency lighting. It is bullet-proof.

Riot police, using special plastic shields, waged a pitched battle with striking farm workers in Rome. Mass violence has made this "new look" necessary for personal safety.

one country to another under international agreement. Thus another step is taken to break down national boundaries and pave the way for the Antichrist, to take control of the entire world. (Revelation 13:4-8.)

16. General Agreement on Tariffs and Trades (GATT). The goal of this last-named Agency is the subject of current battles in the United States Congress, the fight to lower, or do away with, all tariffs on foreign imports, leveling national boundaries and destroying national loyalties.

(Basic Source Information: WORLD ALMANAC, 1969).

Apparently many nations feel that in unity there is strength and the complex problems of today may cause many nations to unite.

The nations are becoming desperate. Jesus spoke of a future time of world-wide chaos and desperation:

> Men's hearts failing them for fear, and for looking after those things which are coming on the earth: for the powers of heaven shall be shaken.
> *(Luke 21:26 King James Version)*

Yet Christ also spoke of His redemption which was to soon follow:

> And then shall they see the Son of man coming in a cloud with power and great glory.
> And when these things begin to come to pass, then look up, and lift up your heads; for your redemption draweth nigh.
> *(Luke 21:27,28 King James Version)*

The European Free Trade Association has been modestly successful since its founding in 1959. The idea was that the peripheral states which have not joined the Common Market should band together economically to strengthen their position against the more tightly integrated Common Market.

These Scandinavian countries which include Denmark, Norway, and Sweden, with Finland and Iceland also interested in participating, have created their association in order to become unified in their goals and objectives.

Throughout the world we find 26 different coalitions of nations which include the Common Market in Europe and The Warsaw Pact among the Soviet Conglomerate of nations.

There is even a race by some to break the national barriers of foreign languages.

The United World College of the Atlantic, located on the cliffs of South Wales, has a singular purpose of becoming the world's first international college and attempting to remove many of today's barriers which create problems between nations.

INTERNATIONALIZING MONEY

One of the problems the world is facing is the problem of money.

Paper money of most kinds inspires little confidence in today's market. Gold is eagerly sought after.

Everyone is looking for reform of the money system — but no one seems to know the answer.

In Canada, homebuyers are already having to pay $9\frac{3}{8}\%$ interest on mortgages.

There has been a desire among many nations to achieve an international money system. Already 34 countries have voted in favor of this new international money. But it will take 67 nations for approval and that is still a little ways off.

France has long suffered from the tendency of many of its people to distrust their own currency.

They have taken as their motto, "In gold we trust."

It has been reported that ancient Greece owes much of its glory to money and the ruination of Rome came shortly after the debasing of its own money.

Spain enjoyed her "Golden Age" as explorers brought back gold and silver from colonies in the New World.

Time magazine reports,

In many ways, the U.S. has been penalized in foreign-money markets for doing all the right things — extending $115 billion in foreign aid since 1945, helping capital-starved nations by making loans and investments, permitting American tourists to spend freely abroad. All this has lead to the transfer of billions in U.S. gold to the Europeans.

Inflation is a problem not only in the United States but throughout the world. Perhaps the entire problem of money can be summed up by what a British labor party official recently said regarding Europe's move toward inflation today: "People want their governments to guarantee good times and plenty of jobs . . ."

How true it is that many people worldwide have one basic desire . . . that is of trying to make a heaven here on earth.

Let us look at some of the problems that face each country in trying to make their country and the world a heaven on earth.

AFTER THE MOON – WHAT?

It was about 12 years ago that the then President John F. Kennedy challenged his countrymen to become "pioneers in a space project."

Now some $24 billion dollars later man has reached the moon but there pervades a gloom at the National Aeronautics and Space Administration (NASA) . . . for now that they accomplished this, they wonder "what next?"

From a peak budget of $5.9 billion in 1966 Congress has dwindled their appropriation down to $3.8 billion this year. From a high of 400,000 skilled craftsmen in 1966, it is projected that by 1974 only 30,000 will be assigned to NASA.

As man's space efforts become more successful there is a danger that they will transfer their faith in God to faith in their own ingenuity. After Apollo 10's trio of astronauts streaked back to earth from circling the moon, Eugene A. Cernan remarked: "I've always believed that nothing is impossible and now I'm convinced of it."

In 1971 NASA sent two spacecraft in orbit around Mars and plans later voyages to Venus and Mercury will follow. They also hope to put up a giant "orbiting campus" that will remain in space ten years . . . eventually to house a "faculty" of 100 U.S. and foreign scientists who would be ferried back and forth every 6 months.

German housewife finds it cheaper to burn worthless Marks than to spend them. Scene was 1923, yet an inflationary spiral is again threatening many nations. Another such disaster could pave the way for Antichrist.

THE U.S. AND ITS "SKY SPIES"

Let us look at some of the problems the United States faces today.

In striving for peace, the United States finds that once again Cuba is installing Soviet-built SAM ground-to-air missile sites.

Pentagon intelligence reveals that three such missiles are now at Punta Gorda and three other sites in Cuba.

The United States is also aware of the fact that the Soviets have a super-rocket with 10 to 14 million pounds of thrust. Saturn, the biggest American rocket, rates only 7.5 million pounds.

The United States realizes that with the new emphasis on outer space, not only they, but also Russia have "sky spies!" No country can keep a secret any more because of these sky spies.

At this moment, the United States has a satellite orbiting more than 100 miles over Moscow.

Among the thousands of photographs which this satellite has taken was one recently which shows a Moscow street in considerable detail . . . such detail that one can recognize a Russian citizen walking along this street.

The amazing thing is that these photographs were taken 100 miles in the air above Moscow.

It has been estimated that of the 458 U.S. satellite launchings since 1958—about two-thirds have had military assignments.

It was through the sky spies that former President Lyndon Johnson was able to say, "I know how many missiles the enemy has."

The United States, through its sky spies, can not only estimate how many missiles Russia has but can also tell how advanced the Communist Chinese nuclear bomb project is. These sky spies can also tell how many millions of tons of rice China might expect to harvest this year. Besides this, they can also reveal the wheat fields of central Russia or relate through intelligence whether Russia will face a drought this summer!

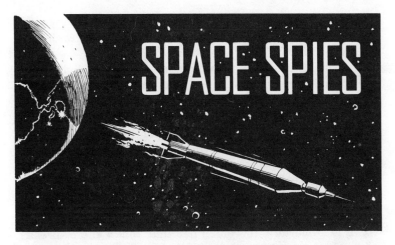

SENTRIES IN SPACE (1957-1969)

		Primarily CIVILIAN satellite launches	Primarily MILITARY satellite launches
The United States can now photograph a Russian citizen walking along a Moscow street. Unusual? YES! Because the photograph is taken by a U.S. SKY SPY satellite orbiting more than *100 miles* over Moscow!	U.S.	174	284
	U.S.S.R.	170*	162*

*Estimated

It has been estimated that the United States has 284 sky spies circling the earth while Russia has 162.

But this figure changes almost every week. These sky spy satellites usually fly for about 8 days and then come down.

But both the United States and Russia are now developing "super-sky spy satellites" (SSSS!) that can stay up for 14 days and perhaps will carry weekly film capsules that can drop from orbit to waiting developing stations below.

We are entering into a sophisticated age when the major countries, through their sky spies, can know what their enemies are doing. Nothing is hidden.

As you read this, can you imagine the power that will be in the hands of Antichrist, when through highly sophisticated spying techniques, he can watch the movements of every individual on earth from space stations above the earth and bring an entire population under his control.

No wonder the mass of the people of that day will say,

Who is like unto the beast [the Antichrist world leader]?
Who is able to make war with him?
(*Revelation 13:4 King James Version*)

It is important to remember that *today* there already exists the basic sky spy system that could make Antichrist powerful in the Last Days.

POLICEMAN FOR THE WORLD

Because of these awesome devices, the United States realizes that it has an obligation to be a world policeman if it hopes to exist in any semblance of peace.

The United States serviceman is stationed not only from coast to coast, but from continent to continent and from sea to sea.

The extent of his presence is vigorously defended by some people and bitterly condemned by others.

There are now more than 1,000,000 U.S. servicemen on military assignment outside our country. One out of five was in the Vietnam area. The total count of U.S. military men in Asia and the Pacific is now about 200,000.

Servicemen in Europe and in the Mediterranean number 320,000. In the western hemisphere, not counting the United States, the number is 230,000. All of these servicemen work for the protection of U.S. interests and the interests of the free world.

36¢ out of every $1 for TAXES

Richard M. Nixon*
1972
$246 BILLION

33¢ out of every $1 for TAXES

Lyndon B. Johnson
1967
$158 BILLION

32¢ out of every $1 for TAXES

John F. Kennedy
1962
$107 BILLION

20¢ out of every $1 for TAXES

Franklin D. Roosevelt
1945
$95 BILLION

Woodrow Wilson
1919
$18 BILLION

Abraham Lincoln
1865
$1.3 BILLION

James Madison
1814
$35 MILLION

George Washington
1789-91
$4 MILLION

THE ROAD TO AN
OVER 200-BILLION BUDGET
Paved with the Mounting Burden of Taxes from George Washington to Richard Nixon

* In 30 years the tax take in the United States has multiplied 17 times. It has soared from 20% of the national income in 1940 to 36% of the national income today. Richard Nixon will be the first President to spend a trillion dollars while in office. By 1974 the national debt will exceed $500 BILLION. Interest on the national debt will become the 3rd largest item on the budget, $22.7 BILLION (or 150% of the 1941 budget of $14 BILLION).

In fact, the United States has engaged in major treaties such as NATO, SEATO, and OAS and has other simple two-country agreements as well which pledge America to defend a total of 42 nations.

This is why it is often referred to as "the world's policeman."

And the cost of equipping these servicemen is increasing —for which the U.S. taxpayer must pick up the bill.

It is estimated that our country spent $79 billion in 1968 for defense alone—almost three times the amount that *all* of our allies spent together.

One of the reasons the United States has come to be the world's policeman is that it is the *only* nation powerful enough to defend the free world.

It is the desire of the United States to stop trouble before, or as soon as, it starts. In defending others, we are actually defending ourselves.

But the cost of the Vietnam war—both in lives and in money—has disheartened many to the point where the United States is becoming more and more cautious before entering into any further conflict.

It is this cautiousness which may cause us simply to give Russia a diplomatic slap on the wrist through the United Nations when Russia finally invades Israel (Ezekiel 38:1-39:16).

U.S. AND THE MIDEAST CRISES

The Institute for Strategic Studies in London stated, "Another Arab-Israeli war would 'almost inevitably' involve the United States and the Soviet Union." In their opinion, Soviet presence in the Mediterranean has made it more difficult for the United States to consider even a partial withdrawal of its forces from this area—particularly since Soviet influence over Egypt has grown far beyond that of the U.S. influence in Israel.

It is estimated that our country spent $79 billion in 1968 for defense alone—almost three times the amount that *all* of our allies spent together.

> For yourselves know perfectly that the day of the Lord
> so cometh as a thief in the night.
> For when they shall say, Peace and safety; then sudden
> destruction cometh upon them, as travail upon a woman
> with child; and they shall not escape. . . .
> For God hath not appointed us to wrath, but to obtain
> salvation by our Lord Jesus Christ.
>
> *(I Thessalonians 5:2,3,9 King James Version)*

On December 23, 1968 *U.S. News & World Report*, started
an article on the Mideast crisis with a headline,

IF THERE'S A WAR IN MIDEAST —
WILL U.S. GET IN IT?

The article points out that Israel has signed no mutual-
security agreement with the United States and it is a member
of no system of alliances that requires the U.S. automatically
to take up arms on Israel's behalf.

There are, of course, statements of policies concerning
Israel which have been issued by American Presidents — every
President since the establishment of Israel just over 20 years
ago.

But most of these statements are to the effect of preserving peace in the Mideast and such statements could favor the
Arab countries as well as Israel — depending on what President was in office and how he interpreted the statements.

Therefore, the promises made to Israel by the United
States also could apply equally to its Arab neighbors.

It was Governor Scranton, sent to the Mideast by President Nixon, who commented that it was important for the
United States to become "more evenhanded" in dealing with
rivals in that part of the world.

Many Arab capitals saw the Scranton mission as a favorable omen, raising the hope that the Nixon Administration
would be more sympathetic to its cause.

Perhaps one of the reasons for this "evenhandedness" is
the fact that the American investment in oil in Arab lands is
estimated at $5 billion.

Already the United States gets over 55% of its oil from Arab land — Europe gets 80%.

One must keep in mind that without the Middle East's oil, European industry would grind to a halt.

In its observations, *U.S. News & World Report* comments, "If any new policy is emerging, State Department officials indicate, it is one that 'leans more heavily' on Israel to avoid renewed war at all costs, and to make more effort toward coming to terms with the Arabs."

In the opinion of the author, such conditions as previously stated would seem to indicate that should a war occur in the Mideast in the End Times, the United States and other European nations will not become involved—their policy being, that it is better to sacrifice one country than to commit an entire world to possible complete destruction. Is this the reason that the Old Testament Prophet Joel, speaking of the final end-time conflagration in Palestine says: ". . . but the Lord will be the hope of his people, and the strength of the children of Israel" (Joel 3:16 King James Version)?

THE U.S. RESERVOIR OF DESTRUCTION

Many people in the United States are unaware of some of the vast resources of destruction it already has at its disposal.

One of the most awesome ones is Nerve Gas. Nerve Gas is being produced in the United States right now in the most secretive of conditions, under the brand name CBW.

Laboratory tests on animals continue almost daily. As an example, a rabbit is subjected to Nerve Gas vapors and within $2\frac{1}{2}$ minutes, the rabbit stops breathing and death occurs.

The United States also has Nerve Gas for people. This gas may be dispensed by aerial bomb, spray or by artillery shells filled with the nerve agent code designation VX. VX is a major weapon in America's arsenal for chemical biological warfare (CBW).

The U.S. Army Arsenal at Pinebluff, Arkansas, which is 35 miles southeast of Little Rock, is one of the places where chemicals for biological warfare are created.

NEW SHOPPING LIST FOR THE UNITED STATES $100 BILLION FOR ARMS

		COST
	C-5A MILITARY CARGO PLANE	4.5 BILLIONS
	SENTINEL ANTIMISSILE SYSTEM	5-40 BILLIONS
	NEW-MODEL DESTROYERS	3 BILLIONS
	LANCE MISSILE	1 BILLION
	NUCLEAR AIRCRAFT CARRIERS	1.8 BILLIONS
	STANDBY LOGISTICS SHIPS	1 BILLION
	AMPHIBIOUS ASSAULT SHIPS	1 BILLION
	NUCLEAR ATTACK SUBMARINES	12 BILLIONS
	F-4 JET FIGHTER-BOMBER	7.4 BILLIONS
	MBT-70 MAIN BATTLE TANK	2 BILLIONS
	F-111 AND VFX SWING-WING JETS	8 BILLIONS
	LATE-MODEL STRATEGIC MISSILES	7 BILLIONS
	NEW-MODEL HELICOPTERS	5-10 BILLIONS

In fact, the Army has spent more than $100 million here on biological warfare facilities. Somewhere on these 15,000 acres there is a germ factory, a pilot plant which is used to produce microbes for war.

And 80 miles southwest of London in Porten, the British have a highly refined biological warfare research center as well.

British scientists have learned how to mass produce germs. Both the British and the United States scientists have learned to combine such germs which cause plague, encephalitis, rabbit fever and others into a sort of germ cocktail that is guaranteed to kill.

Scientists have been able to keep germs alive for as long as 24 hours. This would mean that germs sprayed from enemy airplanes could still cause infection after they had reached the ground.

In fact, any country with a good size brewery could manufacture the germs with essentially the same technology used to now make beer.

The reason the United States and Britain give for the producing of germ warfare and nerve gas is that this is necessary in order to maintain the balance of world power because Russia, they believe, is far ahead of us in the development of both chemical and biological weaponry.

It is believed that the United States spends about $1 million a day on CBW Nerve Gas. After World War II, in great secrecy, the United States went into the nerve gas business.

They built at least two full-scale factories. One is located in the isolated plains of western Indiana, not far from the small farming community of Newport. It is reported that this had cost more than $13 million to construct, and for 9 years it turned out a high quality nerve gas called VX. Then in the fall of 1968, it was decided that the American stock piles of nerve gas were adequate — at least for the present.

Just after the Korean War, a $40 million nerve gas factory was built at the Rocky Mountain Arsenal near Denver. This factory is no longer producing nerve gas and in fact, the Army has removed the supplies to another location.

It has just been revealed that the Army is now testing a lethal strain of encephalitis at the Dugway Proving Grounds in Utah. This is where nerve gas not only killed 6400 sheep, but where it also has destroyed 1700 head of cattle and contaminated 100 square miles of pasture land for as much as two or three years!

Canada also has a nerve gas establishment located in the bleak prairie of Alberta near Calgary.

Here, as in the United States, they are producing a liquid nerve gas. A few drops on the skin or a few deep breaths of this particular concentrate called GB will kill in minutes.

Some of the most unbelievable methods of destruction are now being produced, not only in the United States but also in other parts of the world. With these developments how can man, in all his intelligence, believe that we will ever in our own strength achieve a heaven here on earth!

DUMP POISON GAS INTO SEA

The Army a short time ago shipped 27,000 tons of obsolete deadly Air Force nerve gas and Army mustard gas to New Jersey. From there they hauled these poison gases to the sea and then sunk them.

It took some 800 train cars to carry this deadly cargo from storage facilities in Colorado and Maryland.

Many have questioned whether such dumping will endanger human lives and damage marine life further upsetting the balance of nature. Many protests against such a disposal procedure reached Congress. But, what can be done with these toxic agents designed to kill at the first whiff?

RUSSIA'S HEAVEN ON EARTH

Let's look at Russia and her desires to make heaven here on earth.

Many people do not realize that Russia has a record of broken agreements. Yet, in Congress and throughout the

United States we have individuals who think that they can make a bonafide agreement with Russia to prohibit the use of nuclear weapons and biological warfare.

The problems of peace in this world will not be achieved by making more agreements with the Soviet leaders. One should first strive to get them to live up to the agreements that they have already made—and broken.

It was the Soviets who waited until after we had already defeated Japan before conveniently entering the war.

The Reds' painless extraction of $1 billion in industrial equipment from Manchuria promptly followed.

Chinese Communists have never laid down their arms since the 1930's and the attacks from Java to Saigon are all a part of the same sweeping international aggression carried out by Russia and its Communist counterpart, China.

Former Premier Nikita Khrushchev broke every agreement he had made with President Eisenhower at Camp David. It is a recognized fact that Hanoi (North Vietnam) could not continue the Vietnamese war for 30 days without Soviet support.

But the Soviets have cleverly been able to put only $2 billion a year into continuing this war while the United States was spending over $30 billion a year.

An interesting observation is that while the United States has devoted its chief resources to a moon landing—a quarter million miles away—the Russians have been more interested in developing spaceships for operations within 100 miles of earth.

Why?

In the fall of 1968, the Canadian air-defense camera photographed a Soviet bomb carrier in orbit 100 miles above the earth. This same official commented that, "One orbital bomb, if dropped, could render useless the entire North American air-defense network."

Every month sees new evidence of Soviet military progress in outer space.

In the first 9 months of 1968, Russia orbited 30 military vehicles to 16 for the United States. It is reported that the

Soviets have already perfected an H-bomb carrier that can be brought down to any target on earth by radio signals from Russia.

The United States has nothing comparable to this.

It is true that U.S. spy satellites have become so sophisticated that they can now detect any Soviet intercontinental ballistic missile launching and give about 30 minutes warning time to the military stations throughout the country.

However, even our leaders admit that in the event of nuclear attack, there would be tremendous casualties upwards into the millions in spite of our retaliatory measures.

Military science changes so rapidly that military systems soon become outdated.

In the mid-1950's, the fear of a large fleet of Russian long-range bombers spurred the United States to erect a $25 billion air-defense system. The bomber fleet never materialized and the system is now already obsolete.

Today Russia has developed what is called the SS-9 ICBM (intercontinental ballistic missile).

They have about 1550 ICBM'S and many have an explosive equivalent of 20 million tons of TNT.

There are also smaller missiles which Russia possesses that would be adequate to kill or maim the populations of New York, Washington, and Los Angeles.

The American Security Council has recently warned Congress of the growing might of the Soviets on the high seas.

The sustained growth of their naval forces indicates that within another five years the Soviets will have the capability for naval intervention in the most distant regions of the world. And oddly enough, because Russia has other countries fight its wars for them, it has been able to conserve much of its money. That's why things are looking up for the Russian people.

Pay is better, there is more to buy, and families are even dreaming of owning a car.

The average workweek now in Russia is 41 hours and the average pay is $150 per month, which is up almost 15% over 1966.

While it is true that a Russian must work almost four years to buy a small car (compared with 4 months for the average American), nevertheless, the small car has now for the first time become a possibility for him during this present day and age.

Soviet industry has also surged in the last decade. The steel output has increased 95% since 1958; natural gas has increased by 472%; TV sets have increased by 484%; washing machines have increased by 913% and refrigerators have increased 1094% since 1958. In fact, even color television is now being introduced into Russia.

In 1973, the Soviets plan to be making 200,000 color television sets a year.

One must realize that Russia is a Godless nation and its intentions are totally unlike the intentions of the U.S.

Americans are striving for peace in the world, while Russian Communists believe that conflict between socialists and capitalist nations is the normal state.

Americans give the other fellow the benefit of the doubt and imply a great deal of trust in individuals.

Russian Communists, however, are suspicious of everybody.

Americans would die to preserve individual liberty.

Russian Communists consider individual liberty a potential crime against their society.

THE MIDEAST TINDERBOX

The next war? Where will it be?

Well, it could be anywhere. But the next crucially important war seems to be taking shape in the Middle East.

This is especially significant to Bible students of prophecy — for the final Armageddon struggle of the nations which will be settled only by Christ's judgment from Heaven is a Middle Eastern War over Israel (Revelation 16:13-16; 19:11-21; Joel 3).

And Christ, concerning such end-time events, said:

> And when these things begin to come to pass, then look up, and lift up your heads; for your redemption draweth nigh.
>
> *(Luke 21:28 King James Version)*

The Mideast situation is a problem which worries both Russia and the United States.

LAST 10 YEARS SHOW AMAZING INDUSTRIAL GROWTH IN RUSSIA

Total output	1958	1968	Percentage Increase
Steel (millions of tons)	60.6	117.9	Up 95%
Crude oil (millions of barrels)	790	2,170	Up 175%
Electric power (billions of kilowatt-hours)	235	638	Up 171%
Natural gas (billions of cubic feet)	1,056	6,040	Up 472%
Fertilizer (millions of tons)	13.7	47.8	Up 249%
Cement (millions of tons)	36.7	96.5	Up 163%
Automobiles	122,000	280,000	Up 130%
TV sets	979,000	5,720,000	Up 484%
Washing machines	464,000	4,700,000	Up 913%
Refrigerators	360,000	4,300,000	Up 1094%

But Russia still lags far behind the United States in consumer goods!

Automobiles	....	In Russia: 1 for every 850 people
		In U.S.A.: 1 for every 23
Refrigerators	....	In Russia: 1 for every 55 people
		In U.S.A.: 1 for every 39
TV Sets	....	In Russia: 1 for every 42 people
		In U.S.A.: 1 for every 17

Israel, finding it more difficult to secure arms from other nations, will soon be able to make most of its armaments themselves. It is rumored that Israel is already a nuclear power.

Since the 6-Day war of 1967, the ability of this nation's highly mobile armed forces, equipped with weapons ranging from tanks to missiles, has decisively improved.

Not only are the Israelis becoming better armed, but also the nation's whole economy is booming as never before.

In 1972 industrial exports, principally chemicals, rose by 25%. The output of their electronics industry grew by 55% over the previous year.

The building industry is booming as never before and now accounts for 15% of Israel's labor force.

Even Israel's defense industry has made great strides. Military Industries, a state-owned company formed 20 years ago to make revolvers, now produces all the ammunition used by Israel's armed forces and many of its weapons as well— *and it exports $25 million worth of weapons a year.*

Just 30 miles from Jerusalem, Israel has one of the most advanced aircraft industries in the world...employing 12,000 people!

A constantly repeated remark by Israelis is, "What we are doing is trying to survive."

Much of the success of the Israelis has been because of the financial aid supplied by Jewish people throughout the world. One government official noted, "We're a nation of 3 million residents and 12.5 million taxpayers," referring to contributions that come from Jewish people all over the world.

ISRAEL . . . IT'S CHANGING FACE!

In the last 2 years, this writer has been to the Holy Land 3 times.

And one thing is very evident.

The face of the Holy Land is rapidly changing . . . geographically.

The hills and valleys and quaint little Judean towns may soon become a thing of the past . . . doomed to progress. For almost 2000 years little change has occurred in the topography in the land where Jesus walked.

After the Six-Day war Israel accelerated its industrialization of the country and is moving at a feverish rate to meet the demands of its economy.

Out of necessity, much of its economy is geared to maintaining a strong army. Another large portion of its economy is devoted to building of apartment houses to house the influx of refugees of Jewish heritage and immigrants.

Once bare mountainsides are now becoming filled with concrete apartment complex units.

Throughout the whole of Israel one can find huge cement mills and industrial plants. Once beautiful Haifa is suffering from the penalty of progress. Several miles before you reach Haifa the visitor will see large cement mills with smokestacks spouting forth vast volumes of industrial waste. So intense is this air pollution that on some days it is impossible to see the harbor of Haifa.

Air pollution is becoming an unwanted byproduct of Israel's industrialization. And with the United States paying little attention to its own air pollution problems, it is no wonder that Israel, struggling for survival, has little time for such concern.

Where dirt or single lane roads once were, Israel has built 4 lane superhighways and thruways.

Recognizing the need for maintaining forests they have planted and non-commercialized areas, nevertheless, Israel finds it must make good use of its some 8000 square miles to meet the need of its 3 million people. Because of wise use of water sources Israel has been able to more than double its arable land since 1948.

Its heavy industry includes manufacture of armament, food processing, textiles, chemicals, leather products and plastic. It even assembles automobiles and will soon have some 3000 miles of railway.

The rapid growth of Tel Aviv is making that city a miniature New York City and Haifa is fast becoming another Miami Beach.

For those who wish to see the Holy Land as it was they should plan a trip within the next two years . . . for the face of the Holy Land is changing.

Many people think because the Jews are returning to Israel that there is a resurgence towards the things of God. This is furthermost from the truth. Only 15% of the Jews in Israel are active religiously. And it will not be until the Tribulation Period that the Jewish people will turn to Christ in large numbers.

The Middle East is a place of wonder but it is also the sight of future conflicts.

From a moral standpoint, people are divided over who actually owns the land.

> The land that is now the modern state of Israel was populated mostly by Arabs and other non-Jews for most of the time between A.D. 70 and the early years of the 20th Century. The conflict that has arisen is because the Jewish people have also considered this land their own for 4000 years and today the existence of the state of Israel is a 21-year-old fact.
>
> The Arabs believe that some sort of statue of limitations should apply. That the Hebrews lived in Palestine for 2000 years before Christ should not entitle them to a perpetual title to part of it, any more than the American Indians are entitled to a perpetual title to North America. Territories have changed hands through all of history, and there is no such thing as an eternal lease.

The above was the observation made in a special report made by *The National Observer* recently.

The Israelis see it otherwise. In their opinion, the land that is now Israel has always been Israel—at least since Abraham and his kinsmen moved there from what is now Iraq 4000 years ago.

For centuries the idea of a Jewish national home has been part of the Jewish consciousness and the awful persecution of European Jews by Hitler brought this desire to a climax. Thus we have what perhaps is the crux of the Arab-Israeli dispute.

ARAB vs. ISRAELI FORCES THE TINDERBOX OF THE WORLD

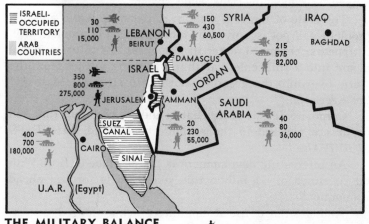

THE MILITARY BALANCE
Arab vs. Israeli Forces

👤TROOPS ▄▄▄ TANKS ✈ PLANES

Russia has been extremely interested in the Middle East and prophetically, Christians who know prophecy (Ezekiel 38:1-39:16) can understand why.

Russia would like to expand its influence in the Middle East and will give aid to anyone who asks for it. It is now building naval facilities in Egypt to service its vast fleet.

The United States has attempted to help both Arabs and Jews alike, although many Arabs feel that such help has been one-sided in favor of Israel.

A study will show that U.S. economic aid to Israel from 1948-1969 totals $1.1 billion. U.S. aid to four recipient Arab countries in that same period totals $3.7 billion.

From a population standpoint, nevertheless, the United States has been more generous to Israel with its population of 2,000,000; than to the Arab states of Jordan, Morocco, Tunisia, and the United Arab Republic, which have a combined population of 52,000,000.

It must also be remembered that Israel has benefited greatly from the generosity of American Jews. Contributions to the United Jewish Appeal have exceeded $3 billion since

1948. And sales in the United States of Israel bonds have topped $2 billion over the same span.

The state of Israel is a thorn to the Arab world and this problem will not be solved by mere man. This problem will, it appears, become greater in proportion. Eventually it will bloom into a full-scale war that will bring armies from the world over into the greatest show-down struggle this world has ever seen.

Complete details of this battle and the problems that will occur are covered in the author's book titled, *GUIDE TO SURVIVAL.*

An interesting development is taking place in Iran. With oil revenues of $1 billion this year Iran is forging ahead economically.

And a strange friendship, rarely acknowledged or discussed, has developed between Iran and Israel. It is reported that some training of Iranian soldiers by Israelis is taking place. The Shah of Iran has emphasized that Israel, contrary to other Arab country viewpoints, has a right to exist. And a mysterious Israeli 42-inch pipeline just opened from Eilat at the southern tip of Israel to the Mediterranean is puzzling Arab countries. And in 1972, President Nixon visited Iran.

Russia has already invested some $5 billion dollars in the last 3 years in aid to the Arab world.

And by contrast, the total U.S. military and economic aid to all nations amounted to only $3.8 billion this year.

The author's parents were both born in Lebanon, a relatively small, prosperous country, with a population of close to 3 million people.

Lebanon is situated at the eastern edge of the Mediterranean Sea and is bordered on the north and east by Syria and on the south by Israel and on the west by the Mediterranean Sea. It was here the Phoenicians reached their peak of prosperity about 1000 BC. In 1945, Lebanon finally won its independence and joined the United Nations.

Perhaps unique in government structure, Lebanon is governed by a Christian President and a Sunni Muslim Prime Minister.

And Lebanon's standard of living is the highest of any Arab country. It is known as the business capital of the Middle East.

Since the 6-Day war, while Israel has prospered, Lebanon has felt a drop in economic prosperity. What worsened relations between these two countries was that Lebanon (of all nations the most friendly towards Israel) within a few minutes suddenly found a major part of its commercial air fleet wiped out by an Israeli air strike.

While Israel came up with many reasons for justifying such an attack, it was this action which, probably more than anything else, caused people in the United States to weigh both sides of the Arab-Israeli problem.

ARAB GUERRILLA WARFARE

Just as the Vietnam war has become difficult because of guerrilla warfare, there is now a growing Arab force, Palestinian commandos, which are dedicated to block any Arab-Israeli peace, which would deprive them of what they believe is their land.

Israeli officials admit that in 1960 alone, 235 of their soldiers and civilians were killed as a result of these guerrilla operations.

One guerrilla leader remarked, "We're not doing very much yet, but give us time — we'll grow."

Their primary objective is to demand the re-establishment of their entire homeland, with a Palestinian government in charge, replacing the Israeli government. And they believe that this can only be done through force.

There are four major resistance groups in the Arab world. The largest and perhaps most active is the Palestine Liberation Movement, commonly known as "Al Fatah." This movement began 13 years ago.

The most ruthless group is the Black September terrorists. They triggered the Munich Olympic tragedy of 1972.

To show you how complex this problem is — if you ask why Palestinians do not settle down in other Arab countries, they point to the Jews as an example, "The Jews didn't forget about their homeland after 2000 years. Why should we forget after only 20?"

As one further studies the Arab-Israeli problems, one realizes how increasingly impossible it is to arrive at a just and a mutually acceptable solution.

It has become one of growing terror between two different peoples.

It is true that there have been massacres and uncalled for killings by the Arabs. But one must realize that there have also been similar actions by the Israelis.

It was Israeli's Defense Minister, Moshe Dayan who is reported to have said when faced with reports of Israeli soldiers' terror and torture, "We are not angels."

The Daily Star, the English speaking newspaper in Beirut, Lebanon on Sunday, April 6, 1969 describes the terror and torture of some of the prisoners now in Israeli prisons. In such a tinderbox, there will always be inequalities and terror.

PAWNS IN A BITTER STRUGGLE

Arab-Israeli tension is increasing with each new day.

And in its wake the children become pawns in the bitter struggle.

For Israel the "silent" war has taken on a new face—it is a 6-day war that has erupted into a 365-day war.

On Saturday, October 6, 1973, the "Yom Kippur" War broke out between Israel and Arab forces. In the first 100 hours, Israel suffered $1 Billion in equipment losses alone!

Prior to this "all-out" war Arab guerrillas kept the flames of tension hot through border clashes, hijackings and terrorism.

Sabotage activities are growing even in the heart of Jerusalem. And guerrilla war is a war that is hard to stop. The U.S. has learned this bitter lesson in Vietnam.

The anti-Arab riots in Jerusalem last fall are a growing indication of the concern Jews have for the safety of their homeland.

Guerrillas are growing and many are enlisted from the refugee camps that dot Jordan and the other Arab countries.

Just as the Israelis determined to stay in Palestine, the Arab commandos (El Fatah) are just as eager to see that they don't. Above is an El Fatah poster which proclaims: "THIS IS THE WAY TO LIBERATION OF MY HOMELAND. AND SO, MY BROTHERS, I'LL FIGHT ON."

Refugees with much time on their hands . . . with fresh wounds of having to leave their homes . . . are eager to join in the fray in the hope that they can regain Nazareth, Jerusalem, Jericho and Bethlehem.

Guerrillas are getting better organized, better trained. They are getting money from rich Arab countries. They are getting equipment from Russia. This means that guerrillas can not only now get arms, but also they can pay their recruits.

This could spark war—an all-out war because Palestine commandos have never accepted the idea that a political settlement with Israel is even worth trying for. They have a fatalistic attitude that, "We have nothing to lose."

The Arabs outnumber the Israelis by 50 to 1 . . . and while the Israeli's have had a much more capable armed force . . . recent arms and technological aid from the Soviet are enabling the Arabs to close the gap.

The Arab viewpoint is that the Israelis can beat the Arabs 12 times and lose the 13th time, and that's enough. The Israelis can afford to lose only once; the Arabs can lose 12 times, if the 13th time they win.

What does this mean?

President Nixon and world leaders are working against insurmountable odds in trying to resolve the Arab-Israeli conflict. The displaced persons and refugee camps of today, however, are minute in problems compared to the tragedies that will occur in the Holy Land during the reign of Antichrist (Jeremiah 30:7; Daniel 12:1; Matthew 24:21; Revelation 12 and 13).

How imperative it is for Christians to work now, harder than before, to spread the Gospel Message while there is still time in these countries. Many avenues are open through first aiding in relieving human suffering. Jews are showing a greater interest in the New Testament and prophecy. Such an opportunity for witness may end quickly!

NO SIESTA IN SOUTH AMERICA

However, the Middle East is not the only area where the

'All-Out War' Erupts in Mideast

Egypt Storms Across Suez

Israeli Troops
Counter Attack:

Israeli Troops Pull Back in Sinai;
Egyptians Claim Key Victories

Included in the ranks of the Fedayeen (Arab commandos) are young Arab girls . . . like this attractive guerrilla practicing her rifle shooting. These commandos are well-equipped and their goal is to reclaim Palestine.

world is facing problems. Both Brazil and Peru are facing monumental problems.

In the year 2000 the city of Sao Paulo is looking forward to a growth of 20 million people! And it lacks money necessary to provide for this growth. Its economy is at a critical stage.

In Peru, the United States is heading towards a diplomatic showdown. This could be a showdown that would produce grave repercussions not only in this country but in other neighboring countries of Latin America.

The growing hostility of South America to the U.S. was evidenced when Governor Rockefeller made his fact-finding tour in June, 1969.

INDIA'S GROWING PAINS

India too, is having her share of problems. In India the rats eat up to 12% of the grain harvest. And after billions in aid and years of experiments and planning, India still is on the edge of disaster.

India is the home of one-seventh of the entire human race!

The President of the United States finds himself on the horns of a dilemma. Should he continue to pour millions of dollars a year in economic aid to India when hardly anything can be seen as a result for the many millions that have already poured into this country?

After 21 years of independence, India can neither support nor defend itself without outside help. While India is the tenth richest country in the world, its resources and wealth must be spread among so many millions of people that the general standard of living is close to poverty.

Since its independence, India has doubled the number of grade schools and tripled the number of teachers. There are more than 10,000 factories, and malaria has been cut to 87,000 cases a year from the previous 85 million cases.

But the important thing to remember is that food consumption by Indians has barely increased in 20 years, and for most people hunger is never far away.

Here are some things to remember. In India a baby is

India—
The Giant
in Trouble

WEALTH
Tenth wealthiest country in the world
(Gross national product of more than
37 BILLION dollars)
BUT
because this wealth must be spread among
520 MILLION people . . . the general standard
of living is close to POVERTY!

SCHOOLS
Since its independence 21 years ago India has
DOUBLED the number of grade schools
(to more than ½ million)
TRIPLED the number of teachers
(to more than 2 million)

HEALTH
Malaria has been cut to 87,000 cases a year
from 85 MILLION

POPULATION
A baby is born every 1½ seconds!
(While you read this . . . a baby was born!)

Every year India adds 13 million more people—
more than live in the state of Pennsylvania!

born every 1½ seconds — less time than it takes to read this sentence. In fact, India adds 13 million people every year, or annually more than those who live in the state of Pennsylvania. And the major foreign source of weapons for India comes from Russia.

THE THREAT OF RED CHINA

Someone once observed that if the Chinese increase at the present rate, in 10 years time there will be 1000 million Chinese! And if nothing happens to check the birth rate, by the end of this century one person in every three in the world will be Chinese.

Red China, with its unbridled advocacy of Cultural Revolution and of International Communistic Revolution, is a constant threat to peace in today's world. It is certainly a threat in the attempts of the United States and other nations to make the world a heaven here on earth.

In November, 1971 Communist China was admitted to the United Nations. Deputy Foreign Minister Chiao Kuanhua's first speech was one of condemnation of the United States.

It is estimated that by 1974, China will be able to begin stockpiling nuclear weapons. And they will test fire some of these weapons this year. China is a land of bewildering contrasts and even the Russians have problems coexisting with their Communist brothers.

China is Asia's largest military machine and yet, when a peasant takes a pig to market he still uses a pole balanced across his shoulder or an old wooden-wheel barrow.

A village in China today is not unlike a village of 100 years ago. The art of primitive medicine still continues.

China today is a nation of discontent and frustration.

It was more than five years ago that youthful "Red Guard" roaming bands totally disrupted the educational system of China and it is still not back on its feet.

It has been reported that education has been set back at least 10 years by the so-called "Great Cultural Revolution."

It is estimated that some 25 million people have been ordered to leave the cities of China and go back to work in the countryside. It is not unusual for husbands to work in one locale and wives in another.

AFRICA

Africa has one problem after another and is like a stormy, unsettled sea. The Nigeria-Biafra tragedy of 1967 witnessed million killed by war and starvation.

Red Chinese now have thousands of "worker-soldiers" in Zambia and Uganda...building railroads and increasing the industrialization of those countries.

Even Russia is becoming increasingly involved in African affairs showing considerable interest in the Sudan. In the past they have not only provided aircraft but also pilots to keep the flames of war hot in that country.

Red China could well be preparing parts of Africa for a stepping off point for a coming invasion of Israel.

DESTINY DISASTER

How often do we forget the lessons of the past? It was in the 1930's that France constructed a 300 mile Maginot Line from the Swiss border north to Belgium.

By today's atomic age standards, the Maginot Line was not expensive. It cost $480 million. It was to be an inpenetrable barrier against foreign invasions, and it was to assure peace and a heaven on earth for France.

However, it didn't take German tanks long to go around this line and conquer France. Today's methods of weaponry are even more sophisticated.

Intelligence agents visualize "guided missiles in a suitcase" as being the possible starter of the next war. Already a lone American soldier while standing can wipe out a tank with the bazooka-like Redstone heat-seeking rocket.

Ernest Cuneo, who at one time was the liaison officer between the OSS and British Intelligence, the FBI, the State Department, and the White House, recently commented in an article on how the next war might start,

> Here is a thumbnail sketch of how intelligence people visualize the start of World War III:
>
> A confrontation takes place. At its peak, the Russian ambassador asks for an appointment with the President of the United States, top priority, and it is granted.
>
> The Russian ambassador then takes from his pocket a slip of paper on which is written a street address in an American metropolis, say 821 East Zelch St., New York City. He hands this to the President and asks him to have the FBI enter the house and report back immediately.
>
> The FBI reports that the house contains a fully assembled H-bomb.
>
> The Russian ambassador then informs the President that all major American cities have been "seeded" with nuclear weapons in a similar manner, and in fact, await only a master signal to blow the country apart.
>
> He gives the President an ultimatum, "surrender or die," and a half hour to make up his mind.
>
> How did the bombs get there? It is a comparatively simple operation to bring in the parts across America's tens of thousands of miles of seacoasts, or even across customs points, part by part.

Mr. Cuneo goes on to say that just a flue and an electric fan blowing out deadly germs from a dark cellar, could within 24 hours, infect millions of city dwellers with the bubonic plague or some other deadly disease. This certainly is a chaotic world and a world that makes it impossible for man to achieve world peace.

SCATTERED OBSERVATIONS

Where incomes have been so high in Kuwait, there are 120,000 cars in this country which has a population of 500,000 ... but Kuwait housewives and young people will no longer be given driving licenses because of congestion and the high accident rate.

THE FRIGHTENING ARMS RACE BETWEEN UNITED STATES AND RUSSIA

Where RUSSIA is AHEAD

Space-Bombardment PLATFORMS	U.S.	None
	Russia	TESTING a system that will soon be OPERATIONAL
Antimissile MISSILES	U.S.	Not Yet Started
	Russia	Already installed around Moscow and possibly elsewhere

Where the U.S. is AHEAD

Submarine-Launched MISSILES	U.S.	656
	Russia	580
Intercontinental-Range BOMBERS	U.S.	646
	Russia	150

Where the race is Neck and Neck

Intercontinental Ballistic MISSILES (ICBM)	U.S.	1054
	Russia	1550*

(*By 1975 it is expected that Russia will have 2000 ICBM's. The U.S. has frozen its production, remaining at 1054. It is seeking to improve its present system.)

WHAT THIS ALL MEANS: Each country, the U.S. and Russia, have enough nuclear power in just the ICBM's to kill 90 million citizens!

And on British television, an attempt was made to give Jesus Christ a new image.

He was depicted as a wild-eyed desert prophet with tangled hair who snarled "use your flaming heads" at His disciples.

In another scene, Peter told Christ: "Go on, get out of here, you nut case." And Christ replied "Nut case? You're right—I bloody am."

At one time it was only people called "religous fanatics" who were saying, "The world is coming to an end."

Now we have respectable scientists who are also making this statement. They too agree that the world will come to an end . . .

> (1) unless we avoid famine, (2) unless we can limit birth rates, (3) unless we can avoid irritating ourselves to death with the waste products of nuclear power plants, (4) unless we can stop poisoning ourselves with pesticides, (5) unless we can avoid heating up the atmosphere to a point where the Antarctic icecaps melt and flood coastal cities, (6) unless we can preserve the oxygen balance in the world and not suffocate to death, (7) unless we can stop air and water pollution, (8) unless we can preserve the ecological system of plant and animal life.

These were some of the observations made by Donald C. Drake and Patricia McBroom in a series of articles on science and medicine.

It was Herodotus who said the wise but now questionable words, "No one is fool enough to choose war instead of peace. For in peace sons bury fathers, but in war fathers bury sons."

Yes, the world is seeking to build a heaven here on earth.

But as one seriously studies not only the problems that presently beset the world, but also the complex problems it will soon face in coming years, one realizes that man in his own might, can never build a heaven on earth.

Peace only rules the day when Christ rules the mind.

And peace will only begin after the terrible tragedy of the Tribulation Period. Then at last the 1000 year Millennial Period with its universal peace will begin.

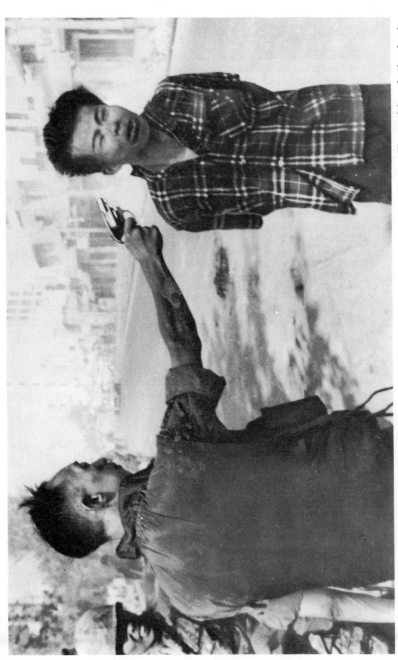

South Vietnamese police chief Brig. Gen. Nguyen Ngoc Loan is shown executing a Viet Cong officer with a single pistol shot in the head. The Viet Cong officer grimaces at the impact of the fatal bullet. Gen. Loan, himself was later wounded and is no longer police chief.

Immediately after the tribulation of those days shall the sun be darkened, and the moon shall not give her light, and the stars shall fall from Heaven, and the powers of the Heavens shall be shaken:

And then shall appear the sign of the Son of man in Heaven: and then shall all the tribes of the earth mourn, and they shall see the Son of man coming in the clouds of Heaven with power and great glory.

(Matthew 24:29,30)

When the Son of man shall come in His glory, and all the holy angels with Him, then shall He sit upon the throne of His glory:

And before Him shall be gathered all nations: and he shall separate them one from another, as a shepherd divideth his sheep from the goats:

And He shall set the sheep on His right hand, but the goats on the left.

Then shall the King say unto them on His right hand, Come ye blessed of my Father, inherit the kingdom prepared for you from the foundation of the world . . .

Then shall He say also unto them on the left hand, Depart from me, ye cursed, into everlasting fire, prepared for the devil and his angels . . .

(Matthew 25:31-34,41)

The wolf also shall dwell with the lamb, and the leopard shall lie down with the kid; and the calf and the young lion and the fatling together; and a little child shall lead them.

And the cow and the bear shall feed; their young ones shall lie down together: and the lion shall eat straw like the ox.

And the sucking child shall play on the hole of the asp, and the weaned child shall put his hand on the cockatrice' (adder's) den.

They shall not hurt nor destroy in all my holy mountain: for the earth shall be full of the knowledge of the Lord, as the waters cover the sea.

And in that day there shall be a root of Jesse, which shall stand for an ensign of the people; to it shall the Gentiles seek: and his rest shall be glorious.

(Isaiah 11:6-10) (All quotations King James Version)

Chapter 8
A Heartbeat Away

Can Man Make Heaven? • What Next? • Is Prophecy a
Dream? • No Private Interpretation • Can Anyone Rise
Again? • Where Are the Unbelieving Dead Now? • The Dead
in Christ—Where Are They Now? • Do Christians in Heaven
Know Each Other? • Can Our Loved Ones in Heaven Ob-
serve Us Now? • Can a Loving God Send People to Hell?

As man advances in this scientific age to strange new
wonders . . . he also creates deadly new problems.

Man, because of the marvelous advances of science now
daily inhales small amounts of poison in the 15,000 quarts of
air he breathes each day.

Man has come a long way in his medical knowledge from
the time when crocodile blood was recommended for failing
eyesight.

And to add to God's creation Americans annually lavish
some $150 million on lipsticks and $140 million on face
powder while paying some $450 million on reducing aids to
combat over-indulgence.

God gave man a miraculous body! Imagine a structure
made up of some 206 bones anchored firmly to muscles so
created that they shield the vital organs of the body . . . with
sizes and shapes you and I could have never dreamed of . . .
bones that can take up to 20,000 pounds of pressure per
square inch!

Imagine 600-odd muscles designed like cables whose pull on bones makes motion possible! And each muscle is inter-related so that one contraction usually involves many others.

And through this maze of muscle and bone run some 60,000 miles of tubing . . . tubing that carries blood to every part of your body!

Triggering all this into action is a nervous system care-fully sheathed in the spinal cord . . . a complex system that channels and coordinates through a three-pound brain a huge traffic of messages . . . moving as fast as 350 feet per second. Just look at this: An electronic computer designed to perform as efficiently as your brain would have to occupy a space as big as a skyscraper!

And who can forget the heart! The heart pumps so steadily and powerfully that in a single day it pushes 10 pints of blood in the average adult body through more than 1000 complete circuits . . . thus actually pumping 5000 to 6000 quarts of blood a day in all!

Yes, God gave man a miraculous body! Then why can't he live FOREVER! Can it be that our ears which can detect sound at the rate of 15 to 15,000 vibrations per second are deaf?

> For the time will come when . . . after their own lusts shall they heap to themselves teachers, having itching ears; and they shall turn away their ears from the truth, and shall be turned to fables.
>
> (II Timothy 4:3,4)

Can it be that our eyes which are so sensitive they can detect light as feeble as a 100-trillionth of a watt are really blind?

> Having eyes, see ye not? . . .
>
> (Mark 8:18)

We are God's marvelous creation . . . yet for many

> . . . their ears are dull of hearing, and their eyes they have closed; lest at any time they should see with their eyes and hear with their ears, and should understand with their heart, and should be converted, and I should heal them.
>
> (Matthew 13:15 King James Version)

Why can't we live forever? We can! And everyone will! But!

While you are reading this . . . and without any thought on your part your heart is automatically pumping, giving you physical life.

But this life must end.

And it's only a heartbeat away!

If you reject Christ as your personal Saviour and Lord . . . at your last heartbeat you will enter immediately into an everlasting separation from God.

If you accept Christ as your personal Saviour and Lord . . . at your last heartbeat you will enter immediately into the presence of the Lord and His heavenly Kingdom (II Corinthians 5:6-10).

You have eyes to see and ears to hear . . . but do you?

CAN MAN MAKE HEAVEN?

In the previous chapters we have examined this earth to see if there is any possibility that man in his finite wisdom could create a heaven here on earth . . . all by himself!

We do know he is trying very hard. But will he succeed? After reading these chapters that answer should be very evident!

Young people are seeking a heaven on earth—
    and find only hypocrisy and inequality.
The business world is seeking to build a heaven on
    earth but find half their "angels" are on strike
    and the only thing high is prices.
Individuals realizing that they can't find heaven on
    earth are merrily "living" till they die.
The United States diligently seeking to be all things
    to all people is realizing that this can't be
    heaven.
The World, nesting together in protective coalitions of
    governments, is fearful that its little heaven

will blow up in a nuclear holocaust.
And sad to say, many clergymen, who should know
the only way to Heaven
   are leading their congregations and world leaders
   straight down the path to everlasting destruction!

Can this be heaven? With the population growth and the complexities of living this will bring, with the poisons growing in the air, with the more catastropic methods of war . . . can man ever hope, in himself, to achieve heaven here on earth?
   The answer is, NO!
   But many men, intelligent men, think so. Their ears are dull of hearing and their eyes are closed to reality and to the Word of God.

WHAT NEXT?

In our book GUIDE TO SURVIVAL we covered in great detail how this present world would end.
   We showed how the Bible tells us that "in the twinkling of an eye" millions of people would suddenly disappear from this earth in what we call the RAPTURE (I Thess. 4:13-18).
   This event would then usher in the 7 year Tribulation Period when a dictatorial world leader would appear on the scenes. He will be called the Antichrist or imitation Christ. His associate to help him fool the world will be called the False Prophet (Daniel 9:27; Revelation 13).
   The first 3½ years of this Tribulation Period will usher in peace for Israel and there will be amid a world of troubles a time of relative calm . . . a calm that will lull many people into thinking that heaven may yet soon arrive.
   But in the last 3½ years of this Tribulation Period, Antichrist will seek revenge on the Jewish people and on anyone not wearing his mark (the number of which is 666) on either their hand or forehead (Revelation 12:1-6,13-17; 13:16-18).
   Coalitions of nations will be formed at this time. Major ones will be a Federated States of Europe which quite pos-

MAN'S STEPS TO HEAVEN

Philippine men allow themselves to be tortured believing that such steps will atone them for their sins and assure them a place in Heaven.

sibly will include the United States and the Armies of the North which will be Russia and her communistic allies.

Russia, determined to acquire the mineral and natural wealth of Israel will invade Israel and through the intervention of God, Russia will be defeated in a tremendous blood bath (Ezekiel 38:1-39:16).

This action will place Antichrist in an even stronger dictatorial position. More persecutions will follow.

Then, the armies of all the world will head towards Israel to destroy this nation. Armegeddon will be the scene of this great world battle. The Lord Jesus Christ will come down from Heaven and vanquish the combined armies of more than 200 million men . . . and the blood bath will cover over 185 miles of Israel (Joel 3; Revelation 16:16; 14; 19:11-21).

At this time Antichrist and the False Prophet are thrown into the Lake of Fire (Revelation 19:20).

And Satan is bound in the bottomless pit for 1000 years (Revelation 20:1-3).

For those wishing the complete background of these events we would recommend you read our initial book titled GUIDE TO SURVIVAL. This very graphically covers the events of the Tribulation Period.

It is at this time that the 1000 year MILLENNIAL KINGDOM is ushered in by Christ himself. This is sometimes referred to as the 1000 year reign of Christ.

This 1000 year reign will take place right here on earth!

Millennial prophecies indicate that many changes will occur on the earth's surface.

In the battle of Armageddon which occurs at the end of the 7 year Tribulation Period, Christ will come down from Heaven and His feet will stand upon the Mount of Olives and here is what will happen:

> And His feet shall stand in that day upon the Mount of Olives . . . and the Mount of Olives shall be split in two from the east to the west by a great valley; and half of the mountain shall remove toward the north, and half of it toward the south. . . .
>
> (Zechariah 14:4 Amplified Bible)

We further learn

> ... that living waters shall go out from Jerusalem, half of them to the eastern (Dead) Sea, and half of them to the western (Mediterranean) Sea; in summer and in winter shall it be.
>
> *(Zechariah 14:8 Amplified Bible)*

This, in itself is a marvel to anyone who has seen the Dead Sea!

For the Dead Sea has no exit for its waters except by evaporation. The present Dead Sea is 53 miles long, 9 to 10 miles wide and lies 1286 feet below sea level.

The Jordan River, which is the main body of water which feeds the Dead Sea, flows SOUTH to the Dead Sea. When it reaches here – there is no exit!

Now look at this: Scriptures tell us, as just quoted, that these waters will go out from Jerusalem – half of them EAST to the Dead Sea and half of them WEST to the Mediterranean Sea.

And we are further told in that same verse (Zechariah 14:8) that these waters shall go out from Jerusalem.

In today's Jerusalem THERE IS NO RIVER!

But at the ushering in of the Millennial 1000 year age, when Christ stands on the Mount of Olives and brings judgment at the battle of Armageddon at the end of the Tribulation Period . . . the Mount of Olives will be split in two and this change of the earth's surface will occur!

With this dramatic flow to the Dead Sea, Christ says:

> ... the waters shall be healed and made fresh. And wherever the double river shall go ... there will be a great number of fish . . . The fishermen shall stand on the banks of the Dead Sea . . . and on the banks of the river on both its sides, there shall grow all kinds of trees for food; their leaf shall not fade, nor shall their fruit fail . . .
>
> *(Ezekiel 47:8,9,10,12 Amplified Bible)*

This is the beginning of JOYS as we enter the 1000 year Millennial Period.

IS PROPHECY A DREAM?

In understanding the prophetic Word of God . . . it is important to remember that prophecy must be interpreted REALISTICALLY. Men cannot assume that the Biblical prophecies are mere meaningless stories . . . or meaningless speech figures . . . thus when the Bowls of God's wrath are poured out in the end-times upon a wicked earth (Revelation 16) actual physical destruction will take place all over this earth.

Think of this a minute!

Without the hope of our Lord's return . . . what future do any of us have? Certainly man is incapable of providing us with eternal life. It's enough of a struggle for man to devise even a table whose shape will satisfy everyone at the Paris peace talks!

Therefore if we cannot place our hope in man . . . we must place our complete faith and hope in GOD and what GOD SAYS!

NO PRIVATE INTERPRETATION

Charles Feinberg very adequately points out: "The Scripture itself lays down the first and most essential rule of all. Peter tells us in his second letter that 'no prophecy of the Scripture is of any private interpretation.' By this it is not meant that no private individual can interpret prophecy . . ." (II Peter 1:20). No, this verse teaches rather that the entire prophetic Word is interrelated and is part of a wonderful unified plan of God—thus no one can give his own "private interpretation" aside from God's intended meaning to any Scripture. Prophecy is written for all to understand and in understanding, there is an opportunity to believe.

CAN ANYONE RISE AGAIN?

This is a question everyone wants to know. And perhaps, more important, what will happen to you the moment you die?

Will you go into a deep sleep? Will you come back as an elephant or a kangaroo or a sacred cow? Will you simply vanish and just no longer exist? Will you come back as a Knight at King Arthur's round table or a Man from Mars in the year 2000?

Just what does happen? Not since the days of the Lord has there been any record of anyone dying, then coming back to report on his new location. And this mystery baffles many. Too soon the dead are forgotten . . . for out-of-sight . . . out-of-mind.

Many people are now questioning:

> . . . How are the dead raised up? and with what body do they come?
>
> (I Corinthians 15:35)

It was the ancient heathen who complained that the sun went down at night, and arose in the morning, but their friends went down in the gloomy darkness of death, and rose no more!

The very idea of living forever has been termed false by many simply because it is a mystery they don't understand . . . and they don't want to literally believe in the Scriptures.

Others don't believe because they say it is against the laws of science. But scientific advance has affirmed the Word of God. And as William Munsey wrote so well many years ago: "To go to science to settle matters of faith, is like going to a dictionary to learn history, or to geology to learn mathematics."

Others don't believe the body can rise again because it is contrary to our experience. Yet someone living in the heart of Africa has never experienced a snow storm but this does not mean there is no snow. Neither does it follow because we never saw a man raised from the dead, that the apostles did not see it.

Another reason for disbelief of a resurrection (a coming to life again) is that it is contrary to the seeming immutability (never changing) of the laws of nature. However, one thing these doubters forget is this: The resurrection is not to be brought about by the regular action of the laws of nature, but by supernatural power!

WHERE ARE THE UNBELIEVING DEAD NOW?

First, let's get some background by turning to Ecclesiastes 12:7 in the Bible. It tells us: "The dust returneth to the earth as it was, and the spirit returneth unto God who gave it."

God gave you a body and a freedom of choice. During your lifetime on earth that freedom is exercised by you either to reject Christ as Lord or accept Christ.

At the end of that lifetime, your body returns to dust but your spirit returns to God . . . who originally gave it to you.

What then happens to the unbelieving dead?

First, it must be remembered that the Great White Throne Judgment—which is the final judgment time for the unbeliever does NOT OCCUR until after the Millennium (1000 year) reign of Christ with His Saints (Revelation 20). Then, if this is so, what happens to the unbelieving dead in the meantime?

The Bible gives us some revelation of their state. Basically the unbelieving dead descend to a place of torment, from which there is no escape. The most graphic account of this given in the Scriptures is of an unbeliever who was very wealthy and a poor beggar, a believer, who both died. The beggar went to Paradise (Heaven) . . . the unbeliever went to hell. The unbeliever's life in hell is described in Luke 16:23,24:

> And in Hades (hell, the realm of the unbelieving dead), being in torment, he lifted up his eyes and saw Abraham far away and Lazarus (the beggar) in his bosom.
> And he cried out and said, Father Abraham, have pity and mercy upon me, and send Lazarus to dip the tip of his finger in water and cool my tongue; for I am in anguish in this flame.
>
> *Luke 16:23,24 (Amplified Bible)*

This tells us some basic things:

1. The unbelieving dead descend to a place of continual torment.

THE RESURRECTIONS

Heaven

Resurrection and Ascension of Christ into Heaven

(Matthew 27:52-53 tells of others who were resurrected after Christ—these were the wave-sheaf of the harvest to come. Leviticus 23:10-11.)

Acts 1:1-11
Matthew 27:50-53

Paradise

Believers who have died before the Rapture. Present in a celestial, spiritual body.*

"And Jesus said unto him, Verily, I say unto thee, To-day shalt thou be with me in paradise."
Luke 23:43

"We are confident, I say, and willing rather to be absent from the body, and to be present with the Lord."
2 Corinthians 5:8

Rapture

Believers meet with Christ in the air
1 Thessalonians 4:16

"...the dead in Christ shall rise First:..."

"Then we which are alive and remain shall be caught up together with them in the clouds to meet the Lord in the air:..." 1 Thessalonians 4:16-17

Judgment Seat of Christ

"For we must all appear before the judgment seat of Christ:...."
2 Corinthians 5:10

Believers now in New Bodies
Philippians 3:20-21

Resurrection of Tribulation Saints
Daniel 12:1-2

Marriage of the Lamb
Revelation 19:7-9

Christ Returns to Earth with His Saints
1 Thessalonians 3:13; Zechariah 14:4

"And I saw the dead, small and great, stand before God; and the books were opened: and another book was opened, which is the book of life: and the dead were judged out of those things which were written in the books, according to their works.
And the sea gave up the dead which were in it; and death and hell delivered up the dead which were in them: and they were judged every man according to their works." Revelation 20:12-13

Great White Throne

"And whosoever was not found written in the Book of Life was cast into the Lake of Fire."
Revelation 20:15

Unbelievers cast into Lake of Fire eternally

Resurrection of the Dead Unbelievers
Revelation 20:11-13; Jude 6

About A.D. 30   This Present Age   A.D.?   Rapture   Seven Year Tribulation Period   Mount of Olives Armageddon   1000 Year Millennial Age   With Satan Antichrist and False Prophet

*Physical body remains in grave awaiting Rapture

2. There is an unimaginable anguish and thirst in that place.

And further we read:

> ... between us (the saved) and you (the rich man in hell) there is a great chasm fixed in order that those who want to pass from this (place—Paradise) to you (in hell) may not be able, and no one may pass from there (hell) to us.
>
> *Luke 16:26 (Amplified Bible)*

This tells us:

1. Once one descends into hell . . . there is NO ESCAPE.
2. Even loved ones who are believers in Heaven cannot offer comfort to those in hell!

We can see that hell, sometimes referred to as Hades, is a place of real torment.

There is no intermediate state as purgatory. Nowhere in Scriptures is such a doctrine pronounced. In fact, just the opposite is stated.

The Bible makes it clear that Christ's SINGLE atonement on the cross has forever ONCE-AND-FOREVER cleansed believers from their sins so that they can go straight to Heaven *immediately* upon death. No purgatorial intermediary fire cleansing is necessary. Thus the New Testament declares,

> ... in accordance with this will (of God) we have been made holy through the offering made once for all of the body of Jesus Christ, the Anointed One.
>
> Furthermore, every (human) priest stands (at his altar of service) ministering daily, offering the same sacrifices over and over again, which never are able to strip (from every side of us) the sins (that envelop us), and take them away.
>
> Whereas this One (Christ), after He had offered a SINGLE SACRIFICE FOR OUR SINS (that shall avail) FOR ALL TIME, SAT DOWN AT THE RIGHT HAND OF GOD. . . .
>
> FOR BY A SINGLE OFFERING HE HAS FOREVER COMPLETELY CLEANSED AND PERFECTED THOSE WHO ARE CONSECRATED and MADE HOLY. . . .
>
> *(Hebrews 10:10,11,12,14 Amplified Bible)*

Therefore, the unbelieving dead go immediately to hell. The believing dead are immediately with Christ (II Corinthians 5:6-10). The souls of the unbelieving dead (those who have not accepted Christ as personal Saviour and Lord) will remain in hell until the Final Judgment at the Great White Throne Judgment. This will occur after the 1000 year Millennium reign of Christ with His Saints (Believers).

In another chapter we will discuss what occurs during this White Throne Judgment.

THE DEAD IN CHRIST — WHERE ARE THEY NOW?

If the unbeliever goes immediately to hell . . . where does the believer go?

Death for the Christian does not mean he enters into a sleep . . . although some would have you believe this.

Death for the Christian does not mean a darkness for a time. In fact, just the opposite.

Remember God's revelation of Heaven to the dying thief on the cross.

The repentant thief turned to Jesus and said,

> Lord, remember me when You come into Your Kingdom! And He answered him, Truly, I tell you, today you shall be with Me in Paradise.
> *(Luke 23:42,43 Amplified Bible)*

Here was a thief whose life, up to the last moment, was wasted in sin. But in that last moment he accepted and Christ promised that *TODAY* . . . immediately . . . this repentant thief would be with Him in Paradise.

There are other evidences in Scripture that reveal that Heaven immediately follows death for the Christian.

In the Bible, II Kings 2:11 (Amplified Version) we read:

> As they still went on (Elisha and Elijah), and talked, behold, a chariot of fire and horses of fire parted the two of them; and Elijah went up by a WHIRLWIND INTO HEAVEN.

In the Bible, II Corinthians 5:8 (King James Version), we read:

> We are confident, I say, and willing rather to be absent from the body, and to be PRESENT WITH THE LORD.

Whether you use the Catholic Douay Version of the Bible, the King James Version, the Amplified Bible, the American Standard Version or any other reputable translation . . . God's Word is the same.

From time to time in this book we quote from various versions . . . simply because, for the layman, it is the opinion of the author that one particular version may more clearly reveal the truth of the original Greek to the reader.

DO CHRISTIANS IN HEAVEN KNOW EACH OTHER?

Most certainly they do!

In our previously quoted Scripture you will recall that the rich man in Hell recognized Lazarus who was in Heaven. On the Mount of Transfiguration the disciples recognized Moses and Elijah (Matthew 17:1-13). So in Heaven, apparently, we shall likewise be able to recognize others.

Perhaps I Corinthians 13:12 gives us the clearest indication that Saints in Heaven have knowledge beyond what they had on earth:

> For now we see through a glass, darkly; but then face to face: now I know in part; but then shall I know even as also I am known.
>
> *(King James Version)*

Though their bodies are still in the grave, both unbelievers and believers will retain their senses and will be able to see, hear and speak! This should not surprise the believer for God Himself is a Spirit and He can see and hear! (John 4:24).

CAN OUR LOVED ONES IN HEAVEN OBSERVE US NOW?

This is a question over which Bible students differ. God has chosen to emphasize that when the believer departs from this life he will be *at once* in the presence of His wonderful Lord. Beyond this, the lesser details are not yet clear. It is like a sea captain telling an inexperienced crew member that he will get him safely to Hawaii, which is a joyous and wonderful place, and beyond this he describes few of the details of life in Hawaii. The details can wait; now the important thing is to have confidence in the safe arrival. So it is with the details of Heaven.

Nevertheless, on this difficult topic let us at least make some observations as follows:

You will recall when Samuel died that Saul was King. Not content to be in the will of God he sought out the witch of Endor and asked the witch to bring back Samuel so he could ask him some questions.

Samuel was in Heaven . . . but God permitted him to converse with Saul and not only reveal what was happening at that time but also what would happen THE NEXT DAY to Saul.

> Samuel said, Why then do you ask of me, seeing the Lord has turned from you and has become your enemy? . . .
> Because you did not obey the voice of the Lord, or execute His fierce wrath upon Amalek, therefore the Lord has done this thing to you this day (The Philistines went to war against King Saul).
> Moreover the Lord will also give Israel with you into the hand of the Philistines; and tomorrow you and your sons shall be with me. The Lord also will give the army of Israel into the hand of the Philistines.
> *(I Samuel 28:16,18,19 Amplified Bible)*

Thus, *at least on this unique occasion* a prophet who had gone to Paradise, Samuel, knew what was happening on earth. Also the rich man in Hell was concerned about the affairs on earth (Luke 16)! For the rich man considered his 5 brothers and wanted to warn them that (a) there is a Hell and (b) that it is a place of torment. See Luke 16:17-31.

And do you remember Abraham's most astounding answer to the rich man who wanted to convey a warning to those on earth?

He said, ". . . if they hear not Moses and the prophets, neither will they be persuaded, THOUGH ONE ROSE FROM THE DEAD" (Luke 16:31).

What a perfect picture of today's "ears-that-do-not-hear" world so engulfed in self-gratification and worldly pleasures! Even a miracle will not phase them!

Then, remember when Moses and Elijah met Jesus at the Mount of Transfiguration. Their conversation with Christ and the disciples centered around the death of Christ on the cross —*an event that had not yet occured!* (Luke 9:27-36).

The Scriptures in Luke 15:7 also reveal a joyful concern in Heaven over the sinner who repents. This is observed in Luke 15:7

> I say unto you, that likewise joy shall be in heaven over one sinner that repenteth, more than over ninety and nine just persons, which need no repentance.
> *(King James Version)*

Another factor to consider is that the Scriptures make clear the precious truth that death for the Christian is not loss . . . but GAIN!

> For to me to live is Christ, and to die is GAIN. But if I live in the flesh, this is the fruit of my labour; yet what I shall choose I wot not (I do not know).
> For I am in a strait betwixt two, having a desire to depart, and to be with Christ; which is far better.
> *(Philippians 1:21-23 King James Version)*

Thus even though we do not find revealed exactly how much those in Heaven are aware of what is transpiring on earth, we do see in the Bible verses that indicate that they do have at least some degree of concern and awareness. So too, in Revelation 6:10 we read this question of the martyrs in Heaven: ". . . they cried with a loud voice, saying, How long, O Lord, holy and true, dost thou not judge and avenge our blood on them that dwell on the earth?" (King James Version)

THREE HEAVENS

The word *heaven* is used hundreds of times in the Bible. The primary meaning of *heaven* is *"that which is above."* In God's Word *heaven* refers to one of three major realms as noted below.

THE HEAVENS	WHERE IS IT	SOME REFERENCES IN SCRIPTURE
THE ATMOSPHERIC HEAVENS	The atmosphere which surrounds the globe. Our troposphere is a blanket of air around earth. It is no higher than 20 miles above the earth. Most clouds are within 7 miles of the earth.	The Israelites were told that the land they were to possess "is a land of hills and valleys and drinketh water of the rain from heaven" (Deut. 11:11). See also Deut. 11:17, II Chron. 7:13, Isa. 55:9-11, Psalm 147:8, Matthew 24:30, Zach. 2:6.
THE CELESTIAL HEAVENS	This is the sphere in which the sun and moon and stars appear. I Kings 8:27 speaks of the Celestial Heavens when it says, "Behold, the heaven of heavens cannot contain God."	"And God said, Let there be lights in the firmament of the heaven to divide the day from the night..." (Genesis 1:14). "...Look now toward heaven, and tell the stars, if thou be able to number them..." (Genesis 15:5). See also Hebrews 1:10, Psalm 33:6, Isaiah 14:12, Amos 5:26 and Jeremiah 23:24.
THE BELIEVERS HEAVEN (The Abode of God)	This is characterized by holiness because God dwells there. Believers also will dwell in God's heaven because they have been made holy by the grace of God. Jesus assured us of the *reality* of this place (John 14:2).	"...I dwell in the high and holy place, with him also that is of a contrite and humble spirit..." (Isaiah 57:15). "Look down from heaven, and behold from the habitation of thy holiness and of thy glory..." (Isaiah 63:15). See also Exodus 20:22, Deut. 4:36, Matthew 3:17, Matthew 14:19, Acts 7:55 and John 3:27.

For a fuller treatment of this subject we recommend: THE BIBLICAL DOCTRINE OF HEAVEN, Wilbur M. Smith, Published by MOODY PRESS, Chicago, Illinois

The chief thing for us to remember, however, is that for the departed believers in Heaven their souls rest from life's fierce competition, its unending toil, its sorrow, its pain and its sin (Revelation 14:13).

Yet in this resting and rejoicing they see Christ's face (Revelation 22:4) and they live with Christ (Revelation 3:12; 3:21; 4:4) . . . and most important they REIGN with Christ . . . sharing with Him in His royal glory!

It would be foolish for the believer to try to read into Scriptures what is not there regarding their loved ones in Heaven.

One who has lost a loved one certainly seeks to know all that is possible about Heaven. And this is understandable.

But God, in His wisdom has not chosen to reveal all. Paul in II Corinthians 12:4 tells of a man who "was caught up into paradise, and heard unspeakable words, which it is not lawful for a man to utter."

What these words were we do not know. It is sufficient for us as Christians to be content with the limits which God has prescribed in his written Word!

One can be sure of this . . . our loved ones in Heaven are rejoicing in their eternal home and our loss is their Kingly gain!

> There is a land of pure delight,
> Where saints immortal reign;
> Infinite day excludes the night
> And pleasures banish pain.

CAN A LOVING GOD SEND PEOPLE TO HELL?

It was William Munsey who best expressed the answer to a question many, many people ask: "How can a God of Love send people to an eternal Hell?" Munsey observed:

> God hates sin in the same proportion He loves virtue.
> Love of the good is of itself hatred of the evil.
> They are the same.
> The eternal punishment of the wicked is not inconsistent
>   with the divine goodness.

If God did not make men capable of sinning, He could not make them capable of being righteous.

If God did not make men capable of sinning and therefore liable to punishment, He could not make them capable of being righteous and therefore of being happy.

After all that divine goodness has done for man, if he, with his eyes open, and as a matter of choice, sins against God, abuses God's love, grieves God's Spirit and disappoints all the agencies God has appointed at so much cost to make him happy, and then, after God is willing to forgive him all, REFUSES in his pride and rebellion to ask God to do so, he certainly does deserve eternal punishment.

In Genesis 1:27 God created man in his own image.

God created you . . . and gave you a will . . . a body, a soul and a spirit. Compared to an endless eternity your present life on this earth is fleeting vapor:

> . . . ye know not what shall be on the morrow. For what is your life? It is even a vapour, that appeareth for a little time, and then vanisheth away.
>
> *(James 4:14 King James Version)*

Therefore how important it is for us to

> deny . . . ungodliness and worldly lusts . . . live soberly, righteously, and godly in this present world;
>
> Looking for that blessed hope, and glorious appearing of the great God and our Saviour Jesus Christ;
>
> Who gave himself for us that He might redeem us from all iniquity. . . .
>
> *(Titus 2:12-14)*

But don't be misled.

While life on this earth is but a fleeting vapor . . . you will exist forever!

Where you live—whether it be in Heaven or in Hell—depends on your decision . . . or rather lack of decision.

For if you as a lost sinner do not choose Christ and accept Him as personal Saviour you are automatically assigning yourself to an eternity in a real, tormenting Hell!

And an eternity in Hell is a long, long, everlasting time.

It was Thomas Mann who quite descriptively observed:

> Time has no divisions to mark its passage, there is never a thunderstorm or blare of trumpets to announce the beginning of a new month or year. Even when a new century begins it is only we mortals who ring bells and fire off pistols.

600-odd muscles, 60,000 miles of tubing, a heart that pushes 10 pints of blood through more than 1000 complete circuits a day . . . and a 3 pound brain that can coordinate a huge traffic of messages moving as fast as 350 feet per second . . . a message center that if man were to duplicate would have to occupy a space as big as a skyscraper.

How thankful are you that God created you . . . and gave you a heart that beats and keeps you alive . . . automatically . . . but gave you an opportunity to decide . . . (after viewing this earth and seeing its inability to provide for you a Heaven here on earth) to decide on eternal life . . . in Heaven or in Hell?

That eternity for you is just a heartbeat away.

> The angels from their thrones on high
> Look down on us with wondering eye,
> That where we are but passing guests
> We build such strong and solid nests,
> And where we hope to dwell for aye
> We scarce take heed a stone to lay!

Chapter 9

How to Live 1000 Years and More

God's Plan for Tomorrow • Surviving the Tribulation • What an Inheritance! • Where is the Millennium Location? • Resurrected Believers and Living Believers . . . The Difference • The Final Temple • Israel's Role in the Millennium • Unrest and Revolt

Fresh from the barricades of Northern Ireland, a five-foot slip of a girl stormed the mother of Parliaments in London with a biting Irish brogue and a political passion for "the oppressed people I represent."

The house was packed. The usually bored gallery attendants leaned forward to see her. Prime Minister Harold Wilson turned around his front bench to get a better view.

She was Bernadette Devlin, Britain's youngest member of Parliament. When an aristocratic member told of his experiences of one night of Irish riots, Miss Devlin waved her fist and said, "This is what I saw in the Bogside, not one night of broken glass, but 50 years of stark human misery. There is no place for us, the ordinary peasant, in Northern Ireland. There is no place for us in the society of the landlord, because we are the have-nots and they are the haves."

The have-nots and the haves! What a picture of this present world in which we live. And the situation gets more critical as our scientific age progresses!

Inequality and suffering are a part of this world . . . strive as man may to change the course of events.

265

But one day, man will live 1000 years in a world of peace, of love, free from pain, sorrow and trials. And yet, even in this 1000 year life, many still will not be satisfied.

This is referred to as the 1000 YEAR REIGN OF CHRIST, sometimes commonly known as the MILLENNIUM.

But before we delve into the Millennium . . . let's get an overall view of the things to come . . . so you will understand them in their proper perspective.

GOD'S PLAN FOR TOMORROW

Here are the future events that will occur *in the sequence they will occur:*

1. RAPTURE
   When Believers meet Christ in the sky. No future prophecy needs to be fulfilled. The Rapture can occur any hour, any day *(I Thessalonians 4:13-18).*

2. TRIBULATION PERIOD
   7 years of time when Antichrist and the False Prophet reign and cause world disaster. It is a period of judgment and tribulation on the earth.
   (Daniel 9:27; Matthew 24:21)

3. MILLENNIUM (1000) Reign of Christ
   When all the believers of all the ages reign with Christ. Here on earth the Old Testament promised Kingdom prophecies of world peace will at last come true.
   (Isaiah 11)

4. THE FINAL TEST FOR THOSE ON EARTH
   When Satan for a brief period at the close of the 1000 years has a last opportunity to deceive people and is thrown into the Lake of Fire forever.
   (Revelation 20:7-10)

5. GREAT WHITE THRONE JUDGMENT
   When the unsaved, non-believers, are judged before God and condemned forever to the Lake of Fire. Both living and dead unsaved are judged here. Those previously dead, up to this point, have already been in hell in torment, awaiting this final Judgment Day.
   (Revelation 20:11-15)

6. EARTH BURNS UP
   To purify this earth God sets it afire with a fervent heat.
   (II Peter 3:7,10)

7. THE NEW HEAVEN AND THE NEW EARTH
All Christians finally reach the ultimate in glory reigning forever with Christ in a new heaven and a new, purged, earth.

(Revelation 21)

This briefly is the sequence of events. They will be explained in detail, of course.

SURVIVING THE TRIBULATION

What happens to the Christians who are living during the Tribulation Period and survive . . . still being alive when it is time for the 1000 year Millennial Age to be ushered in by Christ?

And also, what happens to the non-believers who are living during the Tribulation and survive the Tribulation judgments of God?

Scriptures seem to indicate that although one-third of those on earth during the Tribulation may be killed (Revelation 9:15) . . . still two-thirds will remain. An insight into what occurs then is found in Matthew 25:32-46.

Here we find Christ relating the judgment of the sheep and goats. To the goats; that is to those who have in the Tribulation period rejected Christ by unbelief and who have manifested this by refusing to help Christ's persecuted brethren during this period, our Lord says:

> . . . Be gone from Me, you cursed, into the eternal fire prepared for the devil and his angels! . . .
> Then they will go away into eternal punishment . . .
> *(Matthew 25:41,46 Amplified Bible)*

To the sheep; that is, those living in the Tribulation period who have manifested a love for Christ by aiding His persecuted brethren, . . . to these will come the invitation:

> Come, you blessed of my Father, inherit—receive as your own—the kingdom prepared for you from the foundation of the world. . . .
> *(Matthew 25:34 Amplified Bible)*

THREE VIEWS ON THE RAPTURE*

These are NOT millennial positions but merely three of the views on the exact time of Christ's return within the PRE-MILLENNIAL camp. Correctness on these positions have nothing to do with the salvation of a sinner.

THE RAPTURE POSITIONS	WHAT DOES IT MEAN	WHAT EACH GROUP BELIEVES	WHY MANY BELIEVERS HOLD TO THE PRE-TRIBULATION RAPTURE VIEW
POST TRIBULATION RAPTURE	The Church (believers) will be raptured AFTER the 7 year Tribulation Period.	The Church will go through the awful Tribulation (Matthew 24:21).	
MID TRIBULATION RAPTURE	The Church (believers) will be raptured in the midst of the 7 year Tribulation Period.	The Church will be saved only from the last 3½ year "Great Tribulation" (Matthew 24:21).	The Church is to be spared God's wrath (Romans 9:5). Since the entire 7 year Tribulation Period is a pouring out of God's wrath (Revelation 6:17), the Rapture must remove the Church before this pouring out occurs. Genesis 19:22 shows this principle. The angel could not begin to destroy Sodom until Lot was safely removed from the area!
PRE TRIBULATION RAPTURE	The Church (believers) will be raptured before the 7 year Tribulation Period starts.	The Church will be saved from the entire 7 year Tribulation (Matthew 24:21).	

On the time of the RAPTURE, which is a complex topic, interested readers should refer to:
KEPT FROM THE HOUR, Gerald B. Stanton (Toronto: Evangelical Publishers, 1964);
THINGS TO COME, J. Dwight Pentecost (Grand Rapids, Michigan: Zondervan Publishing Company, 1958);
THE RAPTURE QUESTION, John F. Walvoord (Grand Rapids, Michigan: Zondervan Publishing Company, 1957);
UNDERSTANDING REVELATION, Gary G. Cohen (Faith Theological Seminary: 920 Spring, Elkins Park, Pa. 1968).

*RAPTURE: This refers to the time when believing Christians (both dead and alive) will "in the twinkling of an eye" rise up to meet Christ in the air (I Thessalonians 4:13-18).

THREE VIEWS ON THE MILLENNIUM

THE MILLENNIUM POSITIONS	WHAT DOES IT MEAN	WHAT EACH GROUP BELIEVES	OBJECTION OR SUPPORT
POST MILLENNIALISM	Christ will come to establish His Kingdom on Earth AFTER (Post) the 1000 Years (Millennium).	The earth will get better and better through the spread of the Gospel, and Christ will come to claim His Kingdom after 1000 years of peace has transpired.	Naïve. The earth is not getting better; and the Bible does not teach that it is (II Timothy 3:1-7).
A MILLENNIALISM	There will be NO FUTURE Earthly 1000 year Reign (Millennium). (In Greek "A" at the beginning of a word means "NO.")	The Millennium is NOW! Peace on earth exists in the Church; and Satan is NOW bound so that he cannot prevent the spread of the Gospel.	Revelation 20:3 says that Satan goes to prison "that he should deceive the nations no more." Look at Cuba, China and Russia. Satan is not NOW in prison.
PRE MILLENNIALISM	Christ will come personally to judge the wicked and to establish His Kingdom BEFORE (Pre) the 1000 years (Millennium) begins.	The earth is getting worse, and the Kingdom age cannot begin until Christ comes to destroy the wicked.	This is the teaching of the Bible. Christ will come (Revelation 19: 11-21) and then the Kingdom will be set up (Revelation 20).

THESE POSITIONS HAVE *NOTHING* TO DO WITH THE SALVATION OF A SINNER.

This judgment must occur before Christ begins the 1000 year MILLENNIUM period . . . for the still living non-believers have no right to enter this 1000 year reign with Christ and the saved.

But note the blessed promise for the one who has turned to Christ and who has lived through the Tribulation Period . . . and for Christians of all ages as well. In this last passage Christ is telling you that way back in eternity when the foundations of the world were made . . . this eternal Kingdom was prepared for you.

WHAT AN INHERITANCE!

Life in the Millennium

All of the wonderful things which man has vainly sought in his own strength, without God, will at last be poured out in the kingdom of His Son during the 1000 year MILLENNIUM.

With Satan imprisoned during this time (Revelation 20:1-7) . . . the Millennium Period will be one of

1. PEACE
   Because there will be no war, nations will not have to devote a great part of their budget to war materials. There will be an economic prosperity such as never before has been experienced.
                                                       (Isaiah 11:6-9)

   Perhaps the most well-known verse in relation to this is:
   And He shall judge between the nations, and shall decide (disputes) for many people; and they shall beat their swords into plowshares, and their spears into pruning hooks; nation shall not lift up sword against nation, neither shall they learn war any more.
                                       (Isaiah 2:4 Amplified Bible)

   Many political leaders use this verse referring to the goals of this present world. However this verse refers to the MILLENNIUM 1000 YEAR AGE . . . not to this present age.

2. HAPPINESS
This will be the fulfillment of happiness because there will be no more war nor will there be the multitude of sorrows now present to man on this earth.
(Revelation 20:3; Isaiah 11:6-9)

Therefore with joy will you draw water from the wells of salvation.
(Isaiah 12:3 Amplified Bible)

3. LONG LIFE AND HEALTH
Here in the 1000 year Millennial Period both sickness and death will be well nigh removed. Death will not be banished completely, however, during this period. Open sin may cause some to die because the Millennial Period, while filled with multiple blessings is still not the end of God's final judgments.
(Isaiah 65:20)

Keep these things in mind, however:

A. The DEFORMED will be HEALED
And in that day shall the deaf hear the words of the book, and out of obscurity and gloom and darkness the eyes of the blind shall see."
(Isaiah 29:18 Amplified Bible; also read Isaiah 35:5,6)

B. SICKNESS will be REMOVED
And no inhabitant will say, I am sick. . . .
(Isaiah 33:24 Amplified Bible)

C. SEXUAL REPRODUCTION will EXIST
Those saints who live through the Tribulation Period and enter the 1000 MILLENNIUM in their natural bodies will be able to have children throughout this 1000 year age. In fact the population of the earth will increase rapidly.

But it must be kept in mind that those who are born DURING the 1000 year Millennial Age will have a sin nature and it WILL be necessary for them to accept Christ if they are to participate in the final and continuing eternity that begins after this 1000 year period.

Here are two more verses to help you understand this wonderful blessing:

Out of them shall come songs of thanksgiving and the voices of those who make merry. And I will multiply them, and they shall not be few; I will also glorify them, and they shall not be small.

Their children too shall be as in former times. . . .
(Jeremiah 30:19,20 Amplified Bible)

4. PROSPERITY

The Millennium Period will be one of unequalled prosperity. There will be such an abundance that there will be no want.

Perhaps the most familiar verse . . . and one we hear quoted as referring to today . . . is the verse below, which actually refers to the 1000 year MILLENNIUM PERIOD:

The wilderness and the dry land shall be glad, the desert shall rejoice and blossom as the rose and the autumn crocus.
It shall blossom abundantly, and rejoice even with joy and singing; the glory of Lebanon shall be given to it, the excellency of Mount Carmel and the plain of Sharon. . . .

(Isaiah 35:1,2 Amplified Bible)

Think about this for a moment!

Here will be a desert that will have all the *glory of Lebanon* given to it! The glory of Lebanon is found in the strength and stateliness of its cedars. *The excellency of Carmel and Sharon*, which consisted of corn and cattle, will likewise then characterize this transformed desert!

5. A JOY IN LABOR

Under the direction of Christ there will be a perfect economic system in which people will work in complete joy and desire to provide the necessities of life.
They shall build houses and inhabit them, and they shall plant vineyards and eat the fruit of them . . . My chosen and elect shall long make use of and enjoy the work of their hands.

(Isaiah 65:21,22 Amplified Bible)

6. LANGUAGE WILL BE PURE

In this blessed period language will not be used for taking God's name in vain or for other wrong purposes. Lips will glorify and praise God. Perhaps the language of the earth will at this time be unified.

For then I will give to the people a clear and pure speech from pure lips . . .

(Zephaniah 3:9 Amplified Bible)

7. GOD WILL BE PRESENT

This will be a time when we can fellowship with God and enjoy His manifested presence in a special way.

My tabernacle or dwelling place also shall be with them; and I will be their God. . . .

The abode of God is with men, and He will live among them, and they shall be His people and God shall personally be with them and be their God.
(Ezekiel 37:27, Revelation 21:3 Amplified Bible)

WHERE IS THE MILLENNIUM LOCATION?

The 1000 year Millennium Period will take place *right here* on earth. The earthly center of this Reign with Christ will be in Jerusalem.

The Millennium will not yet be Heaven (Compare Isaiah 65:20 with Revelation 21:4 to see this).

It will be a theocracy.

A theocracy is a government in which God is recognized as the supreme civil ruler and His laws are taken as the laws of the state.

And the Lord will choose Jerusalem to be the center of all spiritual blessing.

And the Lord shall inherit Judah as His portion in the holy land, and shall again choose Jerusalem ... Yes, many peoples and numerous nations shall come to seek the Lord of hosts at Jerusalem and to entreat favor of the Lord ...

Everyone that is left of all the nations that came against Jerusalem shall go up from year to year to worship the king, the Lord of Hosts.
(Zechariah 2:12; 8:22,14:16 King James Version)

Who will be in the Millennium?
The people will include:

1. All the saved of Israel alive at the end of the Tribulation Period;
2. All the saved of the Gentiles alive at the end of the Tribulation Period *(They will have natural bodies in the Millennium Period)*; plus
3. The Believers who have died before the Rapture. These resurrected saints will have positions of responsibility in the Millennium.
(Matthew 19:28; Luke 19:12-27)

(*Note:* It is only fair to here note that while the Bible teaches that the saints who have believed in Christ and who have died will rule with Christ in the 1000 year Millennial Kingdom (Matthew 19:28; Revelation 20:6), yet many excellent Bible teachers believe that this will be a reign in Heaven and not on the Millennial earth. The Bible is clear that they will indeed reign! Whether in Heaven or earth is certainly a lesser question. From Matthew 19:28, which see, amazing as it may sound, it does in fact *appear* that the resurrected believers will actually reign on earth with Christ during the 1000 years.)

RESURRECTED BELIEVERS AND LIVING BELIEVERS . . . THE DIFFERENCE

In our context above the *living believers* are those who are still alive at the time the Millennium Period is ushered in right after the Tribulation. These have survived the Tribulation Period.

These living believers, during the Millennium 1000 year period, will marry and be given in marriage. The women will reproduce and have children. These believers will have natural bodies!

But what about the saints who died and those who were living on the earth immediately prior to the Tribulation Period?

These saints—called the resurrected believers—meet Christ in the air at the RAPTURE!

They are given heavenly bodies and Scripture tells us that they:

Which shall be accounted worthy to obtain that world (heaven), and the resurrection from the dead, neither marry, nor are given in marriage:
Neither can they die any more: for they are equal unto the angels; and are the children of God. . . .
(Luke 20:35,36 King James Version)

Therefore, during the 1000 year Millennium Reign with Christ there will exist, it appears, two classes of believers, having two different bodies:

The Living Believers—in natural bodies.
The Resurrected Believers—in glorified resurrection bodies.

THE FINAL TEMPLE

In the Millennial 1000 year age ... the final TEMPLE will apparently be built in Jerusalem. There will, however, be NO TEMPLE built by man's hands in the New Heaven and New Earth which follows the Millennium ... and more about this in a later chapter.

While even in this present earthly age an architect in Philadelphia, Pennsylvania has drawn plans for a Temple to be erected on or near the present site of the Moslem Mosque of Omar in Jerusalem ... this will NOT be the final Temple.

The FINAL TEMPLE constructed is built in the 1000 year MILLENNIUM Kingdom.

A pictorial description of this final TEMPLE appears with this chapter. The Temple will be located on the top of the mountain of the Lord, apparently in Jerusalem (Zechariah 8:22).

This is the sacred Mount Moriah, where Abraham had brought Isaac to offer him (Genesis 22:2). This is the Holy mountain-hill of the Lord (Psalm 24:3), and here Solomon built the Temple (II Chronicles 3:1). Of this mountain it is written:

... it shall come to pass, that the mountain of the house of the Lord shall be established as the highest of the mountains ... and people shall flow to it.
And many nations shall come, and say, Come, let us go up to the mountain of the Lord ... that He may teach us His ways and we may walk in His paths. ...
(Micah 4:1,2 Amplified Bible)

ISRAEL'S ROLE IN THE MILLENNIUM

During the Tribulation Period, Israel will have suffered persecutions of the greatest intensity (Revelation 12; Jeremiah 30:7). This finally will break her and in humbleness they "shall turn their faces toward me (Christ) whom they have pierced, and they shall mourn for Him as one mourns for his only son . . ." (Zechariah 12:10 Amplified Bible).

Then will the Scriptures be fulfilled in Matthew 23:39 which say: "You will not see me henceforth until you shall say, Blessed be the one who comes in the name of the Lord."

It will be a day of great grief in Jerusalem when the Jew finally accepts Christ, whom he detested . . . when he realizes all the lost blessing that could have been his. Yet,

> He will feed His flock like a shepherd, He will gather the lambs in His arm, He will carry them in His bosom, and gently lead those that have their young.
> *(Isaiah 40:11 Amplified Bible)*

Can you picture the tenderness and compassion of this scene. Christ, rejected for centuries by His own people – the Jews – with a forgiving heart tenderly feeds his flock and carries His lambs in His bosom. What greater love!

Israel can finally rejoice and God will delegate to Israel the opportunity to become His emissaries to the entire Millennial 1000 year Kingdom world.

> But you shall be called the priests of the Lord; people will speak of you as the ministers of our God. You shall eat the wealth of the nations, and the glory (once that of your captors) shall be yours.
> *(Isaiah 61:6 Amplified Bible)*

Thus, in the Millennial Kingdom Israel will once again be reunited as a nation. And Israel will be exalted even above the nations in this period!

> The sons of those who afflicted you shall come bending low to you, and all those who despised you shall bow down at your feet . . .
> *(Isaiah 60:14 Amplified Bible)*

Thus Israel is finally CONVERTED (Zechariah 12:10; Romans 11:26), REGATHERED (Jeremiah 23:7,8), and RESTORED. Both the Northern Ten Tribes, Israel, and the Southern Tribe of Judah will be RESTORED to their Promised Land safe at last (Ezekiel 37:15-28). Then the words of Zechariah 8:22,23 shall be fulfilled:

> Yea, many people and strong nations shall come to seek the Lord of hosts in Jerusalem, and to pray before the Lord.
> Thus saith the Lord of hosts; In those days it shall come to pass, that ten men shall take hold out of all languages of the nations, even shall take hold of the skirt of him that is a Jew, saying, We will go with you: for we have heard that God is with you.
>
> *(King James Version)*

Now can you better understand that verse in Genesis 12:3 which warns us Gentiles concerning Abraham and his children (the Jews):

> . . . I will bless them that bless thee, and curse him that curseth thee: and in thee (the Jew), shall all families of the earth be blessed.
>
> *(King James Version)*

Thus Jew and Gentile will live together in harmony in the 1000 year Millennium period.

When the nations during this period have been won to Christ and the conversion and the restoration of Israel is a reality . . . then will be accomplished the words of Isaiah:

> The earth will be filled with the knowledge of the Lord as the depth of the sea by the waters which cover it.
>
> *(Isaiah 11:9 King James Version)*

UNREST AND REVOLT

This general conversion of nations unfortunately does not mean that every last individual will come to Christ and accept Him as personal Saviour and Lord during the 1000 years.

THE MINISTRY OF ANGELS

THE NATURE OF ANGELS

They are spirits, normally without bodies. At times, however, they assume bodily form (Ezekiel 9:2; Genesis 18:2).

They are holy (Mark 8:38).

They are sexless and innumerable. In Matthew 26:53 Christ could have called 72,000 angels in the Garden of Gethsemane. See also Hebrews 12:22, Matthew 22:30.

At the time of Christ's earthly ministry they did not know the time of His Second Coming (Rapture). "But of that day and hour knoweth no man, no, not the angels for heaven, but my Father only" (Matthew 24:36).

The Bible reveals that the angels, like mankind, also experienced a moral testing. It appears that ⅓ of the angels fell with Satan (Revelation 12:7-9 and 12:4 where "stars" here seem to figuratively represent angels which once glistened in glory; Job 38:7). That not all of the angelic host fell, but only ⅓, is possible because they, unlike mankind, are apparently not a race but individual sons of God (Job 38:7).

"Angel" primarily means "messenger." Angels bear a relationship in some ways similar to sonship because of having their origin from Him. Because of their personal nearness to God they enjoy His special friendship and love. Read Psalm 91:11.

ARCHANGELS

Only two archangels are revealed to us in Scriptures by their names: Gabriel (Name in Hebrew means, "Strong One of God") who announced the birth of Christ; Michael (Name in Hebrew means, "Who is like God") who predicts the Tribulation Period (Daniel 12:1).

Archangels are believed to be rulers of large groups of angels.

CHERUBIM AND SERAPHIM

Cherubims are first mentioned in Genesis when God drives man out from the Garden of Eden and ". . . He placed at the east of the garden of Eden Cherubims, and a flaming sword which turned every way, to keep the way of the tree of life" (Genesis 3:24). Both J. G. Murphy and Wilbur M. Smith as well as other evangelical scholars believe Cherubims are real creatures, not symbols, with a special office in the general administration of the divine will of God.

The Cherubim is closely related to the Seraphim. See Isaiah 6. *Saraph* in Hebrew means "to burn" and it may be that they impart a cleansing fire from God (Isaiah 6:5, 6).

THE MINISTRY OF ANGELS

MAJOR ANGELIC ACTIVITIES	EXAMPLES IN THE SCRIPTURES	SCRIPTURE REFERENCES
REVEAL THINGS TO COME	More of the activities of angels are seen in Revelation than in any other book of the Bible.	Revelation 1:1,2 10:2 14:6-8 17:7
	"The Revelation of Jesus Christ, which God gave unto him, to show unto his servants things which must shortly come to pass; and he sent and signified it by his *angel* unto his servant John" (Revelation 1:1).	
	An angel reveals the vision of the New Heaven and New Earth.	21:9,15
	There are 12 angels at the 12 gates of the Holy City.	21:12
EXECUTORS IN CARRYING OUT JUDGMENTS OF GOD	Seven angels announce the seven Trumpet judgments. Two angels participate in harvest of souls of men.	Revelation 8:1-9:1, 13-14 14:7-8
	An angel looses other angels at the sound of the Sixth Trumpet Judgment. These latter angels (perhaps Satan's?) slay ⅓ of men.	9:13-15
	In the battle of Armageddon an angel beckons the birds to feast on the flesh of men on the battlefield.	19:17-18
	An angel binds Satan in prison for 1000 years during the Millennial Reign of Christ on Earth.	20:1

For a fuller treatment of this subject we recommend:
THE BIBLICAL DOCTRINE OF HEAVEN, Wilbur M. Smith, Published by MOODY PRESS, Chicago, Illinois.

Remember now, while all those at the very beginning of the 1000 year Millennium are believers . . . there are people born during the Millennium to the living saints who endured the Tribulation Period. And each of those born during the Millennial Period will have to individually decide either to accept Christ or reject Him.

Some will reject Him! This is possible because sin will still be possible during this 1000 years! In Zechariah 14:17-19 we are told that certain families and certain nations will refuse "to go up to Jerusalem to worship before the Lord."

And this will usher in . . . at the end of the 1000 year Millennium Period . . . Satan's final folly!

Bernadette Devlin, Britain's youngest member of Parliament, in her first speech in April 1969, told of her homeland, Ireland, suffering "50 years of stark human misery."

But you and I as Christians will have 1000 years of blissful joy. Not 1000 years, though . . . but an eternity thereafter.

That's how to live 1000 years or more . . . by accepting Christ as your personal Saviour and Lord.

There's a popular song making the rounds which begins:

> "I want to live, live, live
> Till I get old. . . ."

This is the message of the world.

But for the Christian, he will live 1000 years and in eternity he will dwell forever in a land where he'll never grow old!

Chapter 10
Satan's Final Folly

Why Loose Satan? • The Big Moment Arrives • What Is Gog and Magog?

There's a familiar hymn, the words of which include

> I am satisfied . . .
> I am satisfied with Jesus

and it expresses so fully the contentment that a Christian finds in his Saviour and Lord.

And another hymn which says . . .

> Content to let the world go by
> To know no gain nor loss

Imagine, living in the 1000 year Millennium Period with every need supplied, all sorrows erased, joy everlasting, death eliminated, no sickness . . . abundant harvests . . . and yet there will still be some who will not be content!

One author noted: "He who isn't contented with what he has wouldn't be contented with what he would like to have." In a recent newspaper column the headline read:

YOU SPELL SUCCESS WITH DOLLAR SIGNS

The article told of a well-known movie tycoon who makes sex films. His record 20 films in 11 years!

In this current permissive climate his films are now being widely sought after by theater chains who previously turned thumbs down on such movies.

"I'm not making dirty movies," he was quoted as saying, "I'm in the entertainment business. . . ."

He continued, "I think sex is here to stay as a movie commodity. . . ."

The overpowering desire of many in this world is the desire to accumulate riches.

But the Bible warns:

> For what is a man profited, if he shall gain the whole world, and lose his own soul?
> *(Matthew 16:26 King James Version)*

In a recent interview with the wife of a TV star who lives in the plush United Nations Plaza, this well-known personality commented: "This is a building of high achievers. People who live here are not climbing. They have arrived!"

Financially, perhaps, yes . . . for they pay from $75,000 for a one-bedroom apartment up to $275,000 for a nine-room duplex plus maintenance charges of as much as $2000 a month!

She further commented, "It's your own private little utopia. My theory is that you can stay in this building and never leave it. . . ." Two years later she left it — divorced!

While some would seek riches as a private utopia (an ideal heaven) . . . others strive to keep forever young.

The furrowed brow, the wrinkled cheek, the baggy eyelid apparently have no place in America these days.

To correct such things people are willing to undergo a plastic surgery where the face is swabbed with a phenol solution which burns away outer layers of skin. This gives the appearance of second-degree burns and takes two months to return to normal.

For this people are willing to pay $1000 to $2500 for a face lifting operation!

And in Las Vegas, the municipality's sign reads:

KEEP LAS VEGAS GREEN. BRING MONEY

And to make it easy to gamble on this so-called "heaven" on earth the sidewalk curbs have been leveled in front of the downtown casinos ... making it possible to shuffle in and play without even raising your foot!

Some of these gambling dens cost $25 million dollars to erect.

The world ... in its greed for wealth ... will use any means to achieve its goals. This is how powerful the encompassing network of sin is!

One of Satan's methods of operation is to instill in the hearts of men a longing for more ... and more ... and more ... a lust for wealth and pleasure that never seems to be satisfied.

And this desire will in some part account for the unrest that comes at the end of the 1000 year Millennium Period when Satan is once again let loose.

And he that plants thorns must never expect to gather roses!

WHY LOOSE SATAN?

About 1000 years before the Millennium, and right after the 7 year Tribulation Period, Satan will be cast into a prison especially made for him by God (Revelation 20:1-3).

Then will follow a heaven here on earth—1000 years of seemingly endless happiness and contentment.

Why couldn't this go on forever?

Why does God want to release Satan from his prison and allow him to once again run rampant throughout the earth ... causing sin and death to abound?

This is a question many have asked.

And there is an answer!

You will recall that during this 1000 year Millennial Period that all the nations submitted to a theocratic government —an authoritarian government ruled solely by God.

And Christ rules this world during the 1000 years with an "iron rod."

> And He shall rule them with a rod (scepter) of iron. . . .
> *(Revelation 2:27 King James Version)*

As Dr. J. Dwight Pentecost so clearly points out in his book, THINGS TO COME, a book we highly recommend:

> The government (of the millennial period) will *deal summarily with any outbreak of sin.*

Scripture references to substantiate this are found in Psalm 2:9 and Zechariah 14:16-21. Also

> But with righteousness shall He judge the poor, and reprove with equity for the meek of the earth; and He shall smite the earth with the rod of His mouth, and with the breath of his lips shall he slay the wicked.
> *(Isaiah 11:4 King James Version)*

Can it be that there are wicked on the earth during the 1000 year Millennium Period? Yes!

While it seems to be true that the population of the Millennium consists of the New Testament saints (those since the death of Christ on the Cross) and the Old Testament saints . . . it must also be kept in mind that there is another segment to the population at that time.

This is composed of those saints who lived during the 7 year Tribulation Period . . . just prior to the 1000 year Millennium . . . and who did not die in the Tribulation.

These Tribulation survivors will enter the 1000 year Millennium Period in their *natural* bodies . . . bodies such as you and I have right now.

They will be able to continue the normal marriage activities and through these have children. Their children are not automatically redeemed to eternal life. They are subject to sin and to be assured of an eternity in Heaven . . . must accept Christ as personal Saviour and Lord.

Note the Scriptures which here tell us that some will refuse to worship during the yearly pilgrimage to the Temple of the Lord.

And it shall come to pass, that every one that is left of all the nations which came against Jerusalem shall even go up from year to year to worship the King, the Lord. . . .
. . . whoso will not come up . . . upon them shall be no rain . . . there shall be the plague, wherewith the Lord will smite the heathen that come not up to keep the feast of the tabernacles.

(Zechariah 14:16-18 King James Version)

Therefore, there will be disobedience during the 1000 year Millennium Period. Thus this is still not the perfect eternal state but only a stepping stone to the final eternal Heaven for the believer.

Reflecting on this, it is easier for us to understand at least one reason why Satan must be let loose for a little while . . . so that the Kingdom of God can be made perfect.

Under the iron rod of Christ all will be obligated to obey. And because of this . . . because it is not an uncompelled-choice decision . . . a minority of individuals will accept this very impatiently. Some will yield outwardly but inwardly will rebel. Some will rebel outwardly, for example, by not making the yearly pilgrimage to worship the King (Zechariah 14:16-18).

Perhaps Dr. René Pache describes this best in his excellent book, THE RETURN OF JESUS CHRIST, when he says:

Now the time comes when eternity is going to seal the final outcome of each one. God, who knows the most secret thoughts, could very well send into eternal Hell the hearts which have rebelled against His grace. But would there not be temptation for such men to say,

"Lord, what have we done to merit such punishment?

Have we not conformed ourselves like the others?

And have we not always been obedient?"

In order to take away from them every pretext of speaking thus and to give them the occasion of manifesting the depth of their wicked heart, God will permit them to be tempted.

As Dr. Pache further observes:

> . . . temptation is for the creature the price of liberty.
> God does not wish to be served by slaves but by beings who
> have freely chosen to love Him and to obey Him.

It must be kept in mind that all of us have received from
God the gift of a will . . . and all of us have been tempted. We
are by creation free agents, we can make choices.

It may surprise some to realize that even angels have
been tempted and even Christ was tempted! (Matthew 4:1-11;
Hebrews 4:15; Jude 6).

THE BIG MOMENT ARRIVES

So now the final stage for Satan has been set. Just one
more time . . . that's all he asks . . . just one more time to
achieve his sinful goals.

You will recall that he was thrown into a prison made for
him by God after the Tribulation Period so he could no longer
have his sway with the nations of the world. This ushered in
the 1000 year Millennium Period of peace and prosperity.

In the LIVING NEW TESTAMENT, a paraphrased, easy-
to-read Bible, this time period is related as follows:

> Then I saw an angel come down from heaven with the
> key to the bottomless pit and a heavy chain in his hand.
>
> He seized the Dragon – that old Serpent, the Devil, Satan
> – and bound him in chains for 1000 years,
> And threw him into the bottomless pit, which he then
> shut and locked, so that he could not fool the nations any
> more until the thousand years were finished. Afterwards he
> would be released again for a little while.
> *(Revelation 20:1-3 Living New Testament)*

Up to this point the 1000 year Millennium Period has
been a Golden Age.

It appears that those who will be deceived when Satan is
once again loosed will be some of the children born during
this Millennial Age.

And here is the tragedy!

> . . . when the thousand years are expired, Satan shall be loosed out of his prison,
> And shall go out to deceive the nations which are in the four quarters of the earth, Gog and Magog, to gather them together to battle: the number of whom is as the sand of the sea.
>
> *(Revelation 20:7,8 King James Version)*

THINK OF IT! Satan will gather an army so big . . . the number of whom is as the *sand of the sea.*

The gathering so rapidly of an army by a formerly great leader who has just fled from prison, here Satan, is not without its historic parallels. When the once great and then imprisoned Napoleon Bonaparte fled his prison of Elbe Isle, army upon army at once rejoined him. He was again in 1815 in power and on the march for "a little season," before his soon final defeat at Waterloo.

After living in 1000 years of prosperity, wealth, without sickness and very little death, with an abundance of everything . . . SOME ARE STILL NOT SATISFIED. And Satan deceives them into believing he can offer them something better! And so clever is his deception that he musters an army AS NUMEROUS AS THE SAND OF THE SEA!

Read that over again! Can you . . . after living 1000 years in a Golden Age . . . imagine this? What a heartache God must have and what patience with mortal man!

Is it no wonder that the NEW HEAVEN and NEW EARTH do not begin until this final weeding out of the chaff is accomplished!

Now, perhaps you can understand why Satan is once again let loose . . . for there is waiting a host of people to join him — a host as numerous as the sand of the sea!

How much sand is there in the sea? Well, this might help you visualize the vastness of Satan's following. The sea occupies 70.8% of the surface of the earth! And with much of the sea's shore and bottom surface covered with sand . . . those that join Satan must represent a very large group . . . yet they probably represent only a minority of the Millennial Kingdom.

One may wonder where all the people come from! However, it must be kept in mind that during the 1000 year Millennial reign war, suffering and even death will have been held in check and mankind will multiply profusely. And with God blessing the ground to give an abundant harvest the earth will be able to support such a large population.

Thus, we see the ingratitude and blindness of millions who have tasted for a thousand years the blessings of Heaven . . . but as soon as they can escape this authority . . . they rush to the folly of Satan.

WHAT IS GOG AND MAGOG?

You will recall that in the last Scripture verse we quoted (Revelation 20:8) there was a reference to the nations of Gog and Magog joining Satan.

This can be confusing to the new Christian since these same names, Gog and Magog, appear in Ezekiel 39:1,2.

In Ezekiel, Gog of the country of Magog refers to the great enemy of the North who shall rush toward Palestine before or during the Tribulation 7 years. Most evangelicals believe this is Russia.

However, in Revelation 20:8, this mention of Gog and Magog refers to those who from the *four corners of the earth* (not just Russia) let themselves be led in the last battle against God.

The event mentioned in Revelation 20:8 occurs at the end of the 1000 year MILLENNIUM Period.

It must be kept in mind that the rebellion of Satan and his followers does *not* occur in the 1000 year Millennial Period, but rather, it *follows* it!

And when the thousand years are expired, Satan shall be loosed. . . .

(Revelation 20:7 King James Version)

And as in previous history that will have long since passed . . . Satan's prime attack will again be directed against the believers (of Christ) and His city, Jerusalem!

The Scriptures tell us:

> And they (Satan and his army) swarmed up over the broad plain of the earth and encircled the fortress (camp) of God's people (the saints) and the beloved city (Jerusalem). . . .
> *(Revelation 20:9 Amplified Bible)*

It is not difficult to understand why Satan first wants to strike Jerusalem. Driven from Heaven long before, Satan is anxious to strike at the heart of God's throne and sanctuary.

But though Satan gathers his rebel following "to battle," there is no battle!

What occurs next—the most tragic occurrence beyond the scope of man's wildest finite imagination—brings an end to Satan's final folly!

And for his followers, "the number of whom is as the sand of the sea," even God's love will never, never reach them! It was Charles F. Kettering who remarked:

> My interest is in the future because I am going to spend the rest of my life there.

Do you spell success with dollar signs? Those who, in this age and at the end of the Millennial Age, follow selfish desires and join Satan's army will find themselves destined to a tragic unending end!

Chapter 11

The Night That Never Ends

The Final War • The Final Defeat • Satan's Crushed Hopes •
The Most Tragic Moment of Tomorrow • What Is Hell Like? •
Hell's Fury • 1. A Place of Consciousness • 2. A Place of
Torment • 3. A Place of Darkness • 4. Eternal Separation
from Loved Ones • 5. Not the Slightest Hope of Release •
6. The Torment of Memory in Hell • 7. The Torment of Un-
satisfied Lustful Cravings • The Unsaved Dead *Before* Their
Judgment Day

In the previous chapter we described life as it will be in
the 1000 year Millennial period, a time of fulfilled joy for the
Christian.

We also pointed out that at the end of this Millennial period, many people, as numerous as the sands of the sea, would
join with Satan in a final revolt against God and His people.

The scene has been set!

This vast, extremely vast, army represents the dregs of
civilization still determined that they can achieve a world far
better than God in His infinite wisdom.

How often in the past has man sought to take things in his
own hands and boast of his accomplishments . . . accomplishments that in reality were possible only because God permitted them.

Not even the abundance of the Millennium 1000 year period was good enough for them.

And, unfortunately, these people did not learn their lesson from the events at the end of the Tribulation Period when Antichrist and the False Prophet sought to wipe out Israel. For it was at that time that God intervened and wiped out a combined army whose size seemed to approach some 200 million men . . . leaving a blood bath that covered 185 miles of Israel! (Revelation 14:20).

It was at that time that Antichrist and the False Prophet were cast into the Lake of Fire and Satan was bound there for 1000 years!

Now Satan is on the march again. Apparently the 1000 years in the Lake of Fire has not reformed him . . . but made him more sinister in character.

Then, for a brief season, the divine restraint will be relaxed. One purpose of this is to provide one last and supreme demonstration of the appalling wickedness of the non-believing human heart!

THE FINAL WAR

With all his men, more numerous than the sands of the sea, one would think Satan would make some dent in his invasion of the area around Jerusalem.

And, were it not for God . . . he could and would. But something unusual occurs!

God causes a spectacular phenomenon to take place.

Here's how the Bible describes it:

> . . . fire came down from God out of Heaven, and devoured them!
> (Revelation 20:9 King James Version)

Think of it! Multiple thousands, in fact millions of people, in a flashing moment, are suddenly consumed by fire that came thundering down from Heaven. Sounds unbelievable, doesn't it?

But reflect on this a moment. Isn't this holocaust possible even today with inventions man has been allowed by God to create? Of course! Nuclear warheads today—dropped from planes from the sky can consume millions in a moment. Napalm—the jelly-like liquid is now being dropped from planes both in Vietnam and by Israel over Arab countries. This is fire from the sky!

Is it any more strange that the God of creation can bring down FIRE FROM ABOVE to wipe out millions who turn against Him and His people? Of course not!

Now, in the light of these nuclear discoveries just over the past few years . . . can you see why these times are even more perilous than the times of 20 years ago . . . and why we ARE in the Last Days as warned in the Scriptures (II Timothy 3:1).

At this point in history . . . a point in history that never before has been achieved by man . . . we can almost duplicate many of the judgments God has reserved for the 7 year Tribulation Period and the final judgment of Satan at the end of the 1000 year Millennial reign of Christ!

Many people are unaware that right now there exists in Washington, D.C., just a few minutes from the White House, the Capitol, and the Pentagon a new Communications Center.

This Center has already made it possible to connect 40 cities into a network of TV communication that will be viewed simultaneously by those seated in auditoriums throughout these cities.

With this has been created electronically the facilities for simultaneous translation for as many as four languages. This will make it possible for one leader in Washington to reach 40 cities, conveying his thoughts and wishes . . . at one time with inter-communcation between these cities. And this closed circuit TV projection system also provides a color television image from ANYWHERE IN THE WORLD, via satellite on a big 16 x 20 foot screen.

You will recognize in this that round-the-world interconnections such as this one will enable instant communication and population control.

And this method may be one of the ways used by Satan, either in the Tribulation Period or later at the end of the 1000 year Millennium Period, to exhort his followers and challenge them to action.

This is all said to make this point: There exists *now* the inventions that can usher in the End-Time.

THE FINAL DEFEAT

Where did it all begin? It began after Genesis 1:31 which reads:

> And God saw every thing that he had made, and behold, it was very good. . . .
>
> *(Genesis 1:31 King James Version)*

It was after this that the fall of Satan must have taken place. It was Satan who caused the fall of the human race. Read Genesis 3. And God predicted his judgment in Eden in Genesis 3:15 and this was accomplished on the cross (John 12:31-33).

Satan's power was second only to God. What was Satan's inheritance? God tells us in Ezekiel 28:11-19 when He here speaks to the wicked King of Tyre who is indwelt by Satan as was Judas (John 13:27). Hence God's words here are aimed directly at Satan.

> You were in Eden, the garden of God; every precious stone was your covering . . . You were the annointed cherub . . . You were blameless in your ways from the day you were created, until iniquity and guilt were found in you. . . .
> . . . you were filled with lawlessness and violence . . . your heart was very proud . . . you corrupted your wisdom for the sake of your splendor. I cast you to the ground; I lay you before kings that they might gaze at you.
> You have profaned your sanctuaries by the multitude of your iniquities . . . Therefore I have brought forth a fire from your midst; it has consumed you, and I have reduced you to ashes upon the earth in the sight of all who looked at you. . . .
> . . . you have come to a horrible end and shall never return to being. . . .
>
> *(Ezekiel 28:13-19 Amplified Bible)*

Ezekiel 28:16 is quite prophetic of today's world . . . especially the phrase that says, "you were filled with lawlessness and violence . . ."

Isn't this a picture of our condition right now, especially on many of our university and college campuses!

Now that we have examined the exalted position Satan once had . . . we can now go further into his judgment by God.

This is the end of the line for Satan . . . and for his followers. For God's judgment in the form of fire from above consumes them. And as related in Ezekiel 28:19 . . . "you have come to a horrible end. . . ."

SATAN'S CRUSHED HOPES

Lewis Sperry Chafer commenting on Isaiah 14:4-23, a passage which addresses Satan through the Satanicly indwelt wicked King of Babylon, notes:

. . . Lucifer's sin consisted in five awful *I will's* against the will of God. . . .

Let's look at these *"I will's"* (See Isaiah 14:12-15).

1. I will ascend into Heaven . . .
2. I will exalt my throne above the stars of God . . .
3. I will sit also upon the mount of the congregation, in the sides of the north. . . .
4. I will ascend above the heights of the clouds . . .
5. I will be like the most High.

(Amplified Bible)

With Satan, the originator of sin, not satisfied to be second to Christ in majesty and glory . . . but seeking to rebel against God and "exalt my throne *above* the stars of God" . . . is it any wonder the world today defies and denies God?

And can you now see why that God, through Solomon, wrote:

. . . there is no new thing under the sun.

(Ecclesiastes 1:9 King James Version)

So Satan's ambitions, generated sometime early in the earth beginnings and nurtured through all time until the end of the 1000 year Millennial Period . . . are finally once and for all CRUSHED by God. In one swift judgment — related in the English Bible in just 12 short words — in just one-third of one Scripture verse God, in effect says to Satan's ambitions, "Satan, THIS IS THE END!"

12 words crush Satan's hopes:

> . . . and fire came down from God out of Heaven, and devoured them.
>
> *(Revelation 20:9 King James Version)*

THE MOST TRAGIC MOMENT OF TOMORROW

What happens next?

Is Satan dead? Are his millions of followers dead and forgotten? No. Their harvest of sin has been sown. Now is the time they will reap their "rewards."

First God takes care of Satan whose deception caused millions to abandon Christ.

> And the devil (Satan) that deceived them was cast into the lake of fire and brimstone, where the beast (Antichrist) and the false prophet are, and shall be tormented day and night for ever and ever.
>
> *(Revelation 20:10 King James Version)*

There are some who will read this passage and laugh. "Thrown into the lake of fire . . . what a fairy tale . . . an allegory . . . surely a God of love could not do this . . . and how can one be tormented day and night forever and ever?"

Perhaps you, as mere man, don't believe. But think about this for a moment. Satan and his angels believe! Turn to James 2:19

> . . . the devils also believe and tremble.
>
> *(James 2:19 King James Version)*

If Satan and his angels believe . . . and in believing . . . tremble . . . should you any less believe that when God says something . . . He means it!

Satan is thus judged and cast into the lake of fire with Antichrist and the False Prophet who have already been there a 1000 years.

Now comes the most tragic moment of this world.

> Then I saw a great white throne and the One Who was seated upon it, from Whose presence and from the sight of Whose face earth and sky fled away and no place was found for them.
>
> *(Revelation 20:11 Amplified Bible)*

Apparently the awesomeness of this occasion is so tragic it is hard for anyone to fully comprehend . . . "the earth and sky" even flee from it.

In your study of the Scripture you may recall that at the start of the Tribulation Period a throne of judgment was set in Heaven. Of this throne we read,

> . . . and there was a rainbow round about the throne. . . .
>
> *(Revelation 4:3 King James Version)*

The significance of the rainbow about this throne is that in the midst of the seven years of Tribulation judgments, God will show mercy and many will be saved (Revelation 7 shows this to be so). So Genesis 9:11-13 shows the bow to be the sign of God's covenant that He will not again destroy all flesh.

But to the unbelievers . . . when their time of judgment comes before God, God sits on his Great White Throne and *no rainbow* encircles the Throne! It will be a most frightening occasion—far more frightening than anything man could conjure.

The throne is pure WHITE representing God's absolute Holiness! Its glistening whiteness cries out in judgment against all sin and sinners.

Sin needs to be put away! Sinners must be punished. The WHITE THRONE cries out with Holiness and Justice against

JUDGMENT DAYS

JUDGMENT OF UNBELIEVERS

BOOK OF LIFE

THE BOOKS OPENED

"And whosoever was not found written in the book of life was cast into the Lake of Fire." (Rev. 20:15)

LAKE OF FIRE

...the tares are the children of the wicked one; The enemy that sowed them is the devil; the harvest is the end of the world; and the reapers are the angels. As therefore the tares are gathered and burned in the fire; so shall it be in the end of this world." (Matthew 13:38-40)

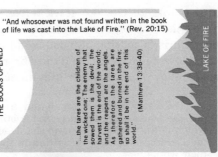

1000 YEAR MILLENNIUM

REWARD JUDGMENTS FOR BELIEVERS

"and I will dwell in the house of the Lord for ever." (Psalm 23:6)

INCORRUPTIBLE CROWN (Victor's Crown)
"... every man that striveth for the mastery is temperate in all things ... they do it to obtain a corruptible crown; we an INCORRUPTIBLE." (I Corinthians 9:25)

CROWN OF REJOICING (Soul Winner's Crown)
"... what is our hope ... or crown of rejoicing? Are not even ye in the presence of our Lord Jesus Christ at His coming? For ye are our glory and joy." (I Thessalonians 2:19, 20)

CROWN OF RIGHTEOUSNESS
"Henceforth there is laid up for me a crown of righteousness, which the Lord, the righteous judge, shall give me at that day: and not to me only, but unto all them also that love His appearing." (II Timothy 4:8)

CROWN OF GLORY (Crown for Service)
"Feed the flock of God which is among you ... (be) examples to the flock ... And when the chief Shepherd shall appear, ye shall receive a crown of glory that fadeth not away." (I Peter 5:2-4)

CROWN OF LIFE (Martyr's Crown)
"... the devil shall cast some of you into prison, that ye may be tried ... be thou faithful unto death, and I will give thee a crown of life." (Revelation 2:10)

"Every man's work shall be made manifest ... because it shall be revealed by fire ... if any man's work abide ... he shall receive a reward ... if any man's work shall be burned, he shall suffer loss: but he himself shall be saved; yet so as by fire." (I Corinthians 3:13-15)

WOOD HAY STUBBLE

| SILVER | GOLD | PRECIOUS STONES |

RAPTURE
BELIEVERS meet CHRIST in the air

sinful mankind. Oh, the stark terror of those who are here before this Throne, for they would not turn to God so that in mercy Christ's sacrificial blood could have washed their sins away. Now it is too late! And the Throne is all White and there is no rainbow. The time for judgment has arrived!

> And I saw the dead, small and great, stand before God; and the books were opened: and another book was opened, which is the book of life: and the dead were judged out of those things which were written in the books according to their works.
> And the sea gave up the dead which were in it; and death and hell delivered up the dead which were in them: and they were judged every man according to their works.
> *(Revelation 20:12,13 King James Version)*

Here is the saddest roll call in history! No matter how poor or how rich you are in today's world . . . money does *not* buy your way into Heaven . . . no more so than good works!

And both small and great now have to give an accounting of themselves—the small and the great who did not accept Jesus Christ as personal Saviour and Lord in their heart!

This resurrection after the 1000 year Millennial period is called the Resurrection of the LOST. The Christians—those who have accepted Christ—are NOT dead at this time. They were raised at the Rapture prior to the 7 year Tribulation Period. That was called the First Resurrection. This Resurrection of the Lost is called the Second Resurrection.

That is why Christ says:

> Blessed and holy is he that hath part in the first resurrection: on such the second death hath no power. . . .
> *(Revelation 20:6 King James Version)*

Thus the unsaved DEAD (and these are the only people who are dead at this time) are raised up from the dead! This includes the millions who were consumed by fire in their rebellion against God immediately after the 1000 year Millennial Period!

It does not include Satan, however, who was immediately after this Period, thrown into the Lake of Fire.

This Great White Throne Judgment seals the eternal separation of the unsaved wicked from God.

Note that in Revelation 20:13 we are told that every man was judged according to his works.

First, keep this in mind, all the unbelievers will go to Hell! None will go to Heaven!

But all unbelievers will not receive the same punishment. Their punishment will be eternal, forever and forever, but the degree of punishment will vary with each individual . . . according to his works!

Christ relates this truth through Luke in the form of a parable when He says:

> The Master . . . will come on a day when he does not expect him and at an hour of which he does not know, and will punish him and cut him off and assign his lot with the unfaithful.
> And that servant who knew his master's will, but did not get ready . . . shall be beaten with many lashes.
> But he who did not know and did things worthy of a beating shall be beaten with few lashes. . . .
> *(Luke 12:46-48 Amplified Bible)*

The Gospel of Christ has been preached in the United States perhaps more profusely than in any other part of the world. Some of the greatest evangelists in the world have had their biggest audiences right here in the United States. The Gospel reaches out not only through the printed Word but through a flood of radio broadcasts and now even coast-to-coast network television broadcasts.

Those in America certainly know "His master's will" and if they do not respond by accepting Christ . . . are automatically commiting themselves to a judgment of many lashes eternally in Hell.

So now it is finished . . . or rather just beginning . . . for the dead — the unbelievers.

Now comes a judgment related in our English Bible in only 18 words that will condemn them forever to a real, everlasting Hell:

AND WHOSOEVER WAS NOT FOUND WRITTEN
IN THE BOOK OF LIFE WAS CAST INTO THE LAKE
OF FIRE.
(Revelation 20:15 King James Version)

There is an English proverb which says

Hell is paved with good intentions.

And here at last, many will wish they had put their good
intentions into action . . . but it will be too late! There is no
second chance. The opportunity for you who are living today
is NOW! If you do not accept Christ NOW while you are living
. . . then your destination is Hell.

Remember this one important fact:

IT DOES *NOT* REQUIRE A DECISION TO GO TO HELL
but
IT DOES REQUIRE A DECISION TO GO TO HEAVEN

Thus ends . . . and begins . . . the most tragic moment in
history . . . a moment that for the unbeliever will be an eternity
in constant torment in Hell.

WHAT IS HELL LIKE?

Is there a real Hell? YES! Is there real torment? YES!
Is it everlasting? YES!

Look at Matthew 25:41 where the Lord, who neither lied
nor exaggerated, says to the unbelievers:

. . . Depart from me, ye cursed, into everlasting fire,
prepared for the devil and his angels:
(for) these shall go away into everlasting punishment:
but the righteous into life eternal.
(Matthew 25:41,46 King James Version)

Dr. J. Dwight Pentecost in his book THINGS TO COME
points out that in the phrase in Matthew 25:41 which says
"prepared for the devil and his angels . . ."

The word "prepared" literally is "having been pre-pared," suggesting that the lake of fire is *already* in existence and awaiting its occupants.

It is of interest to note that C. T. Schwarze, formerly of New York University, wrote in a thesis that such a place as a lake of fire is actually known to science today.

The word *lake* must connote a body of matter having liquid form. Therefore, if Scripture is truth, this eternal fire must be in liquid form.

. . . .

. . . the very simple proof of the portions of Scripture we have been discussing *lies in the existence of the singular phenomena of the skies known as midget or white dwarf stars!* . . . a midget star is one which, because of some things which have happened to it (not quite clear at this time), should be roughly 5,000 or more *times* as big as it really is! Applying this idea for illustration to such a planet as the earth, you must conceive the earth as having shrunk to such an extent that its diameter would be about 400 miles . . . instead of being 8,000 miles in diameter as it really is.

. . . .

This enormous density . . . has a great deal to do with our subject. . . . Most people know the sun, our nearest star is rather hot . . . there is general agreement that the tempera-ture at or near the center of stars is between 25 million and 30 million degrees Fahrenheit! . . . at such temperatures, much can happen, like the bursting of atoms, which helps to explain the phenomenon of the white dwarf. . . .

. . . .

. . . a temperature of 30,000,000 degrees Fahrenheit could explode atoms. . . .
It would cause the atoms to lose their electrons even though the attraction between nucleus and electrons is an octillion . . . times the attraction of gravity. The separated parts could then be better packed in, particularly under such great pressure. . . . With the constant activity of X-rays, atom walls could not be reformed; therefore enormous densities, such as are found in the midgets, can be attained. Now, please note, at such high temperatures all matter would be in the form of gas . . . in a white dwarf the pressure is so great that gasses become compressed to the consistency of a liquid although they may still respond to the character-istics of a gas. . . .

. . . .

. . . Before such a star could cool off and gradually be-come dark it would have to expand to normal proportions. That is, it would have to get to be more than 5,000 times its present size. Here is the difficulty. Such expansion would cause enormous heat which, in turn, would absolutely keep the star compressed, so that, *insofar as astronomers and physicists know, the midget stars can never cool off!* . . . The white dwarf, to all intents, *can never burn out.*

. . . may I summarize to show that the Bible, God's Word, is scientifically accurate? We find, first, an eternal fire which cannot burn out. Being of a liquid consistency it is, secondly, a lake of fire. In the third place, it cannot be quenched, for any quenching material, such as water, would immediately have its atoms stripped of electrons and be packed in with the rest. In the fourth place, since astronomers have been, and still are, studying this strange phenomenon, it is only too evident that the lake of fire *has been prepared* and is now ready. Although we cannot say that God will actually use these lakes of fire in fulfilling His Word, the answer to the skeptic is in the heavens where there *are* lakes of fire. . . .

The final judgment of Hell is certainly an awesome one. Yet many make light of Hell . . . saying, "If there is a Hell, I'll be so busy shaking hands with my friends I won't have time for anything else."

But what will be occurring in Hell?

HELL'S FURY

All the non-believers, with Satan, with Antichrist and with the False Prophet and Satan's angels will be together in Hell. It will *not* be a time for grand reunions. It *will* be a time for eternal torment!

1. A PLACE OF CONSCIOUSNESS

You will recall in a previous chapter we related the Scriptures concerning a certain rich man and Lazarus, a beggar. The rich man was conscious in Hell and he was in torment:

And in Hades (the realm of the dead, Hell), being in torment, he lifted up his eyes . . . and cried out. . . .
(Luke 16:23,24 Amplified Bible)

This Scripture indicates that the unsaved dead are CONSCIOUS.

2. A PLACE OF TORMENT

Both in the above verse just quoted and in verse 28 of Luke 16:

> . . . warn them (the rich man's 5 brothers) . . . lest they too come into this place of torment.

we have an indication from God that Hell is a real place of torment. . . . Also Hell, from these Scriptures, is shown as a hot place for the rich man asks that Lazarus (the beggar who went to Heaven) "dip the tip of his finger in water and cool my tongue; for I am in anguish in this flame" (Luke 16:24 Amplified Bible).

Can you imagine the intense suffering from an unbearable heat? Anyone who has been to Vietnam or other hot climates where the suffocating humidity envelops you along with the intense heat can appreciate this scene.

Also picture the desperateness of the occasion when the rich man would welcome the beggar Lazarus to get water on his finger to alleviate the suffering!

Hell is truly a place of real torment!

3. A PLACE OF DARKNESS

We are told in Matthew that the unsaved

> . . . will be driven out into the darkness outside, where there will be weeping and grinding of teeth.
> *(Matthew 8:12 Amplified Bible)*

Also
> . . . throw him (the unsaved) into the darkness outside (of Heaven); there will be weeping and grinding of teeth.
> *(Matthew 22:13 Amplified Bible)*

And in Jude 13 we are told that the "gloom of darkness'
has been "reserved forever" for those outside of Christ. What
a picture of hopelessness!

4. ETERNAL SEPARATION FROM LOVED ONES

Think about this for a moment. If you are an unbeliever
and some of your best friends and loved relatives ... perhaps
even a husband or wife are BELIEVERS . . . they will go to
Heaven . . . and you will be eternally separated from them!

> There shall be weeping and gnashing of teeth, when ye
> shall see Abraham, and Isaac, and Jacob, and all the proph-
> ets, in the kingdom of God, and you yourselves thrust out.
> *(Luke 13:28 King James Version)*

What a tragedy to enter Hell and then to realize that you
are now eternally separated from those whom you loved so
much on this earth!

5. NOT THE SLIGHTEST HOPE OF RELEASE

Many places in Scripture tell of Hell being a place of
eternal judgment from which there is no turning back. In
Hebrews 6:2 we learn that Hell is a place of "eternal judgment." In Matthew 25:46 it is revealed that the unbeliever
will "go away into everlasting punishment. . . ."

6. THE TORMENT OF MEMORY IN HELL

This, perhaps could be the most agonizing aspect of those
in Hell . . . the torment of a memory . . . a memory that will
evoke continual anguish. This is brought out so clearly in
Luke 16:27,28 where the rich man implores Abraham to:

> . . . send him (Lazarus, who is in Heaven) to my father's
> house:

> For I have five brethren; that he may testify unto them,
> lest they also come into this place of torment.
>
> *(Luke 16:27,28 King James Version)*

What an insight into Hell! Imagine if those unsaved dead right now could speak to us for just a moment . . . what a warning they would give . . . and yet, sad to say, would anyone pay attention?

How pointedly Abraham replied . . . and how prophetically when he said,

> . . . If they hear not Moses and the prophets, neither will they be persuaded, THOUGH ONE ROSE FROM THE DEAD.
>
> *(Luke 16:31 King James Version)*

Thus, the unbeliever in Hell must go through an eternity in torment with a searing, ever-present memory!

7. THE TORMENT OF UNSATISFIED LUSTFUL CRAVINGS

In Hell the unbeliever will *never gain satisfaction.* Sin will continue in Hell but it will be a constant craving . . . without fulfilling. Thus we read,

> He who is unrighteous (unjust, wicked) let him be unrighteous still, and he that is filthy (vile, impure) let him be filthy still . . .
>
> *(Daniel 12:10 Revelation 22:11 Amplified Bible)*

These words here are referring to the activity in Hell. Can you imagine the surprise that awaits the filth peddlers who on this earth are having a heyday distributing pornographic films and literature.

At least, here on earth this activity brings them barrels of cash while they influence negatively the lives of others.

But in Hell, these filth peddlers will have their cravings and lusts . . . but these will be unfulfilled cravings. Can you imagine the intensity of suffering this will cause!

Perhaps there may even be unfulfilled love in sex, unfulfilled forever in Hell. Someone has said Hell is a place where

> the Belshazzars will not have their wine
> the Ahabs will not have their Naboth's vineyards
> the Felixes will not have their Drusillas
> Herods will not have their sensuous dances
> the Judases will not have their cankered gold!

This will give you some insight on Hell's anguishing fury!

No wonder Jesus said in the Sermon on the Mount (this is for those who say, The Sermon on the Mount is my only creed),

> . . . if thy right eye offend thee, pluck it out, and cast it from thee: for it is profitable for thee that one of thy members should perish, and not that thy whole body should be cast into hell.
> And if thy right hand offend thee, cut it off, and cast it from thee: for it is profitable for thee that one of thy members should perish, and not that thy whole body should be cast into hell.
> *(Matthew 5:29,30 King James Version)*

THE UNSAVED DEAD *BEFORE* THEIR JUDGMENT DAY

What happens to those unbelievers who have already died, who will die today, tomorrow or anytime in the future before the beginning of the 1000 year Millennium?

Dr. J. Dwight Pentecost in his book THINGS TO COME points out that there are four different words used in Scriptures to describe the place of the dead until their resurrection at the Great White Throne Judgment at the close of the Millennium.

These four words do NOT always refer to the eternal state of Hell (which begins after the 1000 year Millennium) but rather often to the temporary place in which the dead await their resurrection. Here are those words:

1. SHEOL
   This is used 65 times in the Old Testament of which 31
   times it is translated "grave."
2. HADES (literally, the "unseen" world.)
   This is used generally to describe the unsaved dead who
   are awaiting the resurrection unto the Great White
   Throne. In every instance but one it is translated as
   "hell."
3. TARTAROS
   This word is only used once in Scripture (2 Peter 2:4)
   and refers to the judgment on the wicked angels.
4. GEHENNA
   This is used 12 times in the New Testament.
   (Matthew 5:22, 29-30, Mark 9:43, etc)

   [In the Hebrew this word literally means "Valley" (*Ge*) "of
   Hennon" (*Henna*). Its fires burning the garbage of Jerusalem provided Christ with the perfect picture of the
   eternal doom of those who are lost.]

Therefore the unbelieving dead are right now in torment
and in misery in their temporary place of punishment — Hades
or Hell, awaiting their final resurrection after the 1000 year
Millennial reign of Christ which will then be immediately followed by the Great White Throne judgment and their eternal
condemnation to the Lake of Fire (Revelation 20:11-15).

Before we saw the Bible's picture of Heaven; now in this
chapter we have seen the Bible's portrait of Hell.

It was Charles H. Spurgeon who told a group of seminary
students, "When you speak of heaven, let your face light up
and be irradiated with a heavenly gleam. Let your eyes shine
with reflected glory."

It was Walt Whitman who wrote:

Roaming in thought over the Universe, I saw the little
that is Good steadily hastening towards immortality,
    And the vast that is Evil I saw hastening to merge itself
and become lost and dead.

The fabric of our life today will determine whether we
wear a cloak of righteousness tomorrow. John Greenleaf
Whittier penned these words:

The tissue of the Life to be
    We weave with colors all our own,
And in the field of Destiny
    We reap as we have sown.

The story has been told of a picture painted by an artist who set the scene in a night background. Across the dark waters of a lonely lake a solitary man could be seen rowing a small boat. A high wind churned the waters of the lake into white-crested billows which raged around the little skiff.

Above was a dark and angry sky. But through the blackness there shone one lone star. Upon this the rower fixed his gaze – and on through the storm he rowed.

He was undismayed by the midnight blackness! Beneath the picture the artist had written: "If I lose that, I am lost!"

How true of life. If one does not follow the Star of our hope – the Lord Jesus Christ . . . he is lost.

In this life the "tissue" of our future life is woven.

We reap as we have sown.

If we sow in unbelief . . . we destine ourself to an eternal, real Hell forever.

On the other hand, if we sow in belief, through the acceptance of Jesus Christ as our Saviour and Lord . . . our harvest is an ETERNITY in Heaven!

How long is eternity?

Try to imagine that this earth upon which we dwell is nothing but sand. Now try to imagine that a little bird could fly from a faraway planet to ours and carry back with him a tiny grain of sand, and the round trip would take a thousand years.

Now try to imagine how long it would take for that little bird to carry away this entire earth, a grain of sand each thousand years.

The time required for this would be but a moment in comparison to eternity.

> And whosoever was not found written in the book of life was cast into the lake of fire.
> (*Revelation 20:15 King James Version*)

Is this where you want to spend ETERNITY, in the Night that NEVER Ends?

Chapter 12

The Day Earth Burns Up

A Fresh Start • The Size of the Universe • Earth's Beginning •
Early Theories • Earth's Form • This Passing Earth • Cali-
fornia Earthquake Serious Threat • The Sea • Tomorrow's
Fire

President Franklin D. Roosevelt, in a prayer on Flag Day
1942, said,

Our earth is but a small star in the great universe. . . .

And Rudyard Kipling wrote:

When Earth's last picture is painted,
    and the tubes are twisted and dried,
When the oldest colours have faded
    and the youngest critic has died,
We shall rest, and, faith, we shall need
    it—lie down for an aeon or two,
Till the Master of All Good Workmen
    shall put us to work anew.

How strange that millions of people reside on this earth
and yet take no interest in knowing about its being . . . and
more important, about where they will go when they leave
this earth!

And it is this same indifference that will condemn many
of them to an everlasting Hell.

In the past chapters we have seen how for 1000 years
people will be living in a near-perfect earth. This will be called

309

the Millennium. This will be a Theocracy ruled by God with "an iron rod" (Revelation 12:5). At the close of this 1000 years, however, Christ will allow Satan to be loosed from his prison . . . because for a 1000 years the nations of the earth have been submitting to an authoritarian regime.

And it is not the desire of Christ to be served by slaves but by people who will freely choose to love Him and to obey Him.

It is now time for those who live in the 1000 year Millennial Age to stand up and be counted—either for God or against Him. All others—*prior* to this 1000 year period have already made this decision!

That is why Satan is allowed to once more enter into the picture.

And you will recall that when he does, a crowd as numerous as "the sand of the sea" will follow him (Revelation 20:7-10).

It is then that God, by fire from above, sweeps down in judgment and kills everyone of these followers of Satan.

The resurrection and judgment of unbelievers then begins and they are cast into the lake of fire for eternal damnation (Revelation 20:11-15).

A FRESH START

Now God desires to wipe the slate entirely clean from every trace of sin . . . and He is going to do it by purging the earth by fire . . . giving His Saints a New Heaven and a New Earth.

But before we discuss how the earth will be burned up, let's get acquainted with this present earth.

THE SIZE OF THE UNIVERSE

Dr. Wilbur M. Smith in his book THE BIBLICAL DOCTRINE OF HEAVEN observes, as others have, the size of the universe.

Our *earth* is one of nine planets revolving around the sun, and has a diameter of 8,000 miles. Its mass is estimated to be 6,600,000,000,000,000,000,000 tons. The distance from the earth to the moon is 238,857 miles; while the average distance to the sun is 93,000,000 miles.

The *sun* has a diameter of 866,500 miles, and a mass 330,000 times that of the earth. The sun – and here the mind begins to stagger at such enormous distances and innumerable masses – is only one star in a galaxy of some one hundred billion other stars (100,000,000,000!), a galaxy that has a mass of about seventy billion times that of the sun.

Distances now become so great that we will find it so cumbersome to use the measure of a *mile* that it is necessary to construct a more practical unit which is called a *light year*. Light travels at the speed of 186,280 miles per second (generally referred to as m.p.s.), or 11,176,800 miles in one minute. (The sun is eight light minutes away.) A *light year,* then, means the distance light will travel in one year, or approximately 6,000,000,000,000 (six trillion) miles. Our solar system has a diameter of 660 light minutes; but the galaxy of which it is a very small part has a diameter of 100,000 light years!

Enormous as is the galaxy in which our solar system moves, it is only one of innumerable other galaxies – possibly one thousand million of them, the nearest of which is the Andromeda galaxy, 1,500,000 light years distant! You can see this supergiant galaxy, called M31 by astronomers, with a small pair of binoculars – if you know where to look.

If in *each* of these thousand million galaxies there are, as astronomers believe, 100,000 million stars, then in the entire universe there are some 150 million million million (150,000,000,000,000,000,000) stars.

On a clear night as many as 2,000 stars can be seen with the naked eye by a person standing at one spot. The total number of stars visible in the entire sky is estimated at about 6,000. With a telescope with a lens one inch in diameter some 225,000 stars can be observed. With the one-hundred-inch telescope about 1,500,000,000 stars. However, with the two-hundred-inch telescope nearly one billion *galaxies* are brought within observation, which includes objects as far away as two billion light years.

Very recently the frontiers of space have been pushed even farther back by Dr. Maarten Schmidt, Professor of Astronomy at California Institute of Technology. He has found five *quasars*, that is, quasi-stellar radio noise sources that are thought to be farther from the earth than any other known object. The most distant of these five quasars is labeled 3C-9. "The light we see from 3C-9," says Professor Schmidt, "left there many billions of years ago, long before the sun and the earth were born, when the expanding universe was only a third as big as it is now."

EARTH'S BEGINNING

The third planet in order of distance from the Sun is our Earth. It is evident that in its early stages it was in a state of much greater heat than at the present time.

How did our Earth start?

In the beginning God created the heavens and the earth.
(Genesis 1:1 King James Version)

Man has tried to devise other beginnings for the Earth but we believe God's Word. God created the Earth.

And we are further told in God's Word that "the earth was without form, and void; and darkness was upon the face of the deep . . ." (Genesis 1:2 King James Version).

Then God brought light . . . dry land . . . and gathered the waters into seas . . . vegetation . . . sun, moon and stars . . . sea and animal life, and finally—man!

How old is Earth? No one knows for sure! We do know the earth is tremendously old. Its age is believed by some scientists, on the basis of the theory of "eternally uniform" radioactivity, to be some 4½ billion years . . . not the traditional 6000 years or so that Archbishop Ussher advocated about three centuries ago.

Some might believe this a contradiction . . . and for you, we would recommend highly that you read THE GENESIS FLOOD, written by two well-known Christians, Henry M. Morris and John C. Whitcomb, Jr. Another excellent treatment on these topics is chapters 9 and 10 of PILGRIM'S PROGRESS IN THE TWENTIETH CENTURY by Dr. Gary G. Cohen.

Scriptures tell us that in the beginning God made heaven and earth. There are those who hold to the "Cataclysm Theory" that between Genesis 1:1 and Genesis 1:2 there was a pre-Adamic earth which God created and then destroyed.

While others point out that the genealogies in the Old Testament in Genesis chapter 5 and 11 very probably purposely include some gaps. An excellent example of this type of genealogy is Matthew 1:1 which tells us:

> . . . Jesus Christ, the son of David, the son of Abraham.
> *(Matthew 1:1 King James Version)*

If we were to follow this as successive genealogy—father, son, grandson—we would be way off as there is a gap of two thousand years between Abraham and Jesus. Thus one cannot use the reporting of the genealogy records in the Scriptures to determine the age of man, much less the age of this earth. Many Bible scholars who are fundamentalists believe that such genealogical gaps permit man to be far older than Archbishop Ussher's 6000 years. And the Earth itself, think they, may quite possibly be as old as the 4½ billion years of recent scientific theory.

However, any attempt to determine the age of the earth is just that—an attempt—and one enters on dangerous ground when one tries to read into Scriptures something that God has chosen not to reveal to us.

Both Scripture and physics agree that (1) no new creation *ex nihilo* (that is "out of nothing") is now taking place on earth, and that (2) decay is evident.

EARLY THEORIES

The Babylonians thought that dry land rose up from endless water; the Greeks considered that battles between the gods started everything. Up until 1600 A.D. some men thought the Earth was flat. Some even thought that the Sun and planets revolved around the Earth along with the moon.

Now man knows for sure how it came to pass that the nine planets, if which Earth is one, are in orbit around the Sun.

EARTH'S FORM

Many scientists *theorize* that Earth was originally in a molten form and that it took 50 million years or more for it to cool to its present state. God may very well have accomplished this in that pause between Genesis 1:1 and 1:2 or between 1:2 and 1:3.

It is further theorized that our planet's crust has been shaped and reshaped over spans of millions of years and that this process of change is still going on.

This shaping and changing occurs through *weathering*, where moisture and gases in the atmosphere decompose rock chemically and dissolve tiny amounts of it.

It also occurs through *erosion*, the destruction and removal of rock by running water, waves, freezing and wind.

It also occurs through *faulting*, when rock masses are displaced causing earthquakes.

Surprisingly enough, the earth's crust is very thin—only about 30 miles thick at its maximum thickness.

THIS PASSING EARTH

Now after having discussed the earth's beginnings and its form, let us survey a few topics which relate to the possible ways of the earth being devastated and destroyed.

With the advent of man into a scientific modern age, the habitation of earth is changing. When explorers first came to North America they found a wilderness community of great size and diversity that stretched across a continent. Wild animals existed in staggering profusion and variety. But today much of the wildlife is in danger of being wiped out. Just in a few brief years of "progress" man has torn apart the fabric of this country—hacked down the forests, plowed up the long-grass prairie, blasted away at the mountains, polluted the streams, and brought water to change the desert.

More than 500,000 square miles of the Earth's surface have been scarred, within historical time, by molten lava, rocks, cinders, ash, or gases expelled by volcanoes. And this may give us some insight on God's final judgment of Earth. There are over 10,000 volcanoes presently known on this Earth!

CALIFORNIA EARTHQUAKES SERIOUS THREAT

In a recent feature article in *Wall Street Journal,* Staff Reporter Frederick Taylor revealed that scientists warn of dangers of earthquakes in California . . . but few seem concerned about it. It was 36 years ago that a powerful earthquake hit Long Beach, killing 120 persons, flattening many unoccupied school buildings. And February 9, 1971 an earthquake in Los Angeles killed over 60 persons.

Yet even today 1500 of the state's schools still don't meet the standards of a California law requiring that all schools be built to withstand quakes.

Experts are certain that a "great earthquake" will hit California sooner or later.

Louis C. Pakiser, a top official of the U.S. Geological Survey "National Center for Earthquake Research" near San Francisco said:

"Between now and the year 2000—only 27 years away— there will be 100,000 earthquakes in the San Francisco Bay area alone.

Of these, only 100 will be strong enough to be felt; 10 will be strong enough to be damaging, and there's a 50-50 chance that one will qualify as a great earthquake."

Peter A. Franken, professor of physics at the University of Michigan, predicts tens of thousands would be killed and tens of thousands injured if San Francisco were struck by an earthquake comparable to the 1964 quake in Alaska.

In the April 22, 1969 edition of the world's leading financial newspaper, *Wall Street Journal,* there appeared the following article:

WAITING FOR THE END

Idea That Cataclysms
Peril Earth Intrigues
Some Men of Science

———————

Will the Antarctic Polar Cap
Slide Into the Sea? Or Will
Cosmic Debris Hit Earth?

———————

Outrunning a Sheet of Ice

Concerned about air pollution? The danger of being mugged in the streets? Forget it; those are niggling worries compared to the bona fide cataclysms (sudden, violent change in earth's surface) that menace the earth and everyone on it.

Ponder, for instance the estimated six million cubic miles of ice that make up the Antarctic polar cap. A substantial portion of this cap might slide precipitously into the sea, causing the levels of the world's seas to rise by up to 75 feet.

Or consider the possibility that a huge chunk of cosmic debris may collide with the earth. There is a crater 37 miles wide in Quebec that scientists believe was caused by just such a collision, generating several million times the energy of the atomic bomb that fell on Hiroshima.

"If a big one landed in the Atlantic Ocean," says Ian Halliday, an astronomer at Canada's Dominion Observatory, "I've heard it said that the resulting tidal wave would wash right over the Appalachian mountains. That sounds like a reasonable estimate."

. . . The ice cap and cosmic collision theories both are the work of respected scientists. . . .

Lloyd Motz, chairman of Columbia University's astronomy department says: "If one is to ponder the ice age and cosmic collision theories, it is just as well to consider the ultimate — and inevitable — disasters. The earth is doomed."

Mr. Motz explains that the tidal drag of the moon is slowing the earth's rotation. In order to keep the gravitational system in balance, the moon inevitably moves away from the earth. Eventually, in this theory, the moon's rotational period will match that of the earth, eliminating tidal "drag."

But the sun will continue to exert tidal pull, further slowing the earth. The sun also will cause the moon to reverse direction and move closer to the earth until the moon is torn apart at a distance of 10,000 miles. By then, however, the moon's tidal drag will have been reasserted with cataclysmic force, and it will have caused chaos on the earth, such as earthquakes and enormous tides.

"Of course, by that time the sun will have made this whole question academic," Mr. Motz says. "It will have become a giant star, many times as large as present, and many times more luminous. Things will have become impossible on the surface of the earth."

The expansion of the sun will, in fact, indicate its advancing age, a prelude to death. Mr. Motz says there already is evidence of fatal decay in the sun, evidence suggesting, for instance, that it was about 10% smaller a billion years ago. He estimates that the expanding sun will make it altogether too hot for life on the earth within another billion years.

By Drew Fetherston
Staff Reporter of the *Wall Street Journal*

The Sun troubles scientists . . . particularly the sunspot cycle, which about every 11 years generates extensive solar flares. These solar flares are vast areas of gases that suddenly brighten—and give MORE LIGHT than the *entire* solar surface. These flares travel at speeds higher than 500 miles per *second* and pour out intense streams of X rays and cosmic rays. The threat lies in the fact that these cosmic rays can destroy cellular processes and cause a holocaust of death here on this earth.

The only thing that shields man now from these rays from the sun is our atmosphere.

THE SEA

You will recall we stated previously that water now covers over 70% of the Earth's surface! In fact, land's tallest mountain, 29,028 foot high Mount Everest, could be sunk without a trace in the ocean's greatest abyss, the 35,800 foot Mariana Trench in the western Pacific.

And look at this fact:

> If all of the irregularities on the earth's surface were to be smoothed out, both above and below the water, so that there were no dents or holes anywhere, NO LAND WOULD SHOW AT ALL. The ocean would cover the entire globe *to a depth of 12,000 feet!*

These facts may help you see clearly how the Flood in the days of Noah was possible and, in fact, did occur.

In fact Scriptures tell us that the flood covered the earth for approximately 371 days.

TOMORROW'S FIRE

One of the most important passages in Scripture relating both to the Flood and to the future destruction of this Earth is found in II Peter:

> Knowing this first, that there shall come in the last days scoffers, walking after their own lusts,
> And saying, Where is the promise of His coming? for since the fathers fell asleep, all things continue as they were from the beginning of creation.
> For this they willingly are ignorant of, that by the Word of God the heavens were of old, and the earth standing out of the water and in the water:
> Whereby the world that then was, being overflowed with water, perished: [The Flood in Noah's time]
> But the heavens and the earth, which are now, by the same word are kept in store, reserved unto fire against the day of judgment and perdition of ungodly men.
> *(II Peter 3:3-7 King James Version)*

What Peter is saying here is that many people are becoming smug and indifferent living under the illusion that "all things continue as they were." And by this statement they show their ignorance of the prophecies and past occurrences in Scripture which reveal (a) that there was a Flood and (b) there will be a fire!

Peter is saying that this earth is being kept until that fire which will occur in that day of judgment—that day being the day when the wicked dead are raised and judged to an eternity in Hell—after the 1000 year Millennial Period.

Peter goes on to tell us in verse 9 of this same 3rd chapter of II Peter that the Lord is not slow or slack regarding His promises . . . even though some people may get this impression . . . but, rather, that He is longsuffering (extraordinarily patient) towards each of us because He is not desirous that any should perish . . . but that all should repent and accept Life Eternal.

But how true a picture this is of today . . . learned men as they become more knowledgeable, more scientifically advanced too often seek corruptible gain and lose their own life. One word becomes their stumbling block. That word is FAITH . . . faith in God based on His divine testimony to us through His Word, the Bible.

So, God, desiring to wipe the slate clean, after the judgment of the unbelieving dead at the close of the 1000 Year Millennial period . . . will create a new heaven and a new earth.

> . . . we, according to His promise, look for new heavens and a new earth, wherein dwelleth righteousness.
> *(II Peter 3:13 King James Version)*

In light of this one reads in Isaiah:

> For, behold, I create new heavens and a new earth: and the former shall not be remembered, nor come into mind.
> *(Isaiah 65:17 King James Version)*

This will be a time of rejoicing for the Christian but it is a catastrophe that many now reading this will not believe it, because of its great magnitude. Nevertheless, it will happen! And here is how it will occur:

> . . . the day of the Lord will come as a thief in the night; in which the heavens shall pass away with a great noise, and the elements shall melt with fervent heat, the earth also and the works that are therein shall be burned up.
> Seeing then that all these things shall be dissolved, what manner of persons ought ye to be in all holy conversation and godliness,

> Looking for and hasting unto the coming of the day of God, wherein the heavens being on fire shall be dissolved, and the elements shall melt with fervent heat. . . .
>
> *(II Peter 3:10-12 King James Version)*

What do these passages of Scripture tell us?

They inform us of the following:

1. This event will occur SUDDENLY
2. The Heavens will pass away WITH A GREAT NOISE
3. The Elements will melt with a FERVENT HEAT
4. The Earth will be BURNED UP
5. Everything on the Earth will be BURNED UP

Has man created or discovered anything that could simulate this condition on a small scale? Yes.

Have you ever heard the sound a jet plane makes when it breaks the sound barrier? It certainly is a great noise!

What about the discovery of the atom and the power of the nuclear bomb that melts everything with fervent heat!

Since God controls the atoms it is entirely possible that He may use this atomic power in the earth's final destruction. These imprisoned energies may be dissolved or released suddenly, without warning and the visible Heavens will vanish and the Earth melt with fervent heat!

Keep in mind that this occurrence will not take place until after the Rapture, Tribulation Period, 1000 Year Millennium, and Great White Throne judgment of the unsaved dead take place. Then, and only then, will God release His judgment on the Earth through FIRE!

Dr. Edward Hitchcock, the first chairman of the Association of American Geologists and Naturalists (1840) made this interesting observation:

> We may infer that Peter did not mean to teach that the matter of the globe would be in the least diminished by the final conflagration (fire).
>
> I doubt not the sufficiency of divine power partially or wholly to annihilate (wipe out) the material universe.
>
> But heat, however intense, has no tendency to do this; it only gives matter a new form.
>
> And heat is the only agency which the apostle represents as employed. . . .

What Dr. Hitchcock is saying here is that while God could completely wipe out the earth . . . these Scriptures indicate that the Earth will burn with fire . . . and fire acts as a purifier in its melting process but does not diminish the totality of the earth's matter but simply gives it a new form.

Thus the world is purified from the contamination of sin and is surrounded by a new atmosphere, new heavens, and will become the residence of the righteous.

Earth has had many natural calamities.

> There have been 63 recorded major *earthquakes,* and these appear to be increasing in frequency ever since 1932. On August 31, 1968 13,000 people were killed in an earthquake in Northeastern Iran.
> There have been 18 recorded major volcanic eruptions.
> And there have been 36 recorded major floods . . . the one in China in 1939 estimated to have caused the deaths of 1 million people!

But Earth's greatest calamity will be its destruction of its present form by FIRE.

Our greatest experience with fire or heat is perhaps that coming from the Sun. The Sun is a typical star and is only one star out of millions within our own SINGLE galaxy . . . and there are millions of galaxies in the universe.

The Sun is 864,00 miles in diameter or just over 100 times the diameter of the earth . . . yet it is only of moderate size when compared to some other stars. The Sun is about 93 million miles from the Earth and yet the Sun provides the primary source of energy for the Earth.

It may be impossible for you to comprehend these statistics but the amount of energy given out by the Sun is immense.

It amounts to

> 4 million tons of matter transformed into heat, light and ultra-violet waves A SECOND!

Its solar flares, that we have previously discussed, throw out particles at such a high speed that they travel the 93 MILLION MILES to reach the earth in just about ½ hour! This is some 50,000 miles a SECOND.

Through God's providence our earth's atmosphere acts as a shield to protect us, at present.

In June, 1946 the Sun sent out an arch of flame that soared above the Sun over ONE MILLION MILES — which is more than the diameter of the Sun!

The surface temperature of the Sun is estimated at 6000 degrees Centigrade but near the center of the Sun it is believed that the temperature must rise between 12 and 15 MILLION degrees Centigrade!

Imagine, if you can, a cake of ice one and one-half miles square and 92,000,000 miles high. It would reach from the earth to the sun. Scientists tell us that this gigantic cake of ice would be completely melted in thirty seconds if the full power of the sun could be focused upon it!

Now, can you see what natural elements now already create a fervent heat . . . a heat, such as this, stands waiting for the moment of God's kindling it. It will be so intense that when God allows it . . . it will in its intensive fire melt all the elements of the earth, burn the earth and set the atmospheric heavens on fire and in that fire . . . dissolve those heavens!

After the 1000 year Millennial reign of Christ . . . after the awesome resurrection of the unsaved dead and their legacy into the Lake of Fire . . . then comes God's final act of judgment upon the earth, the scene of so much sin.

This is the day the Earth burns up!

But for the Christian it is a day of new life:

> We, according to His promise, look for new heavens and a new earth.
>
> (II Peter 3:13 King James Version)

Ten thousand times ten thousand,
In sparkling raiment bright,
The armies of the ransomed saints
Throng up the steeps of light;

'Tis finished — all is finished —
Their fight with death and sin!
Fling open wide the golden gates,
And let the victors in.

Chapter 13

The Day That Never Ends

Our New Body • Where Is the New City? • Earth's Sorrows Are Erased • 1. No Temple • 2. No Night • 3. No Tears . . . No Death • 4. No More Separation • Those Streets of Gold

> He the pearly gates will open
> So that I may enter in,
>
> For He purchased my redemption
> And forgave me all my sin!

There is no chapter that gives me a greater thrill to write than this one. The event that we will now describe will fulfill all of the aspirations of the Old Testament saints, of the New Testament saints and of the Tribulation and Millennial saints.

No earthly pen can hope to convey the completeness of joy and the fullness of peace that will be ours as Christians, born-again believers, in God's New Heaven and New Earth!

But some day, God will reveal our Heavenly inheritance and it will be beyond human words . . .

> The false and empty shadows
> The life of sin, are past—
> God gives me mine inheritance,
> The land of life at last.

In the previous chapters we have seen Satan loosed from his prison at the end of the 1000 year Millennial period; and "numerous as the sands of the sea" are those that follow him, not satisfied with Christ.

And as they encircled Jerusalem, God, in a judgment from Heaven itself, reaches down and slays them (Revelation 20:7-9).

At this point all the unsaved are dead!

Satan is then cast into the Lake of Fire to join Antichrist and the False Prophet forever (Revelation 20:10).

The unsaved dead are then raised from the dead in what is commonly referred to as the "second resurrection" (the first resurrection being when the believers were raised to life eternal with Christ)—(Revelation 20:5-14).

Then—the saddest verse of all:

> And whosoever was not found written in the book of life was cast into the lake of fire.
>
> *(Revelation 20:15 King James Version)*

Then God seeks to purge even the physical earth and heavens of any evidences of sin. He does this by sending a fire so intense that it melts the elements with a fervent heat and burns the earth. The heavens also pass away with a great noise (II Peter 3:10-12).

Now God has rid the universe of the last vestige of man's pollutions through sin.

And now every Christian is about to enter into the greatest glory that God has prepared—the NEW HEAVEN and the NEW EARTH!

One of the first inklings that God gives us about this Divine inheritance for us is found in the Old Testament book of Isaiah:

> For, behold, I create new heavens and a new earth: and the former shall not be remembered, nor come into mind.
>
> *(Isaiah 65:17)*

I wonder if you can grasp the full significance of this verse? What God is revealing to us is that not only is He going to create a New Heaven and a New Earth ... but it will be so wonderful, so breathless in sight that it will occupy all of our thoughts and we will not even remember this old world we call Earth ... nor will we even recall it! It simply will not come into our minds! Can you imagine such peace of mind?

There will be no homesickness for the old things of Earth — such will be the dazzling splendor of this New Earth!

As we mentioned previously the New Heaven and New Earth do *not* come into being until

1. After the battle of Armageddon *(Revelation 19)*
2. After the Millennial reign of Christ *(Revelation 20)*
3. After the judgment of sinners at the Great White Throne *(Revelation 20)*
4. After the present earth is burned up *(II Peter 3; Revelation 21)*

OUR NEW BODY

Scriptures indicate that we will be the same person having the same soul as we now have. We will also have a new glorified body.

The characteristics of this new body will no doubt bear a relationship to our former body much the same as the qualities of Christ's resurrection body bore to His same pre-resurrection body.

The Bible tells us that when we accept Christ as Saviour and Lord we too are spiritually a new creation:

> . . . if any man be in Christ, he is a new creature: old things are passed away; behold, all things are become new.
> *(II Corinthians 5:17 King James Version)*

All will be new in that day . . . New Heavens, New Earth, and New Jerusalem (Revelation 21:1,2).

Here will be a place finally without corruption. No decay, no rust. Many people today think that silver won't rust, but rust, which is iron-oxide, also has its counterpart even in silver-oxide and silver-sulfide. All metals today corrode in one way or another. As an example, for every hour of plane flight in Vietnam, it requires 25 man-hours of anti-corrosion maintenance. NASA and the military together spend $6 billion per year fighting corrosion damage.

God tells us:

> Your gold and silver is cankered; and the rust of them shall be a witness against you. . . .
> *(James 5:3 King James Version)*

Thus, believers, who through acceptance of Christ, are now new creatures, will be completely fulfilled in all of God's glory in the New Heavens and the New Earth.

You will recall that the relationship between Christ and His saints is revealed in Christ's prayer of intercession in Gethsemane when He prayed:

> Father, I will that they also, whom thou hast given me, be with me where I am; that they may behold my glory, which thou hast given me. . . .
> *(John 17:24 King James Version)*

WHERE IS THE NEW CITY?

Let's read in Revelation about our new inheritance:

> And I saw a new heaven and a new earth: for the first heaven and the first earth were passed away; and there was no more sea.
> And I John saw the holy city, new Jerusalem, coming down from God out of heaven, prepared as a bride adorned for her husband.
> *(Revelation 21:1,2 King James Version)*

It is important to remember that this New City, JERU-SALEM, will not be the identical city on this present earth that we know as Jerusalem (For a further study on this subject we would recommend that every Christian read THE BIBLICAL DOCTRINE OF HEAVEN by Dr. Wilbur M. Smith).

> . . . and (He) showed me that great city, the holy Jerusalem, descending out of Heaven from God. . . .
> *(Revelation 21:10 King James Version)*

Here, God is revealing to John, the author of this God-inspired Book of Revelation in the Bible, that great city, Jerusalem, descending out of Heaven.

This New City, Jerusalem, is suspended over the earth as John sees it in the future!

One of the very interesting aspects of these new things is that while God chose to reveal to us in one single verse the creation of the New Heavens and Earth . . . there are at least 25 verses which describe in very great detail the "great city, the holy Jerusalem" (Revelation chapters 21 and 22).

EARTH'S SORROWS ARE ERASED

1. NO TEMPLE

It is hard for man to fathom the characteristics of this New City, Jerusalem. It is also an eternal city WITHOUT a Temple!

You will recall that there will be a Temple in the Millennial earth. But here in the New City, Jerusalem, there will be no need for a Temple. Christ will be that Temple. The entire city will be that Temple – a vast cubical (Revelation 21:16) Holy of Holies wherein God dwells. Since there will be no sin and our conversation and thoughts will be holy we will be dwelling with God in that Holy City.

2. NO NIGHT

There will be no night there. Christ will be the light that illumines that City.

> . . . I am the light of the world: he that followeth me shall not walk in darkness, but shall have the light of life.
> *(John 8:12 King James Version)*

With sin gone and with the saints being in the physical presence of God His light will be our light and there will be no night there.

> . . . for there shall be no night there.
> *(Revelation 21:25 King James Version)*

3. NO TEARS . . . NO DEATH

There will be no more tears in Heaven. There will be no more pain in Heaven. There will be no more sorrow, no crying in Heaven. There will be no more death in Heaven! Hear God's promises to every Christian who has placed his faith and trust in Him:

... God shall wipe away all tears from their eyes; and there shall be no more death, neither sorrow, nor crying, neither shall there be any more pain: FOR THE FORMER THINGS ARE PASSED AWAY.

(Revelation 21:4 King James Version)

What a glorious transformation ... when His blessed face I see ... no more pain and no more sorrow ... O what glory that will be!

4. NO MORE SEPARATION

All the saints of all the ages will be there. No more will friends have to part again. No more will families have to have tearful farewells. What a grand reunion saints in Christ will enjoy forever and forever. As Dr. Wilbur M. Smith has so wonderfully reminded us ... there will be no need to carry photographs of our absent loved ones in order for us to renew our memory of them ... for those who have been absent for years ... will now be ever present. No more disagreements, or misunderstandings, with our loved ones. Together, the believers will rejoice in everlasting joy and companionship.

THOSE STREETS OF GOLD

The Bible tells us the measurements of the New City, JERUSALEM in Revelation 21:16-21.

Size: 1500 miles in each direction[1]

Dr. Wilbur M. Smith, in his book, THE BIBLICAL DOCTRINE OF HEAVEN gives us some insight from an Australian engineer.

The City will give you an area 2,250,000 square miles. This makes it 15,000 times as big as London; 20 times as big as New Zealand; 10 times as big as Germany and 10 times as big as France.

[1] For anyone interested in calculating the "exact" size of the city by the "12,000 furlongs" to each side, Revelation 21:16, see Gary G. Cohen's UNDERSTANDING REVELATION, footnote, pp. 146-47. Here there is a discussion in detail of the exact length of the Greek *stadion*, the unit of length used in Revelation 21:16.

And it is 40 times as big as all England and even much bigger than India!

Taking the number of people to a square mile in the city of London, this Australian engineer, computed that the City Foursquare (the New Jerusalem) could hold 100 thousand MILLIONS — or about 70 times the present population of the globe!

Now it must be kept in mind, however, that this New City, Jerusalem will NOT initially be located on earth, but rather, above the earth. It descends to the New Earth after the New Earth is brought forth by God *(Revelation 21:1,2)*.

Wall: The wall is approximately 216 feet high.

Gates: It will have 12 gates.

The 12 gates are as 12 pearls in appearance, glistening! There are 3 gates facing in each direction. They are guarded by 12 angels. The names of the 12 tribes of Israel are on these gates.

Foundations: There are 12 foundations to the City, each named for one of the Apostles.

For he looked for a city which hath foundations, whose builder and maker is God.
(Hebrews 11:10 King James Version)

Stones in Foundation: (with the meanings traditionally assigned to them).
JASPER, an indication of wisdom
SAPPHIRE, repentance
CHALCEDONY (white agate), drives away sadness
EMERALD, indicating no counterfeits in Heaven
SARDONYX (onyx), married happiness
CHRYSOLITE, freedom from evil passions
BERYL, everlasting happiness
TOPAZ, fidelity and friendship
CHRYSOPRASE (green agate)
JACINTH (a reddish orange gem)
AMETHYST (violet quartz)

The Temple: The Lord God Almighty and the Lamb . . .
The tabernacle of God is with men.
(Revelation 21:22 and 21:3)

The Sunlight: The Glory of God and the Lamb

And the city had no need of the sun, neither of the moon, to shine in it: for the glory of God did lighten it, and the Lamb is the light thereof.
(Revelation 21:23)

The River: A pure river, clear as crystal

This is the river of paradise with its fountain-head being God and the Lamb.
While the streams of earth are polluted, this river of life is pure and clear as crystal.

(Revelation 22:1)

The Tree: The Tree of Life

Through the middle of the broad way of the city; also, on either side of the river, the tree of life with its twelve varieties of fruit, yielding each month its fresh crop. . . .
(Revelation 22:2 Amplified Bible)

Fed by the pure waters of the crystal river, this tree offers 12 varieties of fruit to satisfy every taste. It is never barren.

The Leaves of the Tree: Healing

You may recall in Genesis 2:9 that "out of the ground the Lord God made to grow every tree that is pleasant to the sight or to be desired. . . . *(Amplified Bible)*
But, of course, by disobeying God's law Adam caused sin to enter the world.
Now, this Tree in the New Jerusalem has healing in its leaves, forgiveness to all who believe.

No Temptation: NO MORE CURSE

Satan is no longer present . . . and the curse has been removed as promised:

And there shall be no more curse: but the Throne of God and of the Lamb shall be in it. . . .
(Revelation 22:3 King James Version)

No Night: GOD is the Light

There will be no need for candles, light bulbs or even sunlight for the Lord God will by His very presence illuminate this New Jerusalem *(Revelation 22:5)*.

The City: TRANSPARENT GOLD

This may be hard to imagine now as nothing on earth can presently duplicate a pure gold, clear and transparent like glass.
Yet God showed John in the Revelation a sight of this new city, New Jerusalem, which he could only describe as

having streets of Gold so clear and transparent that it resembled glass *(Revelation 21:18)*.

What a marvelous revelation of our new home! And what a marvelous promise:

> . . . the gates of it shall not be shut at all by day: for there shall be no night there. . . .
> but nothing and no one
> . . . shall ever enter it . . . but they which are written in the Lamb's book of life.
> *(Revelation 21:25,27 King James Version)*

No unsaved person will be in Heaven . . . nothing that would defile this Heavenly Kingdom. How true that old things will have passed away and all things will then be new!

As Dr. J. Dwight Pentecost has so excellently pointed out in his fine book, THINGS TO COME, life in that eternal city of the New Jerusalem will include:

1. A life of fellowship with Him
2. A life of rest
3. A life of full knowledge
4. A life of holiness
5. A life of joy
6. A life of service
7. A life of abundance
8. A life of glory
9. A life of worship

What greater promise is there than that found in I John:

> . . . we know that when He shall appear, we shall be like Him. . . .
> *(I John 3:2 King James Version)*

What is Heaven?

Heaven is a place where Mansions have already been prepared for us:

> In my Father's house are many mansions . . . I go to prepare a place for you . . . that where I am, there ye may be also. . . .
> *(John 14:2,3 King James Version)*

Heaven is a place where all our saved loved ones will be:

> Then we which are alive and remain shall be caught up
> together with them [our saved loved ones] in the clouds,
> to meet the Lord in the air: and so shall we [all of the saved]
> ever be with the Lord.
> (*I Thessalonians 4:17 King James Version*)

Heaven is a place where we shall see God:

> Then we . . . shall be caught up . . . to meet the Lord in
> the air: and so shall we ever be with the Lord.
> (*I Thessalonians 4:17 King James Version*)

Heaven is a place where we will have new bodies:

> So also is the resurrection of the dead, It [the body] is
> sown [planted] in corruption; it is raised in incorruption.
> (*I Corinthians 15:42 King James Version*)

Heaven is a place where we will receive rewards:

> If any man's work abide which he hath built thereupon,
> he shall receive a reward.
> (*I Corinthians 3:14 King James Version*)

Heaven is a place where we will be given wonderful rewards. The Bible describes these as crowns, wreaths of victory (*stephanos* in the Greek), as those given to the winners of the Grecian games.

However the crowns of the Christian are eternal, enduring, and golden.

> Now they [those who participate in the Grecian games]
> do it to obtain a corruptible crown, but we an incorruptible.
> (*I Corinthians 9:25 King James Version*)

Behold the eternal CROWNS:

1. A Crown of Life
   > . . . he (the Christian) shall receive the crown of life,
   > which the Lord hath promised to them that love Him.
   > (*James 1:12 King James Version*)

2. A Crown of Righteousness
Henceforth there is laid up for me a crown of righteousness, which the Lord, the righteous judge, shall
give me at that day: and not to me only, but unto all
them also that love His appearing.
(*II Timothy 4:8 King James Version*)

3. A Crown of Glory
And when the chief Shepherd shall appear, ye shall
receive a crown of glory that fadeth not away.
(*I Peter 5:4 King James Version*)

4. A Crown for Soul Winners
For what is our hope, or joy, or crown of rejoicing — is it
not even yourselves [Paul's converts] — in the presence
of our Lord Jesus at His appearing?
(*I Thessalonians 2:19 From the Greek*)

5. A Crown for Martyrs
. . . behold, the devil shall cast some of you into prison
. . . be thou faithful unto death, and I will give thee a
crown of life.
(*Revelation 2:10 King James Version*)

And Christ promises that He will come quickly to call for
His own, and He thus urges us in the Scriptures to be strong
in the Last Days, not to give in to false doctrine nor to those
who would say, "Where is the promise of His Coming?" But
rather, Christ tells His followers:

. . . hold that fast which thou hast, that no man take thy
crown.

and promises

Him that overcometh will I make a pillar in the temple
of my God. . . .
(*Revelation 3:11,12 King James Version*)

And so overjoyed will we be in this New Jerusalem that
we will cast our crowns at His pierced feet (Revelation 4:10).

And when the battle's over,
We shall wear a crown!
We shall wear a crown!
We shall wear a crown!
And when the battle's over,
We shall wear a crown in the New Jerusalem!

Then we shall be
  where we would be
Then we shall be
  what we should be
Things that are not now
  nor could be
Soon shall be
  our own!

What joy will be ours, eternally, in the Day that Never Ends!

Chapter 14

Your Last Goodbye

This Decaying World • Can Youth Bring Heaven? • Is the
United States Heaven? • A Better World? • The Choice •
Choose Your Future Inheritance • What Will I Do with Jesus?

On a tombstone out West is an inscription:

> Remember, friend, when passing by,
> As you are now, so once was I.
> As I am now, soon you will be,
> Prepare for death and follow me.

To which someone added the phrase:

> To follow you I'm not content
> Until I know which way you went!

And then there was the meek husband of a nagging wife
who willed one-third of his estate to his wife, and the rest to
a fund for stray animals. He stipulated that his widow was to
have carved on his tombstone the words: "He rests in peace."

The angry widow complied, but she added a line of her
own: "Until we meet again."

But seriously, the verdict of death is one that each of us
must someday face . . . unless Christ, in the meantime,
catches believers up to be with Him at the Rapture. Then, of
course, we shall not see death (I Thessalonians 4:13-18).

335

But, for the Christian, death is not a time of sadness . . . for it is not a period, but a comma in the story of life. For with death comes a glorious ushering in, immediately, to God's presence. As believers in Christ we can rejoice with Paul when he said in Philippians 1:23 ". . . to be with Christ . . . is far better."

Someone once said, "We understand death for the first time when He puts his hand upon one whom we love."

To the Christian, death is not extinguishing the light. It is putting out the lamp, because dawn has come!

One day they were burying a rather unsavory character who had never been near a church in his life. The services were being conducted by a minister who had never heard of him.

Carried away by the occasion, he poured on praise for the departed man. After ten minutes of describing the late lamented as a father, husband and employer, the widow, whose expression had grown more and more puzzled, nudged her son and whispered:

Go up there and make sure it's Papa.

No flowery oratory at our funeral will gain us an entrance into Heaven.

For at this point . . . it is TOO LATE!

How true that Americans have more time-saving devices and less time than any other people in the world.

And in this modern 20th Century, we are having less and less time for God!

Americans today are more concerned about earthly pleasures than heavenly treasures!

THIS DECAYING WORLD

What can this world hope to offer?

Can peace ever be achieved in this world?

If you are not a born-again believer in Christ . . . will you think about these things for just a moment.

First. Do you expect to live forever?

If yes . . . then how? No one else on this world has lived forever. All have died . . . even the most rich, the most prominent, the most philanthropic. Are you any different?

There is nothing so certain as change itself. If this were not true the funeral directors would soon be out of business.

Even while you were reading this . . . time passed by . . . time you will never again be able to retrieve . . . time that is bringing you closer and closer and closer to death.

You will recall in the very first chapter of our book we remarked about the fact that "the leaves must fall." One day your leaf will fall. And you don't know what day that will be!

> As for man, his days are as grass: as a flower of the field, so he flourisheth.
> For the wind passeth over it, and it is gone; and the place thereof shall know it no more.
> *(Psalm 103:15,16 King James Version)*

Are you putting your hope in this world?

On what basis?

On the basis of the sex filth that is flooding this nation? Do you think this will build a better world for tomorrow . . . a world that encourages the doing away with the holy institute of marriage . . . and instead, glorifies self gratification of lustful pleasures at the expense of countless disappointed and heartsick young people whose lives have been made shipwreck.

Are you basing your hope in what many ministers who counterfeit the very Word of God, tell you? These direct you to search for "a reorientation of persons in religious transition" . . . or to celebrate communion with a rock and roll mass. While these are obvious departures from the faith, far more dangerous are those clergy who are "having a form of godliness [pious talk], but denying the power thereof [they reject the Biblical testimony that God can do miracles]. . . ." It is against these that Christ warns us ". . . from such turn away" (II Timothy 3:5 King James Version). And, unfortunately, their ranks in the clergy are growing larger every day.

Another sad fact is that even some evangelical publishing houses are trying to imitate the world. Instead of bringing the individual up to the standard of Christ . . . they are lowering Christ down to the standards of the world.

Typical of some of the unfortunate material that is being distributed in some of our evangelical and fundamental churches is this excerpt from a Sunday School take-home paper for high schoolers.

This is from the April 20, 1969 edition Sunday School take-home paper:

Front Cover: A bearded youth

Copy:
Someone you know, with or without a beard, waits for you to sock the gospel to him. In fact, lots of someones in a lot of places.

Page 2:   Headline
SOCK IT TO THE WORLD

(First six paragraphs).
There it is. The world. The rocking, psychedilic headquarters of earth-man. See it there?

Don't worry; a little noise now and then doesn't scare it any. You can sneak up on this baby and it'll never know the difference. That's why we've got this plan, see?

What we do is sock it to it. Really hard.

You're skeptical, right? You say, "For what?" *For God. For the world.* God made a better way for men to live. Not everybody knows about it. Not everybody has felt or seen the difference it makes. So they ought to.

The whole smashing plan is this: we go all out to sock the gospel of Christ to the world – now.

Here's the cool soul of it all: we don't sock it to everyone at one time, exactly I mean, even one man at a time is a good target. And you don't have to wait for the other guy to start. Sure, the big idea is that everybody gets into the rumble before long – everybody that's a Christian, that is. And of course if it all goes like it's supposed to, there'll be more and more Christians to get involved, see? . . .

Do you see the danger the Apostle Paul was warning against when he wrote:

And be not conformed to this world, but be ye transformed. . . .

(Romans 12:2 King James Version)

What I am trying to say is . . . you can't depend on what man will tell you . . . not even many of today's clergy and churches.

Your sole reference and hope must rest completely on the literal Word of God! Man will disappoint you! And if your faith rests on a personality you are on a weak foundation . . . unless it is based on the personality of the Lord Jesus Christ!

Is your faith for a better world based on present environmental conditions? Then look about you at the smothering mountain of air pollution, population explosion, and famine in the world.

Do you think these will improve? Then, talk to scientists and biologists who are specialists in this field and learn of their concern . . . a concern which in most instances is solely theirs because everyone else appears to be "living till I die" and couldn't care less—until one day the full impact of the threat reaches into their very home!

CAN YOUTH BRING HEAVEN?

What about our youth? Is your hope for a heaven here on earth based on them? As sincere as many of them are . . . never before in history have we raised such a crop of drugged young people. Never before has our nation experienced such lawlessness with Presidents of schools being kicked off college campuses by students with rifles and an array of ammunition. And never before have colleges, under pressure, been forced to adapt new standards . . . lower standards, classes on love and sex, classes without grades, courses without purpose.

In many colleges throughout our nation . . . just going to school should qualify one for "hazardous duty" pay!

The youth, understandably so, are fed up with the hypocrisy of this world. We as adults, have handed them a world about to blow up and they are scared! Yet they cannot come up with an answer. They have plenty of demands for what they believe is the answer. But not one of their demands includes GOD!

And the adults have plenty of concern regarding this up-heaval—but not one of their concerns for correcting the situation includes GOD!

Will the youth of tomorrow bring heaven to earth? NO!

IS THE UNITED STATES HEAVEN?

As much as we dearly love our country and have served it in military service . . . the United States cannot provide a heaven here on earth.

We are popularly known among some Europeans as the "assassination center of the world" . . . our President is realizing more and more that the larger we get . . . the more educated we get . . . the more scientifically advanced we get . . . the greater are the problems that beset us.

With the population of the U.S. in the last 10 years going up about 10% . . . crime has risen 88%! And some politicians and clergymen are still telling us that, "Everything is fine; there is nothing to be concerned over."

We are not solving our crime problem. We are not solving our poverty problem. We are not solving our social problems. What most people don't realize is that now with a new problem—outer space—it will take at least an expenditure of $5 BILLION dollars a year just to keep our space effort afloat . . . let alone worrying about better housing and more schools. And even with more schools, New York City last year had to spend $1 MILLION dollars replacing windows broken by irresponsible children! Not only are we breeding a nation of irresponsible children . . . but more tragic . . . irresponsible parents.

United States is the land of the free but many people have not come to the realization that with freedom also comes responsibility—responsibility first to God—then and also to our fellow citizen and to our Nation. We have become so mired in the muck of pornography that I am afraid it is too late to get out of this quagmire of obscenity and onto the Solid Rock, Christ Jesus!

What a tragedy that the leadership of this country we love, in the form of the Supreme Court, through its rulings, makes such filth possible. While the High Court claims to seek true justice it quibbles over technicalities, criminals go free and pornography reigns supreme with the blessing of the state.

Can the United States provide a Heaven here on earth? NO!

A BETTER WORLD?

What about the world? Is our only hope for heaven found here? Here is a world that never before in history has been able to produce so much destruction as today. With its nuclear bombs, its germ warfare, its highly refined and deadly nerve gas . . . a nation can be wiped out virtually overnite . . . almost painlessly.

And yet, many foolish Americans would place their hopes on a Non-Proliferation Treaty with Russia and others. In simple words—non-proliferation—means that the United States will agree not to produce any more nuclear armament. Have you ever been able to make a bargain with the Devil himself . . . and come out a winner? Russia . . . whose leadership denies the existence of God . . . and who has not kept one Treaty yet . . . will not (in spite of *our* good intentions) keep this one!

And since our world must include Russia, Red China, and Cuba—who spout atheism—how can we expect to have this world create for us a Heaven on earth?

In the last decade there has been a greater frequency of wars than in any other period! And the United Nations certainly has not solved the problem!

Just the other day, buried in the middle of a local newspaper was a short report on China's intentions. The Chinese Defense Minister called on Communist China to prepare for nuclear war with both the United States and Russia. And within a year or two it will have the capability to do so!

Look around you. Read the daily newspapers. Does this convey to you a world at peace . . . or the indication that it is headed towards peace?

Can the World provide a heaven here on earth? NO!

THE CHOICE

Somewhere then, there may be an answer. And there is one! The answer is GOD! And before you were born . . . Christ has told us:

> . . . Come, ye blessed of my Father (Believers), inherit the Kingdom prepared for you from the foundation of the world. . . .
> *(Matthew 25:34 King James Version)*

You do not automatically go to Heaven. And your works, no matter how good they are, will not earn your way into Heaven. For you cannot earn your way into Heaven . . . regardless of how good your intentions are!

Eternal life in Heaven is a *gift* of God:

> . . . God commendeth His love toward us, in that, while we were yet sinners, Christ died for us.
> . . . as by one man (Adam) sin entered into the world, and death by sin; and so death passed upon all men, for that all have sinned. . . .
> For as in Adam all die, even so in Christ shall all be made alive. . . .
> For the wages of sin is death; but the gift of God is eternal life through Jesus Christ our Lord.
> *(Romans 5:8,12; I Corinthians 15:22; Romans 6:23)*
> *King James Version*

That gift of eternal life is yours . . . by acceptance of Jesus Christ in your heart as your personal Saviour and Lord. The *wages* you have earned as a sinner is *death*; but the gift which God will give to you if you repent of your sins and turn to Him in faith is *eternal life*.

That is the decision you must make for eternal life. It is the only decision you have to make. Don't fear coming to God, for Jesus has promised, "Him that cometh unto me shall in no wise be cast out" (John 6:37).

If you do not make this decision, your lack of decision automatically leaves you condemned already because of your sins to eternal damnation in a real, tormenting Hell.

It takes NO DECISION on your part to go to Hell!

It does take a DECISION on your part, however, to go to Heaven!

> He that believeth on Him is not condemned: but he that believeth not is condemned already, because he hath not believed in the name of the only begotten Son of God.
>
> *(John 3:18 King James Version)*

One of Satan's greatest weapons is found in 5 letters: D E L A Y.

And he has used this word very successfully in telling millions—"Sure, you must accept Christ as personal Saviour and Lord to get to Heaven. But why spoil things now. Enjoy life first, live it up, there's plenty of time!"

> But now is the only time you own!
> Decide now what you will;
> Place not faith in "tomorrow" for
> The clock may then be still!

Let's look at it from a practical standpoint. What will be your inheritance if you choose Hell? And what will be your inheritance if you choose eternal life in Heaven?

CHOOSE YOUR FUTURE INHERITANCE

HELL	HEAVEN
Eternal Torment in the Lake of Fire for your sin	Eternal bliss in Heaven for your acceptance of Christ
No hope ever for escape	Heaven is yours forever
A place of conscious torment constantly	A place of conscious joy forever

Hell	Heaven
Anguishing torment by fire that is never quenched and never consumes you	No sickness, no sorrow, no death but eternal abundance of life that never ends
Eternal darkness that brings weeping and grinding of teeth	Eternal light for there is no night there . . . singing praises to God
Eternal separation from loved ones who are believers in Christ. No hope of communication between you and those living on earth to warn them of the reality of Hell	Eternal reunion with loved ones who are believers in Christ
The torment of a memory that will add to your constant suffering, realizing that a decision of repentance and faith on your part, while living on earth, could have changed your destination	Eternal happiness in a New Heaven and a New Earth with all the former things passed away and remembered no more
Eternal torment of unsatisfied lustful cravings	Complete fulfillment of all of God's Promises

Just as there is one word Satan uses that is 5 letters — DE-LAY . . . so Christ offers one word that is 5 letters — FAITH.

By delaying your decision you forget that the clock of your life may stop suddenly, and your obstinate clinging to your still unforgiven sin will rob you of your inheritance of Heaven.

And to many in this world, the word FAITH is their biggest stumbling block to acceptance of Christ and an eternity in Heaven.

While they exercise FAITH every day when they cross a bridge, or fly in an airplane, or turn the ignition on of their car . . . they find it impossible to exercise FAITH in the acceptance of Christ as their own personal Saviour and Lord.

And yet,

> . . . without FAITH, it is impossible to please Him: for he that cometh to God must believe that He is, and that He is a rewarder of them that diligently seek Him.
> FAITH is the substance of things hoped for, the EVIDENCE of things not seen.

And we desire that every one of you . . . through FAITH
. . . inherit the promises. . . .

And for this cause He (Christ) is the mediator of the new
testament, that by means of (His) death (on the Cross at
Calvary for our sins), they (the believers) which are called
might receive the promise of eternal inheritance (Heaven).
(Hebrews 11:6; 11:1; 6:11,12; 9:15 King James Version)

Faith in God sees the invisible, believes that which has
been historically validated, and receives that which has been
promised. The action of FAITH in the most plain language
I can convey to you is

F orsaking
A ll
I
T ake
H im

There are thousands of ways of pleasing God, but not one
is possible without first having FAITH.

What about your faith today? Will it be placed in this
world and its feeble attempts to make this a heaven on earth?

Or will you right now, in prayer to God, humbly place your
faith in our Lord Jesus Christ, who at this very moment
stands at your heart's door KNOCKING! By FAITH, will you
let Him in and inherit something this world can never offer,
an eternity with Christ in HEAVEN! Hear His words,

Behold, I stand at the door, and knock: if any man hear
my voice, and open the door, I will come in to him and will
sup with him, and he with me.
(Revelation 3:20 King James Version)

Hell in torment constant OR Heaven in joy eternally?

What will be your destination when it comes time on this
earth for YOUR LAST GOOBYE!

WHAT WILL I DO WITH JESUS?

Will you accept Jesus Christ as your personal Saviour and
Lord or will you reject Him?

This you must decide yourself. No one else can decide that for you. The basis of your decision should be made on God's Word —the Bible.

God tells us the following:

". . . him that cometh to me I will in no wise cast out. (37)

Verily, verily (truly) I say unto you, He that believeth on me (Christ) *hath* everlasting life" (47)— (John 6:37, 47).

He also is a righteous God and a God of indignation to those who reject Him . . . .

" . . . he that believeth not is condemned already, because he hath not believed in the name of the only begotten Son of God"—(John 3:18).

"And whosoever was not found written in the book of life was cast into the lake of fire"—(Revelation 20:15).

YOUR MOST IMPORTANT
DECISION IN LIFE

Because sin entered the world in the days of Adam and Eve and because God hates sin, God sent His Son Jesus Christ to die on the cross to pay the price for your sins and mine.

If you place your trust in Him, God will freely forgive you of your sins.

"For by grace are ye saved through faith; and that not of yourselves: it is the gift of God: (8)

Not of works, lest any man should boast" (9)— (Ephesians 2:8,9).

" . . . He that heareth my word, and believeth on Him that sent me, *hath* everlasting life, and shall not come into condemnation: but is passed from death unto life"—(John 5:24).

What about you? Have you accepted Christ as your personal Saviour?

Do you realize that right now you can know the reality of this new life in Christ Jesus. Right now you can dispel the doubt that is in your mind concerning your future and that of your loved ones. Right now you can ask Christ to come into your heart. And right now you can be assured of eternal life in heaven.

All of your riches here on earth—all of your financial security—all of your material wealth, your houses, your land will crumble into nothingness in a few years.

And as God has told us:

"As it is appointed unto men once to die, but after this the judgment: (27)

So Christ was once offered to bear the sins of many; and unto them that look for Him shall He appear the second time without sin unto salvation" (28)—(Hebrews 9:27,28).

Are you willing to sacrifice an eternity with Christ in Heaven for a few years of questionable material gain that will lead to death and destruction? If you do not accept Christ as your personal Saviour, you have only yourself to blame for the consequences.

Or would you right now, as you are reading these very words of this book, like to know without a shadow of a doubt that you are on the road to Heaven—that death is not the end of life but actually the climactic beginning of the most wonderful existence that will ever be—a life with the Lord Jesus Christ and with your friends, your relatives, and your loved ones who have accepted Christ as their Saviour.

It's not a difficult thing to do. So many religions and so many people have tried to make the simple Gospel message of Christ complex. You can not work your way into heaven—*heaven is the gift of God to those who believe in Jesus Christ.*

No matter how great your works—no matter how kind you are—no matter how philanthropic you are—it means nothing in the sight of God, because in the sight of God, your riches are as filthy rags.

" . . . all our righteousnesses are as filthy rags . . . "
—(Isaiah 64:6).

Christ expects you to come as you are, a sinner, recognizing your need of a Saviour, the Lord Jesus Christ.

Understanding this, why not bow your head right now and give this simple prayer of faith to the Lord.

Say it in your own words. It does not have to be a beautiful oratorical prayer – simply a prayer of humble contrition.

My Personal Decision for CHRIST

"Lord Jesus, I know that I'm a sinner and that I cannot save myself by good works. I believe that you died for me and that you shed your blood for my sins. I believe that you rose again from the dead. And now I am receiving you as my personal Saviour, my Lord, my only hope of salvation. I know that I'm a sinner and deserve to go to Hell. I know that I cannot save myself. Lord, be merciful to me, a sinner, and save me according to the promise of Your Word. I want Christ to come into my heart now to be my Saviour, Lord and Master."

Signed ....

Date ....

If you have signed the above, having just taken Christ as your personal Saviour and Lord . . . I would like to rejoice with you in your new found faith.

Write to me . . . SALEM KIRBAN, Kent Road, Huntingdon Valley, Penna. 19006 . . . and I'll send you a little booklet to help you start living your new life in Christ.